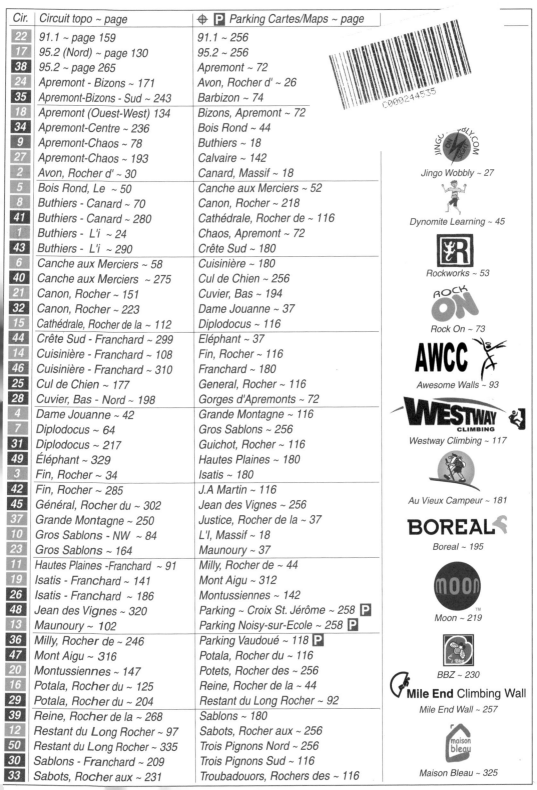

Jingo Wobbly ~ 27

Dynomite Learning ~ 45

Rockworks ~ 53

Rock On ~ 73

Awesome Walls ~ 93

Westway Climbing ~ 117

Au Vieux Campeur ~ 181

BOREAL

Boreal ~ 195

moon

Moon ~ 219

BBZ ~ 230

Mile End Climbing Wall

Mile End Wall ~ 257

maison bleau

Maison Bleau ~ 325

David Atchison-Jones
Editor & Photographer
additional photography by
Carrie Atchison-Jones & James Bacon

FONTAINEBLEAU MAGIQUE
Jingo Wobbly – Topo Guides
First Published in April 2005
By Jingo Wobbly Euro Guides
(An imprint of Vision PC).
Holmwood House, 52 Roxborough Park,
Harrow-on-the-Hill, London. HA1 3AY, Great Britain

Copyright © David Atchison-Jones 2009
Graphics by Botticelli
Image Scanning – The Grain Store
Printing – Fratelli Spada SPA, Roma.

A CIP catalogue record is available from the British Library

ISBN 978-1-873 665 81-7

TRADE DISTRIBUTION
visit
www.jingowobbly.com
for our list of EUROPEAN &
WORLD distribution agents

Cover photos:
T-left photo: Rouge 5 ~ 6a, Franchard Cuisinière; Olivia Hsu
T-right photo: Rouge 47 ~ 5c, 95.2; Trym Seland
B-Left photo: Bleu 34 ~ 5a, Rocher Canon; Fiona Murray
B-right photo: Orange 19 - 5a Restant du Long Rocher Nord; David Atchison-Jones

Title photo: Orange 8 ~ 5a; Grande Montagne, Trois Pignons
Climber; Matt Nicholson

Frontispiece: Orange 16 ~ 3b, Dame Jouanne; Libby Graham

FONTAINEBLEAU

Magique

 JINGO WOBBLY CLIMBING BOOKS – LONDON

I dedicate this book to the memory of Michael Cooper, a climber I met during the making of this book at Isatis, but who unfortunately died several months later in a car accident. Whilst taking photos for the book, I met over 400 different climbers from tiny tots to veterans. Mike was very typical to nearly everyone climbing at Bleau, easy going, happy, liked to smile a lot, but on a problem gave it his all - grimacing unmercifully; he will be missed by many.

A giant thanks to Virginie Percival who has worked so hard on translating the main text into French, an impossible task given the sometimes bizarre thought patterns of the author; Carsten Joiko for the German Intro, and Anna Fubini-Venezia for the Italian intro.

I have to thank Carrie for her wonderful support, and taking many photos with a broken arm for much of the duration of the book. A big thanks to Jim Bacon who has added so much to the photography for the book by cranking hard, and rising at ridiculously early times to get the best of the cool summer mornings.

A big thanks to everyone who helped out with all the photographs and are credited beneath the photos; an additional thank you to anyone that didn't make it into the book but helped in cruising a problem for a snap.

An obvious huge thanks to all the previous guidebook writers to Fontainebleau, and everyone involved in keeping the circuits traced throughout the forest.

Carrie after an extreme Bouldering session!

Carrie back at full strength!!!

Milly-la-Fôret, the picturesque central market.

CONTENTS

Vaudoué

Arbonne-la-Forêt

Fontainebleau est tout simplement La Mecque de l'escalade à blocs. C'est l'arène où les meilleurs grimpeurs mondiaux viennent tester leur habileté sur les passages très connus de Bas Cuvier et de Franchard. Pour ceux qui souhaitent se comparer à eux et se féliciter de grimper sérieusement à 8a, le défi est d'accomplir 10 passages à 8a, chacun sur des sites différents. Pour les autres l'escalade à bloc sur les 300km² de forêt de Fontainebleau est tout simplement divertissante. La taille des blocs varie beaucoup entre des tout petits parfaits pour les enfants, et des géants qui culminent à 15 mètres de haut. La concentration d'excellents sites est assez exceptionnelle et l'accès est facile en particulier grâce à la proximité de Paris. Il y a 3 facteurs principaux qui font que Fontainebleau reste si populaire : la qualité des blocs, les aires de réception excellentes et la possibilité de grimper pendant 365 jours de l'année.

Il est intéressant de comprendre la géologie du grès de Fontainebleau afin de préserver les blocs et d'améliorer votre performance. La formation du grès est partout la même, le sable se dépose pendant des millions d'années en couches qui forment un lit horizontal qui avec chaleur et compression se transforme en roche. Les grains de sable sont rarement petits et la compression est rarement forte, c'est pourquoi la roche qui en résulte s'érode facilement et naturellement. Le grès de Fontainebleau est un peu différent car les grains de sable étaient au départ très petits. Cependant une fois le grès formé, la mer laissa d'autres dépôts qui formèrent une couche supplémentaire cette fois de dépôts de calcium appelés calcaire. Avec la tectonique des plaques, le grès emprisonné devint très compressé contre le calcaire situé au-dessus. Ceci explique pourquoi la roche est si compacte et bien cimentée. Les mouvements de la terre ondulèrent la couche de grès emprisonnée et la cassèrent naturellement en pavés géants. Avec le temps, les petites fentes entre les pavés furent bouchées avec des dépôts de silice. Puis finalement avec le surcroît de pression, de chaleur et de réactions chimiques, les dépôts se transformèrent naturellement en veines de quartz, enfermant chacun des pavés géants. Après des millions d'années, le calcaire disparu et c'est grâce à leur surface de quartz que les blocs purent survivre pendant si longtemps. Malheureusement le quartz blanc et lisse est très glissant pour grimper, mais sans lui les blocs se

seraient érodés il y a de nombreuses années. Les prises les plus glissantes apparaissent là où les grains de sable sont usés et le quartz est laissé apparent. Lorsque vous trouvez une prise très sableuse, faites attention car c'est un signe qu'il n'y a pas de quartz sous-jacent qui cimente la roche et qu'elle risque donc de s'éroder rapidement. C'est pourquoi il est important de nettoyer les semelles de vos chaussons avant chaque passage, d'une part pour améliorer votre performance mais d'autre part pour protéger les rochers contre l'érosion. Malgré l'érosion du paysage par le vent et la pluie, les pavés géants restent intacts, mais reposent pour la plupart sur un simple lit de sable. Dans les secteurs du sud, les escarpements de grès ont très peu de quartz. Bien qu'il soit plus adhérent et plus confortable pour grimper, c'est un grès qui se casse facilement et qui s'use très rapidement. Bien que ces blocs aient de bonnes aires de réception, ne sous-estimez pas les passages très hauts et engagés.

L'accès à la forêt est gratuit et l'escalade y est parfaite en toute saison, la pluie est le seul élément qui vous empêchera de grimper. Notez que le grès humide est très fragile, donc ne grimpez pas si les blocs ne sont pas complètement secs. Les secteurs sur le haut des coteaux sèchent en un instant et ils sont donc parfaits pour les jours d'hiver ensoleillés. Il y a par ailleurs de nombreux sites avec des arbres qui sont mieux adaptés pour le printemps et l'automne. Dans la chaleur de l'été, nous vous conseillons les sites perdus au fin fond de la forêt pour être au frais. Il y a au total 30.000 passages et 30.000 sites différents et avec de bonnes informations, vous trouverez toujours l'endroit parfait pour grimper.

Sur la carte, Fontainebleau est entouré par un massif vert géant. La forêt est en fait constituée de forêts plus petites qui sont cependant toutes gérées par l'Office National des Forêts. Le travail de l'ONF consiste à protéger la forêt et son habitat naturel, mais supporte également l'intégration d'activités récréatives qui n'ont aucun effet adverse sur la forêt. Il y a de nombreux parkings dans la forêt (qui sont pour l'instant gratuits) mais ils sont souvent isolés et ne sont pas surveillés. Certains individus sont prêts à casser les vitres des voitures pour voler ce qu'elles contiennent et si vous êtes au fin fond de la forêt, il vous sera impossible de les arrêter. Donc ne laissez rien dans votre voiture à moins que vous ayez un esprit charitable.

Dans la forêt, le camping sauvage est interdit et il y a ni poubelles, ni toilettes. Camper n'est pas un problème puisqu'il y a plusieurs terrains de camping proches des sites d'escalade. Les poubelles ne sont pas indispensables puisque chacun peut rapporter ses détritus. Les toilettes posent un problème puisque si vous passez la journée dans la forêt, vous aurez besoin d'y aller. C'est la raison pour laquelle les alentours de sites populaires comme Bas Cuvier et Cul de Chien sont devenus dégoûtants. Si vous avez besoin d'aller aux toilettes, respectez la règle qui est de ne pas aller à moins de 50 mètres d'un bloc. Réfléchissez au fait que vous n'apprécieriez pas que l'on utilise votre départ assis comme toilette !

L'érosion naturelle du sol est particulièrement agressive durant les gros orages et il y a régulièrement des chutes de pierre et des glissements de terrain à la Dame Jouanne, Maunoury et Apremont. Ces sites sont placés sur des flancs de coteau qui sont prédisposés à une érosion naturelle. Les blocs peuvent bouger à tout instant alors soyez prudents et réfléchissez avant de vous asseoir sous un bloc – surtout lorsqu'il pleut. Par le simple fait de descendre une pente sableuse, vos pieds peuvent pousser une quantité assez considérable de sable en bas du coteau. Si vous le pouvez, essayez toujours d'utiliser les blocs pour descendre afin d'éviter de créer trop d'érosion ou alternativement faites des zigzags. Lorsque vous sautez ou tombez sur le sol, un trou assez profond apparaît rapidement, mais si vous utilisez un crash pad, vous réduirez nettement les effets de cette action. Si vous le pouvez, remettez de la terre à l'endroit où le trou se crée pour éviter que les blocs basculent. Si le début d'un passage n'est pas assez supporté par la terre qui peu à peu a disparu, cela peut causer beaucoup de tension sur les prises de départ et causer leur cassure. Dans ce cas de la terre doit donc être ajoutée pour réajuster la hauteur du sol. Il est parfois également judicieux de doubler votre crash pad pour réajuster le niveau de difficulté de certains débuts de passage. En été la forêt est très sèche et est très propice aux incendies, donc n'allumez aucun feu. Pour les grimpeurs, le plus grand danger sont les frelons qui font souvent leurs nids dans les trous des blocs. Vous verrez souvent le mot FRELON écrit à la craie en dessous de certains trous. Donc soyez prudents et observez bien chaque prise avant de les utiliser. Vous trouverez des nids en particulier sur les circuits d'Isatis, 91.1 et Cul de Chien.

Rappelez-vous qu'une piqûre de frelon peut vous empêcher de grimper pendant plusieurs jours. Les vipères sont également présentes dans la forêt, mais elles sont en général enfouies dans les sous-bois. Les sangliers vivent également dans la forêt, mais ils sont généralement effrayés par le bruit et les vibrations des crash pad jetés sur le sol. Enfin la forêt est remplie de champignons sauvages, mais avant de les ramasser faites attention car nombre d'entre eux sont vénéneux et parfois même mortels.

Même si vous n'appréciez pas les barrières à l'entrée des terrains de camping, elles sont en fait les bienvenues au vu des nombreuses effractions de voitures. N'oubliez pas d'apporter votre maillot de bain si vous souhaitez utiliser les piscines, mais rappelez-vous que les shorts style boxers ne sont pas autorisés. Vous trouverez sur la carte la location des magasins et sur la page d'index, toute l'information nécessaire sur ces derniers. D'autres guides d'escalade et des cartes IGN sont également disponibles dans les librairies de Milly-la-Forêt et de Fontainebleau. Il est essentiel d'avoir un moyen de transport pour se déplacer puisqu'il n'y a aucun transport en commun autour de la forêt. Une voiture est idéale, mais un vélo peut faire l'affaire. De nombreux grimpeurs louent un gîte pour une semaine puis vont aux différents sites d'escalade en vélo, certains ayant eu l'audacieuse idée de fixer un porte-bagage leur permettant de transporter un crash pad dans le sens de la longueur.

L'escalade à Fontainebleau est totalement différente de l'escalade en salle. Parfois certains passages ne nécessitent que l'utilisation de la force, c'est cependant très rare. En général il faut associer technique et équilibre sur les voies de Fontainebleau. Assurez-vous de toujours bien nettoyer vos chaussons car cela vous permettra de grimper plus aisément et à un niveau plus élevé. Les débuts de passage sont souvent éloignés des aires de réception, donc un petit tapis ou un matelas en plus du crash pad peuvent être utiles. De nombreux grimpeurs utilisent un pof, un chiffon qui contient de la résine en poudre ou colophane. Cette poudre très pratique rend vos doigts collants. Elle est de plus invisible, biodégradable en quelques jours et elle sent bon. Le magnésium de carbonate que l'on appelle magnésie n'est pas très joli à voir sur les rochers, mais il disparaît lorsqu'il pleut. Si vous grimpez au soleil les jours chauds, vous aurez besoin d'en utiliser beaucoup. Il est donc probablement préférable de grimper à l'ombre afin de diminuer son usage. Essayez de choisir le bon site d'escalade selon la température ainsi vous n'aurez pratiquement pas besoin de magnésie. La forêt est pour tout le monde donc il est du devoir de chacun de la protéger. Utilisez le moins de magnésie possible et brossez les prises aussi doucement que possible. Frapper les rochers vigoureusement avec le pof est très traditionnel à Fontainebleau et c'est un bruit que vous entendrez dans toute la forêt. Est-ce que cela force la résine dans la roche ou est-ce que cela décolle le sable des cristaux laissant un quartz lisse ? Le débat reste ouvert. Les meilleures conditions pour grimper des passages à 8b sont en hiver. Cependant faites attention car lorsque les rochers sont chauds et que les températures chutent, les blocs deviennent suants et se couvrent de condensation (de novembre à mars). J'ai vu des grimpeurs faire des 7c et des 8a en août mais à l'ombre et donc au frais. Le plus important pour grimper à Fontainebleau est le choix du site et non le mois de l'année. L'escalade est intense et les petites prises font beaucoup mal à doigts. Il est donc recommandé d'essayer différents passages avec des styles variés afin de grimper plus longtemps. Essayez toujours d'avoir une parade si possible car même une petite chute peut faire très mal. L'hôpital de Fontainebleau est indiqué sur notre carte et le personnel est habitué aux fréquentes visites des grimpeurs (p 143) !

Ce qui rend Fontainebleau unique c'est la création des circuits d'escalade. Ils débutent avec un passage qui indique D-départ puis vous mène vers un autre passage de niveau similaire, et ainsi de suite. Vous pouvez les faire en suivant une succession de petites flèches et de numéros jusqu'au dernier bloc (A-arrivé.) Les circuits sont colorés suivant le niveau de difficulté (comme au ski, bleu, rouge, noir par exemple) et comprennent environ 25 à 75 passages. Certains circuits sont peints alors que d'autres n'ont aucun balisage. Il y a environ 250 circuits balisés dans la forêt et 300 qui ne le sont pas. Un schéma est souvent utile ainsi qu'une bonne interprétation des cartes car même les circuits balisés sont parfois difficiles à suivre. Les circuits non balisés sont souvent envahis par la végétation, mais ils ne sont jamais polis ou usés. Le balisage des circuits est supervisé par COSIROC, une organisation française dont le travail consiste à protéger tous les sites naturels d'escalade

de France. Si vous souhaitez les aider, vous pouvez les contacter par leur site Internet www.cosiroc.org. De nombreux circuits furent créés, il y a 30 ou 50 ans et par le biais d'améliorations et l'apport de variantes, ils changent chaque fois qu'ils sont repeints. Ils sont parfois complètement re-balisés, mais c'est assez rare.

Nous avons choisi probablement les 50 meilleurs circuits de difficulté moyenne (d'orange à bleu) afin de convenir à tous ceux qui grimpent entre 5a et 7a. Il est à noter que la difficulté de chaque circuit varie considérablement, et la couleur d'un passage n'est pas un indicateur de sa difficulté. Lorsque d'autres circuits se mélangent avec les nôtres, nous indiquons les côtations d'origine. Cette information supplémentaire peut-être très utile cependant les passages peuvent être sous évalués du fait de l'érosion, des prises polies, etc. Seulement un minimum de passages supplémentaires illustrés sont indiqués sur les topos pour une utilisation plus facile.

Nous produirons bientôt un autre guide d'escalade: 'FONTAINEBLEAU BLOC'. Il présentera les circuits populaires qui ne figurent pas dans 'FONTAINEBLEAU MAGIQUE' et sera idéal pour tous ceux qui ont un crash pad et qui souhaitent grimper au même endroit toute la journée.

Nous avons utilisé l'échelle de cotation traditionnelle de Fontainebleau (intérieur de la couverture), mais nous n'avons pas copié les cotations d'autres guides d'escalade. Vous découvrirez donc que les nôtres sont assez différentes – parfois plus faciles, parfois plus difficiles. Pour mettre les choses en perspective, j'ai grimpé tous les passages durant un été et à vu. Je mesure 1m83cm et je pèse 74kgs, je suis très souple et assez fort, mais je n'ai pas beaucoup de force dans les doigts. Les cotations de tous les passages dépendent de ces données. J'ai utilisé un procédé assez rudimentaire pour les cotations. Grade 1 est utilisé pour les passages qui peuvent être fait en équilibre sans utiliser les mains. Grade 2 est pour les passages verticaux avec de bonnes prises, mais pour lesquels peu de technique est nécessaire. Grade 3 est pour les passages qui nécessitent une technique particulière comme un rétablissement par exemple. Grade 4 demande de la force dans les doigts. Grade 5 nécessite des bras musclés. Et enfin le grade 6 est pour les passages qui demandent à la fois de la puissance est des doigts forts. Ce n'est pas une science exacte, mais cela permet d'expliquer pourquoi un passage reçoit la cotation 3 ou 4. Pour suivre ce guide, utilisez le plan schématique et consultez les cotations de chaque passage.

Dans nos guides, nous aimons donné d'amples informations que vous pouvez utiliser ou totalement ignorer ! Si vous ne connaissez pas très bien Fontainebleau étudiez les renseignements donnés par les icônes car ils sont très pratiques. Dans la première colonne, nous illustrons la couverture offerte par les arbres pour chaque passage vous permettant ainsi de choisir un circuit adapté au temps de la journée ou de savoir quelle partie du circuit sèche la plus rapidement. Nous donnons la hauteur de chaque passage et je vous promets que 5m peut parfois être très effrayant ! Les icônes pour un crash pad, une parade, un passage très haut ou exposé sont simplement une indication de l'ambiance générale d'un passage. Vous seul déciderez de l'endroit où vous irez grimper, mais utilisez au moins notre expérience avant de vous rendre sur un site. Vous n'arriverez peut-être pas à lire les passages convenablement, mais les informations données par un autre grimpeur peuvent être très utiles. Les icônes à droite des cotations décrivent la meilleure manière d'essayer un passage ou de faire la partie la plus difficile. Nous donnons notre (M) magique pour chaque passage que nous estimons de première classe.

Pour les grimpeurs avec de bonnes aptitudes, nous offrons le Défi du Magicien'. La compétition est personnelle et consiste à grimper un circuit complet en une seule journée avec un maximum de 10 chutes seulement. Après de nombreux essais, nous avons décidé que 10 chutes était une bonne moyenne pour grimper à vu ; pas trop pour être trop facile mais suffisamment pour un bon défi. La colonne de droite a été laissée vide pour vous permettre de noter chaque chute ou un abandon avec retour au sol (un peu comme une compétition en salle.) Certains circuits ont des passages extrêmement difficiles. Notre but cependant est d'offrir un défi sympa et divertissant qui peut-être réalisé par la plupart des grimpeurs. C'est la raison pour laquelle nous avons inscrit un 'X' dans la colonne, pour les passages que nous avons trouvés difficiles et que nous ne souhaitons pas inclure dans notre défi. Cependant nous ne souhaitons pas changer le circuit original et nous l'avons donc conservé complet. Puisque nous avons

grimpé tous les passages du guide nous connaissons ceux qui vous surprendront. C'est pourquoi nous avons indiqué les 10 passages à vu les plus durs pour chaque circuit et nous les avons numérotés par ordre de difficulté, 1 étant le plus difficile. Il n'y a rien à gagner si vous complétez le circuit avec moins de 10 chutes, sinon notre marque d'approbation pour être le Magicien de Fontainebleau. Si vous échouez, vous recevrez le prix du Vieux Chien. Pour rendre les choses plus faciles nous avons arrangé les circuits en ordre ascendant de difficulté. Ne sous estimez pas le défi du magicien, il a réussi à faire chuter un grimpeur top niveau sur un bleu ! C'est pourquoi nous vous conseillons d'essayer tout d'abord les circuits les plus faciles. Vous découvrirez que faire 50 à 60 passages en une seule journée ressemble à un véritable marathon. Si vous ne trouvez pas les 20 premiers passages faciles, vous aurez du mal à terminer le circuit. Nous avons l'exemple d'un ami qui arriva a la fin d'un circuit avec seulement 7 chutes, mais qui rata le défi sur le dernier passage. Un grand avantage avec le défi est que puisque vous essayez la majorité des passages une fois seulement, vous ne travaillez pas et donc ne fatiguez pas les mêmes muscles ce qui est très pratique à Fontainebleau. Pour profiter au maximum de Fontainebleau, je recommande un cycle d'escalade de 3 jours : essayez un circuit complet assez facile le premier jour, puis essayez des passages difficiles le jour suivant, enfin ayez un jour de repos le troisième jour. Cette combinaison vous laisse plein de force le deuxième jour et permet à votre peau de bénéficier de 2 jours de repos entre des sessions difficiles. Il semble peut-être insensé de ne pas grimper pendant une journée entière surtout si vous avez voyagé de loin mais en final, vous comprendrez et approuverez les bénéfices de cette méthode.

Le Château de Fontainebleau

Fontainebleau is simply the world Mecca of bouldering. It is the arena where the top climbers of the world come and test themselves against the famous historic problems at Bas Cuvier and Franchard. If you think you're world class standard, simply choose ten different 8a problems – each from a different outcrop. Only when you have done them all, can you rate as a serious 8a boulderer. For the rest of us, bouldering isn't that intense, it's about fun, enjoying relaxed climbing with your friends and discovering all the blocs in the giant 300sq.km of forest. Some rocks here are tiny and make a perfect challenge for kiddies, yet others are true giant boulders, a breathtaking 15 metres high. The concentration of excellent bouldering areas is quite exceptional, and the close proximity to Paris makes access easy and guarantees popularity. There are however three separate qualities that keeps Fontainebleau bouldering up in the stratosphere; fantastic rock quality, soft sandy landings, and 365 day appeal.

It's worth understanding geologically how the sandstone was formed here. This way you can get the very best from your performance, and also preserve the rock surface. The understanding of sandstone formation is generally well known. Sand gets deposited over millions of years into layers that form a horizontal bed, then with resulting heat and compression, this strata forms into rock. Sand grains are rarely microscopic, and the compacting is rarely powerful; hence the resulting rock is easily eroded by nature again. Fontainebleau is slightly different, because most of the sand grains were very tiny to start with. Critically however, after the sandstone was formed, seas washed over the area leaving further deposits which formed a capping layer of calcium deposits - limestone! This in effect put a giant pressure cap on top of what was to become millions of years later - the Paris area. With minute tectonic plate movement, the trapped sandstone became very highly compressed against the limestone strata above. This explains why the rock is so compact and well cemented as you gain altitude in the forest. The final gem however, was that these earth movements actually rippled the sandstone layer underneath, and naturally broke it up into tightly packed, giant cobbles. Over time, the tiny slits between the cobbles became clogged with silica deposits from the sand. Finally with the addition of

pressure, heat and chemical reaction, the deposits naturally turned to fine veins of quartz, encasing each of the giant cobbled blocks. Over millions of years, the limestone top crust has worn away and has disappeared. It is only the quartz rich surface of the blocs that has allowed them to survive in nature for such a long time. Unfortunately, the milky white and smooth Quartz is heinously slippery to climb on, and is even harder than steel; but without it, the boulders would have eroded a long time ago. Most slippery footholds occur where the sand grains have been worn away, and you are left with a pure quartz surface. Remember, that friction can be generated on two slippery flat surfaces, so long as there is nothing between them. When you find a foothold gritty, be careful since it is a sign that there is no underlying quartz cementing it together, and it will erode very quickly. Cleaning the soles of your shoes before each problem not only enhances your performance by many grades, but also protects the rock against needless erosion. Much less quartz is found in the lower strata, resulting in soft beds of sandstone at lower levels. As the wind and the rain erode the landscape, the giant cobbles remain intact, but now simply rest on a bed of sand in a lot of places. In the southern sectors, you will find the big steep escarpments of sandstone with little quartz. It may be grippy and comfortable to climb on, but it can easily break off in clumps, and is wearing away fast. Even though these boulder landings are sandy and fun, don't underestimate our warnings of highball and deathball.

The forest has free access to the public every day, and the climbing is perfect in any season; it's only the rain that will stop you. Please note, that wet sandstone is weak. Do not pull on it or use it until it is totally dry. The sectors on the top of hills dry out in an instant, which makes them perfect climbing spots for a sunny January day. There are plenty of areas with light tree cover to suit spring or autumn. In the heat of summer, a trip into the deep green forest for secluded but chilled, moss encased boulders is just the ticket. Consequently, there isn't a best time to come here. There are 10,000+ problems & 30,000 different ways to climb them; with good information, you can always find the perfect place to climb.

Fontainebleau is surrounded on the map by a big green clump. This extensive forest actually consists of several different forests with different names, and are managed by the Office National des Forêts (folk in green uniforms). The ONF works exceptionally hard to protect the forest and the natural habitat, but also is highly supportive of integrating recreational activities, on the proviso that they have no adverse effect on the forest. There are many useful parking areas in the forest (which at present are free), but they are lonely and unsupervised. The simple fact is that criminals operate in the area, and will break 'any window' to enter 'any car' they wish, and do! If you are deep in the forest, you will hear nothing, so even locking your car seems pointless. Leaving anything at all in your car, can only be described as charitable.

In the forest, wild camping is not allowed, there are no rubbish bins, and no toilets to be found anywhere. Camping is not a problem since the area is well served with commercial campsites. Climbers don't drop litter, so who needs rubbish bins anyway. No toilets is weird one, since people do actually need to go to the loo if they are out all day. In popular places like Bas Cuvier and Cul de Chien – the surrounding area is disgusting. If you do need to go to the loo in the forest, obey the 50-metre rule, and never dump within 50 metres of a boulder. Think carefully, how would you like it if someone used 'your sit start problem' as a toilet!

Natural erosion to the soft sandy soil is particularly aggressive during mammoth thunderstorms, and there are often rockfalls and landslides at Dame Jouanne, Maunoury and Apremont. These areas are set on hillsides and are particularly susceptible to natural erosion. Any boulder can move at any time, so be cautious and think before you sit under a boulder – especially when it's raining. By simply walking down a sandy slope, your feet can push a considerable amount of sand down the hill; please if you can, always walk downhill on top of large boulders to cause minimal erosion, alternatively take a zig zag route causing less erosion. When you jumping or fall onto bare ground, a deep hole appears relatively quickly, but by using a crash pad, you reduce this effect immensely. If you can, replace soil to these pounded areas so that the boulders don't become undercut and start to topple over. If the start to a problem becomes undercut, it can often put a needless strain on starting hand holds, eventually causing these precious holds to break off. Soil must

be added to restore the height of the ground in these cases. It makes sense to double up your crash pad, to make the starts 'no harder' than the rest of the problem, and is sensible for short climbers anyway. In any summer, the forest dries out and becomes a real fire hazard, so don't even think of lighting a fire. The biggest danger to climbers are hornets (Frelons), which often nest in holes that are just bigger than your hand, and look inviting when you are running out of strength. You often see 'FRELON' written in chalk beneath a hole, so beware. Observe any reasonable holes for a while before attempting a problem that uses one. You will find nests on popular circuits like Isatis, 91.1 and Cul de Chien, and a bite from a hornet can often react and can stop you climbing for several days. It is well known that poisonous viper snakes inhabit most parts of the forest, but they are usually deep in the undergrowth. I did once experience the landing zone from a highball, turn into a somewhat more serious forked tongue arena! Wild boar live in the forest, but are usually scared off by the thwack of the crash pad onto the ground, the ground vibrates as they thunder away. The forest is full of wild mushrooms, but you need to know your stuff since some are lethal.

Property theft from cars is notorious, so the inconvenience of security barriers at some of the campsites is actually a blessing. Swimming pools in France do not allow any fancy costumes or boxer swimming trunks – even made by speedo; only tight slip style costumes are allowed, so make sure you bring yours along. We illustrate shops on our map, and include information on the shop index page. You can generally pick up other climbing guidebooks and IGN maps in the bookshops of Milly-la-Forêt and Fontainebleau. Having your own transport is essential since there are no public transport services around the forest. A car is perfect, but a bicycle is also very good and many climbers simply rent a gite for a week, then cycle to the climbing areas. The smarter climbers have a rack on the bike, to carry a triple crash pad lengthways and therefore avoid wind drag.

You will find Fontainebleau climbing, totally different to indoor bouldering. Some of the problems just require strength – but that is rare, most of the time you need excellent skills in balance and technique. Footwear - if the soles of your rock shoes are jet black and perfectly clean, you will climb around 5 grades

higher – simple. A problem often starts away from
your landing zone, so a small additional carpet or
mat with a waterproof underside is essential. If you
stand on a clean crash pad with clean soles, then
wipe the rock with a cloth – any loose sand will fall
onto the pad and back onto your soles. Stupid! - you
have just dropped back 2 grades. Most local climbers
use a 'pof,' a cloth rag that encloses powdered resin -
colophony (from your local pharmacy). This powder
makes your fingers stickier which is really handy,
sure it's cheating; but on the other hand it's invisible,
biodegradable in days, and smells good. White 'light
magnesium carbonate' that we call 'chalk,' does
makes a big mess - but washes off in the rain. If you
climb in the sun on a hot day you will need tons of
it, but then again – why not climb in the shade on a
hot day and hardly use it. If you pick the right area
for the temperature, you rarely need chalk. If you
repeatedly try a problem time and time again, the
holds will get sweaty and you will need lots of chalk.
In the end, the forest is for everyone, so it is up to
us to denigrate it as little as possible. Simply use as
little chalk as you need to, and brush holds clean as
gently as possible. Thwacking the rock with the pof
is part of 'bleau' history and you hear it everywhere,
does it force the resin into the rock and glue it
together, or does it prise the crystals of sand out and
leave smooth quartz? The open debate continues.
The ultimate friction for climbing 8b problems is
found in the winter months. Beware however, if the
rock is warm and then the temperature drops, the
boulders sweat and become covered in condensation
(Nov-March). Alternatively, I have seen 7c and 8a
problems, easily climbed in August - but at a cool
spot in the shade. It's always the choice of location
that matters, not the time of year. Climbing here is
intense and the small holds will bruise your fingertips
badly. Trying lots of different problems with varying
styles is recommended, since your body will last a lot
longer. Always climb with a spotter where possible,
even falling from a few metres can cause injury. The
Hospital at Fontainebleau is marked on our overview
map, they are used to visiting climbers! Treatment is
generally paid for by your credit card. You need to
keep a document called the 'Feuille de Soins,' and
keep any receipts from the pharmacy or doctors. Up
to date instruction of how to claim back any money
is best sought from the web - www.dh.gov.uk and
does actually work. (You should have a European
health card - free from the gov.)

What makes Fontainebleau unique, is the creation
of bouldering circuits. They start at a D-depart
problem, which then leads to another problem of a
similar standard, and so on. You can climb them by
following a succession of tiny arrows and numbers,
and usually finish on top of the largest block in the
local area (A-arrivé). You then jump up and down
and proclaim your brilliance! The coloured circuits
ascend in set difficulty (like in skiing; blue, red,
black) and can include from 25-75 problems. Some
are marked up with paint, and others are left blank.
There are about 250 marked, and 300 unmarked
circuits in the forest – more than enough for a
lifetime. Even the marked up circuits can still be
fiendish to follow, so a diagram is often essential,
along with a degree in mapinterpretology. Unmarked
circuits are invariably overgrown, but thankfully are
never worn or polished. The marking of circuits is
controlled by COSIROC, a French organisation that
works to protect all the natural climbing areas in
France. Many of the circuits were created 30-50 years
ago; they mutate with improvements or variations
when they get repainted, so beware! You should be
able to follow these circuits even if the numbering has
changed! (Our 'BLOC' book negates this problem).

I have chosen - 'perhaps' the 50 finest mid grade
circuits (Orange-Blue), to suit those climbers
operating at sport grades of 5a-7a. Please note that
the grade range for each circuit is considerable, and
the colour of a problem is not an indicator to its
difficulty. Where other coloured circuits intermingle
with ours, we give the 'HISTORIC CIRCUIT
GRADES' in a coloured box. This extra info can
be very useful; but with erosion, polish, etc. the
problems may be undergraded. I have kept the
number of extra problems actually illustrated on the
topos to a minimum, for ease of use and clarity.

We are soon to produce another guidebook called
FONTAINEBLEAU BLOC. This will include the
popular areas not featured in MAGIQUE, and is
designed as a 'non-circuit' book - ideal if you have a
few crash pads and want to stay in one area all day.

We have used the traditional Fontainebleau scale
of grading for this book (see inside back cover). We
certainly haven't copied any of the grades from any
other guidebooks, so you will find ours different
- some easier, others harder. To gain an equal

perspective, I climbed all the problems in a single summer and mostly onsight. I am 183cm high, 74 kilos, very flexible and reasonably strong, but I hate fingertip pain and have very weak fingertips; therefore all problems are graded accordingly for me, and you know that fingery problems will be easy ticks. I have used a rough scheme for grading. Grade 1, is for problems that can be climbed in balance and not using your hands, fun style. Grade 2, is for vertical climbing with good holds, and where no real climbing technique is required. Grade 3, is when you actually need to do specific climbing moves such as bridging or a mantelshelf. Grade 4 requires you to have fingertip strength. Grade 5 requires arm and upper body power, you might have to lock off on one arm. Grade 6 requires a combination of both power and fingertip strength. It can never be an exact science but it will often explain why a problem gets either grade 3 or 4. To follow the guidebook, simply use the diagrammatic layout plan, and see the grades for each problem.

We like to offer a lot of information in these guidebooks, on the basis that you can either use it, or ignore it! If you don't know Fontainebleau like the back of your hand, you can benefit hugely from a little study of the extra information via the icons. We illustrate tree cover for every problem in the first column, so you can choose a circuit that will suit the weather for the day, or at least know which part of the circuit will dry out the quickest. We give the height for each problem, I can promise that 5m high is often quite scary! Icons for a crash pad, spotter, highball or deathball; are simply a pre-warning to the general aura of a problem. You make your own decision, but at least know of our thoughts before you go there. If I feel the top move is significant, then I usually give a separate grade for it. You may not read the rock properly and come unstuck of course, but information from a previous climber is often useful. The icons to the right of the grade are usually to help describe how the problem is best attempted, or where the difficulty is. We give our magical (M) icon for any problem that is 1st class.

For climbers of good all round ability, we present the amusing 'Magicien Challenge.' The competition is purely personal; to climb a whole circuit in a single day, with a maximum of 10 falls only. After lots of testing, we found that 10 falls was a fair judgement

for onsight climbing; not too many to make it easy, but enough up your sleeve if you have some genuine bad luck. The right hand column is left blank, so you can record each time you take a fall, or back down and touch the ground (the same as an indoor climbing competition). Some circuits have a few outrageously hard problems, as Font aficionados know well! Our aim though is for a nice fun challenge, and one that is perfectly possible for any climber of a reasonable standard. Therefore we put an X in the column for any problems that we think are ridiculously hard on the circuit, and don't include them on our challenge. We don't want to change anything on the original circuit though, and leave it complete as intended. By climbing all the problems in the book first, we know the difficult ones that will catch you out. We warn you about the 10 hardest onsight problems for each circuit, and number them in difficulty, 1 being the hardest. There is nothing to win if you do complete a circuit in under ten falls, apart from our fun accolade as being the Fontainebleau Magicien. If you don't succeed, then you simply get the award of the Vieux Chien – the Old Dog, and your friends will no doubt remind you of your new status in life.

To make life easy, we have arranged the circuits in ascending order of difficulty. You are well advised to attempt the easier circuits first with the Magicien challenge, since I even once saw a world class boulderer fall of a blue problem! So don't underestimate the challenge, it's a good one. You will also find that 50-60 problems in a day is a marathon, I can guarantee that you need to find the first 20 problems quite easy, to stand any chance of making it to the end. We had a friend who got to the last problem with only 7 falls, and then blew it, a laugh you are sure to have. One big advantage with the challenge, is that because you only try most problems once, you never wear the same piece of skin or tire the same muscles - really handy in Font. To get the most out of Font, I recommend a 3 day climbing cycle: Attempt a full easyish circuit on the first day, then apply yourself to hard problems on the following day, then have a rest day. This combination leaves you powerful for the second day, but gives your skin a 2-day rest between really damaging sessions. When you've travelled a long way to come to Font, it may seem crazy not to climb for a day; but in the end - you will agree.

Dieses Buch wurde für Kletterer gemacht, die eine entspannte und lockere Klettereinstellung haben und ist ein ideales Standartwerk für alle, die Sportrouten von 5a bis 7a klettern. Es umfasst 50 Kletterparcours im mittleren Schwierigkeitsgrad mit etwa 2000+ Kletterproblemen. Die bekannten Gebiete sind aufgeführt, aber ebenso die ruhigeren Teile des Waldes, die sich für einen Tagesausflug eignen. Font ist riesig und es gibt ungefähr 30.000 Kletterprobleme – das bedeutet auch 30.000 verschiedene Standorte. Dieser Kletterführer liefert eine enorme Menge an Informationen, aber der Kauf der lokalen IGN-Karte (1-25.00 blau) wird immer empfohlen. Fontainebleau bietet herausragende Klettermöglichkeiten an 365 Tagen im Jahr, einzig und allein der Regen kann einen aufhalten. Bitte beachtet, das nasser Sandstein empfindlich ist, nicht daran ziehen oder Routen nutzen, bevor der Stein vollkommen trocken ist. Sonnige Hügel sind im Winter ideal, leicht schattige Teile eignen sich für Frühling oder Herbst und nordseitig gelegene moosbedeckte Gebiete sind im Sommer ideal.

Orange 13 - 3b+, Isatis; Katia Dore

An natürlicher Erosion kann man nichts ändern, an „menschlicher Erosion" sehr wohl. Nehmt beim Zustieg in Steilstücken kleinwinklige Zick-Zack-Wege und versucht, zum Abstieg große Blöcke zu nehmen, die sich nicht bewegen. Nehmt ein Crash-pad um den Untergrund zu schützen weil überhängende Boulder einen weichen Untergrund haben, der sich schnell abträgt, so dass sie umstürzen. Eine Gefahr für den Kletterer sind Hornissen (Frelons) die oft in Löchern nisten, die etwa handtellergroß sind. Im gesamten Wald ist wildes Campen verboten. Campingplätze, Einkaufsmöglichkeiten usw. findet ihr auf unseren Touristikseiten. Achtung: Schwimmbäder in Frankreich erlauben nur eng anliegende Badeslips, keine Boxershorts, denkt also daran, eine Badehose mitzubringen. Ihr benötigt ein Auto, weil es im gesamten Waldgebiet kein öffentliches Verkehrssystem gibt. Alternativ reicht auch ein Fahrrad, viele Kletterer mieten einfach ein „Gite" für eine Woche und fahren dann mit dem Rad zu den Klettergebieten. Es gibt viele gut gelegene Parkplätze im Waldgebiet, die aber unbewacht sind. Diebe gibt es im gesamten Klettergebiet. Sie

brechen „jedes Fenster" auf um in „jedes Auto" zu gelangen, in das sie wollen. Das Auto abzuschließen scheint fast sinnlos, deshalb niemals irgendetwas im Auto lassen! Im Wald gibt es keine Toiletten, wenn ihr also zum Klo müsst, beachtet die „50-Meter-Regel" und hinterlasst nichts im Umkreis von 50 Metern um einen Boulder. Denkt genau darüber nach, wie ihr euch fühlen würdet, wenn jemand euer „Sitzstartproblem" als Toilette benutzt hätte.

Fontainebleau hat einmalige Kletterparcours. Die Parcoursanfänge sind mit einem D („depart") gekennzeichnet, gefolgt von kleinen Pfeilen mit Nummern. Die Farbe der Pfeile gibt den Schwierigkeitsgrad an (ähnlich wie bei Skiabfahrten) und variiert. Einige Parcours sind farbig markiert, andere nicht. Es gibt ca. 250 markierte und 300 unmarkierte Parcours im gesamten Waldgebiet. Achtung: manchmal kann es auch bei markierten Parcours echt schwer sein, ihnen zu folgen. Das Geheimnis des guten Kletterns in Font sind absolut saubere Schuhsohlen. Bringt (zusätzlich zum Crashpad) unbedingt ein kleines Stück Teppich oder Fußmatte mit. Die meisten Kletterer haben auch „Pof" dabei, einen zusammengebundenen Stofflappen, der zerstoßenes Kolophonium (ein Harz) enthält. Es ist ein klebriges Pulver, das die Hände griffiger macht, aber nicht trocknet. Wenn ihr an einem heißen Tag in der Sonne klettert, werdet ihr also Tonnen von Chalk benötigen. Aber andererseits: warum nicht im Schatten klettern an einem heißen Tag und den Fels sauber lassen? Wenn man sich immer ein „cooles" Problem aussucht, wird man selten Chalk benötigen. Das Klettern ist sehr intensiv hier und kleinste Griffe werden euren Fingerkuppen schwer zusetzen, also empfehlen wir, viele verschiedene Kletterprobleme in unterschiedlichen Stilen zu probieren. Wo immer möglich, solltet ihr mit einem Spotter, einem Kletterpartner, der euren Sturz abbremst klettern. Auch ein Sturz von wenigen Metern kann Verletzungsfolgen haben.

Unser unterhaltsamer „Magicien Challenge": die witzige Idee ist, einen ganzen Parcours in einem Tag zu klettern und dabei maximal 10 Mal zu stürzen. Unser Ziel dabei ist eine nette lustige Herausforderung, die für jeden Kletterer mit mittlerem Standart möglich ist. In der rechten Spalte kann die Zahl der Stürze notiert werden. Lächerlich schwere Probleme sind nicht im „Challenge" enthalten und werden mit einem X markiert. Wir warnen euch vor den 10 schwersten Problemen jedes Parcours und geben sie euch in der Reihenfolge der Schwierigkeit nach an, beginnend mit der 1 als schwierigstem Problem. Es gibt nichts zu gewinnen außer unserem scherzhaften Ritterschlag zum „Fontainebleau Magicien", dem „Zauberer von Fontainebleau". Wenn ihr versagst, bekommt ihr lediglich die Auszeichnung des „Vieux Chien", des alten Hundes, und eure Freunde werden lebenslänglich über euren neuen Titel lachen. Wir haben die Parcours in aufsteigender Reihenfolge der Schwierigkeit nach geordnet und es ist ein guter Rat, zuerst die einfacheren Parcours im Magicien Challenge zu versuchen. Ihr werdet auch bald herausfinden, dass 50-60 Probleme am Tag ein Marathon sind. Ein großer Vorteil des Challenge ist, das ihr euch selten dieselben Hautstellen abschürft oder die gleichen Muskeln ermüdet, weil man die meisten Probleme nur einmal versucht. Es ist eine echt nette Alternative dazu, nur harte Probleme zu klettern.

Ciel au dessus Dame Jouanne

Thunderstorm on its way into Barbizon

Questa guida è specializzata per scalatori che hanno un'attitudine rilassata e piacevole ed è specifica per tutti quelli che scalano vie sportive di 5°-7°. Copre 50 circuiti di roccia di media difficoltà con circa 2000+ problematiche da risolvere. Ci occupiamo delle zone più conosciute ma anche delle zone più tranquille della foresta che sono ideali per una gita piacevole di un giorno. Fontainebleau è molto vasta e ci sono circa 30.000 problematiche, perciò 30.000 località differenti. Questa guida fornisce un'enorme quantità di informazioni, ma raccomandiamo anche l'acquisto di una cartina locale IGN(1-25.000 blu). Fontainebleau offre eccellenti arrampicate 365 giorni all'anno, solo la pioggia potrà fermarvi! Per favore notate che la roccia arenaria bagnata è debole, non tiratevi su e non usatela finchè non è completamente asciutta. Le cime soleggiate sono ideali in inverno, le parti leggermente ombreggiate in primavera ed autunno e le zone a nord, coperte di muschio, sono ideali in estate.

Non si può far nulla per limitare l'erosione naturale, ma per quella causata da esseri umani si può intervenire. Nelle discese ripide, scegliete i sentieri facili a zigzag, sia per salire che per scendere, e cercate di spostarvi su lle pietre più grandi che non si muovono. Usate un 'bouldering mat' per proteggere il terreno dato che i 'undercut boulders' (tagliati sotto) hanno una superficie morbida, si consumano velocemente e spesso cadono. Un pericolo per gli arrampicatori sono i calabroni che spesso nidificano in buchi pressappoco grandi come una mano. Il campeggio libero non è ammesso nella foresta. Per campeggi, negozi ecc. vedere le nostre 'pagine turistiche.' Attenzione: nelle piscine francesi è necessario indossare costumi aderenti tipo slip, perciò non dimenticatelo a casa. Avete bisogno di una automobile, dato che non c'è servizio pubblico nella foresta. Anche la bicicletta è molto utile; molti arrampicatori affittano un gite per una settimana, poi usano la bicicletta per raggiungere la zona da arrampicare. Ci sono molti parcheggi utili nella foresta, ma non sono controllati. Ci sono molti criminali nella zona; spesso rompono i vetri per rubare qualsiasi tipo di automobile. Chiudere a chiave la macchina serve poco, non lasciate nulla nella vostra vettura! Non ci sono gabinetti nella foresta, perciò, se dovete, seguite la regola dei 50 metri, non sporcate entro i 50 metri dal boulder. Pensate attentamente quanto vi piacerebbe se qualcuno usasse la vostra 'problematica con partenza da seduto' come gabinetto!

Fontainebleau ha circuiti di bouldering particolari che iniziano da una problematica di partenza D (Depart), seguita da piccole frecce e numeri. I colori rappresentano varie difficoltà come sulle piste da sci e variano. Alcuni sono marcati con varie pitture, altri sono lasciati vuoti. Ci sono circa 250 circuiti marcati nella foresta e 250 non segnati. Attenzione: anche i circuiti segnati possono essere veramente difficili da seguire. Il segreto per arrampicarsi bene e facilmente in Fontainebleau è di mantenere la suola delle vostre scarpe veramente pulita. Portatevi anche un piccolo tappetino (oltre al bouldering mat).

La maggior parte degli arrampicatori locali usa un "pof," uno straccio che racchiude resina polverizzata (colophony). E' una polvere appiccicosa, biodegradabile, e aiuta (ma non vi asciuga molto bene la pelle). Se vi arrampicate in una zona soleggiata in una giornata molto calda avrete bisogno di una grande quantità di gesso, ma sarebbe meglio arrampicarsi in una zona ombreggiata in una giornata calda e lasciare la roccia pulita. Scegliete sempre una problematica fresca e avrete bisogno del gesso raramente. L'arrampicata qui è intensiva e le piccole prese urtano e spelano male la punta delle dita, perciò è raccomandabile provare problematiche diverse con stili differenti. Arrampicatevi sempre con un osservatore se possibile, anche una caduta di pochi metri può causare ferite.

La nostra divertente "Gara del Mago" (Magicien Challenge). Questa piacevole idea è di arrampicare in una giornata un circuito completo, con un massimo di solo 10 cadute. Noi cerchiamo di organizzare una gara piacevole e divertente, a cui possano partecipare arrampicatori di media abilità. La colonna a destra è per marcare il vostro numero di cadute. Problematiche esageratamente difficili non sono incluse nella gara e sono marcate con X. Vi informiamo sulle 10 più difficili problematiche di ogni circuito e le numeriamo secondo la difficoltà, numero 1 è la più difficile. Non si vince nulla a parte la nostra qualifica di "Mago di Fontainebleau." Se si perde, si ottiene il titolo di Vieux Chien (Vecchio Cane) e i vostri amici rideranno del vostro nuovo titolo. Abbiamo organizzato i circuiti in ordine crescente di difficoltà e vi suggeriamo di provare prima i circuiti più facili della Gara del Mago. Troverete anche che, 50-60 problematiche in un giorno sono come una maratona. Un grande vantaggio della Gara è che, dato che provi la maggior parte delle problematiche soltanto una volta durante la giornata, non consumi mai lo stesso pezzo di pelle o usi e stanchi gli stessi muscoli. E' una piacevole alternativa al cercare di risolvere problematiche difficili.

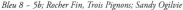

Bleu 8 - 5b; Rocher Fin, Trois Pignons; Sandy Ogilvie

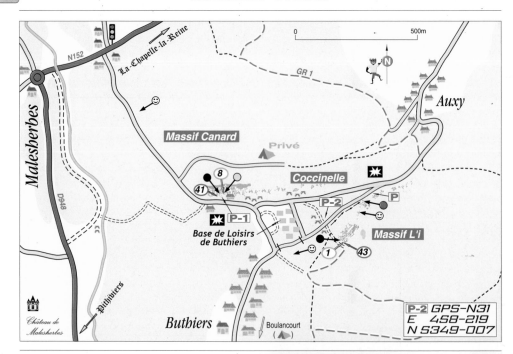

On map: N152, La Chapelle-la-Reine, Malesherbes, D948, D, Massif Canard, Privé, Coccinelle, GR 1, Auxy, P-2, P, Massif L'i, P-1, Base de Loisirs de Buthiers, Château de Malesherbes, Pithiviers, Buthiers, Boulancourt, 0 — 500m, N

P-2 GPS-N31
E 458-219
N S349-007

Circuit	Cot.	Ang.	Prob-Var	Bois	Expo	Info

MASSIF CANARD (p 70 & 280)

Circuit	Cot.	Ang.	Prob-Var	Bois	Expo	Info
☺	ENF	1-2		27		Yum	Fun
	PD-	1a-6a		29		HBall	Cool
	AD	3-4b		34		CP	Cool
	D+	3a-5b		40 & (2)		HBall	
	ED	6b-7a		22		HBall	☺
♦	ABO	6c-8a		14		DBall	Pump

MASSIF DE LA COCCINELLE

| | ABO | 7a-8a | | 25 | Q-D | SS | Pump |

MASSIF L'I (p 24 & 290)

☺	ENF	1-2		25?		Yum	Fun
	AD-	3-4b		44		S	☺
	D+	3a-5b		41 & (2)		HBall	
	TD+	5a-6b		35		Cool	
	ED-	5a-6c		39	Q-D	HBall	Cool
♦	ABO	7a-8a		14		Cool	

Massif L'i, Orange Fun – 2a; Jenny Van Santen

La route des Trois Pignons à Malesherbes, en passant par Vaudoué, est tranquille et belle, et vous permet d'accéder à la zone d'escalade de Buthiers en environ 15 minutes. Il est conseillé de visiter ce massif situé au sud de la forêt car le temps y est souvent meilleur. Il y a à Buthiers une base de plein-air avec courts de tennis, parc à roller, parking et tables de pique-nique, le tout entouré d'un site naturel d'escalade composé de blocs de toutes taille. Il y a 4 secteurs d'escalade variés depuis les circuits pour les enfants jusqu'à des 7c et des 8a extrêmes. Le secteur massif L'I est très compact, les blocs sont proches les uns des autres et les aires de réception sont en général plutôt bonnes. La roche est plus friable qu'à certains autres sites - comme Franchard par exemple - alors soyez prudent avec vos pieds. Dans le Massif L'I il y a 4 circuits, d'orange à noir, offrant des voies accessibles à tous les grimpeurs quel que soit leur niveau. Le circuit orange est une introduction sympa aux passages de moyennes difficultés avec seulement quelques-uns à proscrire aux débutants du fait de leur hauteur. Le circuit est bien ombragé et se suit logiquement dans le sens des aiguilles d'une montre. La plage de sable au milieu de tous ces blocs est idéale pour un pique-nique ou pour un moment de détente entre amis. Le circuit débute de manière plaisante avec de beaux passages, puis s'anime progressivement avec le surplomb (8). Nous avons donné à 5 passages du circuit la cotation de 1c, qui est le niveau de difficulté pour une voie qui peut se faire purement en équilibre sans utiliser les mains. Sympa à essayer. Les (18) et (21) testeront l'habileté des débutants sur les grattons. L'angle géant du (32) doit s'aborder tranquillement, il a de bonnes prises en dépit du quartz très glissant. Certaines flèches manquent au circuit cependant il reste facile à suivre et des variantes peuvent également être ajoutées. Il se termine avec 3 dalles très jolies toutes plaisantes et sympa, comme le reste du circuit.

Orange 30 ~ 3c- ; Wobbly

Orange 7 ~ 3b; La Jeune fille

Orange 5 – 1c+; Jean-luc Laval

BUTHIERS - MASSIF L'I - (AD-/Orange)

The road to Malesherbes from the Trois Pignons forest via Vaudoué is quiet and well made, allowing you to reach the southern climbing areas around Buthiers in around 15 minutes. This detour south is often worthwhile since this area gets fractionally better weather than the boulders to the north of Fontainebleau. The whole area has been developed into a 'Base de Loisirs' (outdoor centre). It has been well thought out with tennis, skateboarding, parking & picnic areas - all interspersed between the rocky outcrops of climbing that remain a natural unorganised chaos of small and high blocks. There are 4 different climbing sectors which offer everything from kiddies circuits up to desperate 7c and 8a problems. The massif L'i sector is very compact with boulders close together and generally good landings. The rock is softer than outcrops such as Franchard, so please be considerate and careful with your feet. There are four circuits from orange-black in the massif L'i, offering something for everyone. The orange circuit is a lovely introduction to climbing in the lower middle grades, with only a couple of problems to be excluded for beginners since they are perhaps a bit too high for comfort and safety. The circuit takes a natural clockwise direction around the outcrop and is nicely shaded by trees. There is a large sandy area enclosed by the boulders shown on our topo, and this makes an ideal spot for a group picnic. The circuit starts pleasantly with some nice and friendly problems, gradually warming up to an energetic punch with the overhang at (8). We give a total of 5 problems on the circuit grade-1c, our grade for a climb that can be done with pure balance, and is possible without using your hands on any of the holds or even touching the rock; it's great fun to try. (18) & (21) will test the crimp strength for most beginners and may prove to be a bit too powerful. The giant corner of (32) needs a cool approach, but does have good holds in spite of the horribly slippery quartz sheet for the feet. There is also a central labyrinth area that makes an ideal spot for trying out chimney technique. Historically, the numbers have been haphazard with some missing, but the circuit is still easy to follow and add your own variations. It finishes with 3 lovely slab climbs, all fun and friendly – the character of this circuit.

Orange 35 ~ 3b; Matt Nicholson

"Sans Mains - No Hands"

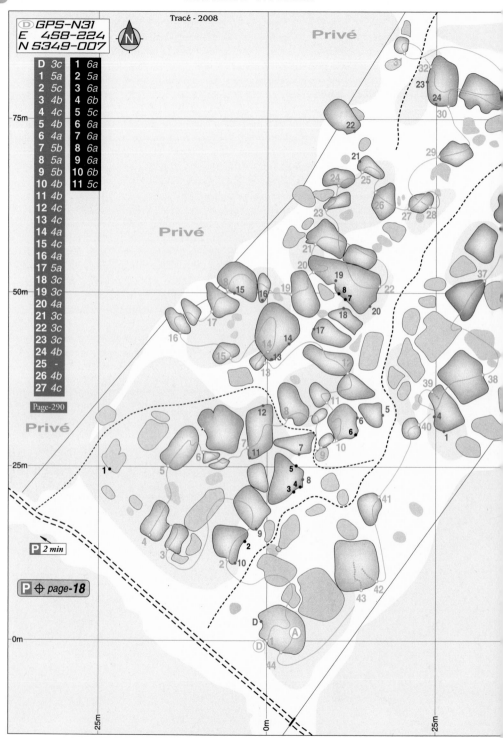

Tracé - 2008

GPS-N31
E 458-224
N 5349-007

D	3c		1	6a
1	5a		2	5a
2	5c		3	6a
3	4b		4	6b
4	4c		5	5c
5	4b		6	6a
6	4a		7	6a
7	5b		8	6a
8	5a		9	6a
9	5b		10	6b
10	4b		11	5c
11	4b			
12	4c			
13	4c			
14	4a			
15	4c			
16	4a			
17	5a			
18	3c			
19	3c			
20	4a			
21	3c			
22	3c			
23	3c			
24	4b			
25	-			
26	4b			
27	4c			

Page-290

Privé

Privé

Privé

75m

50m

25m

0m

P 2 min

P ⊕ page-18

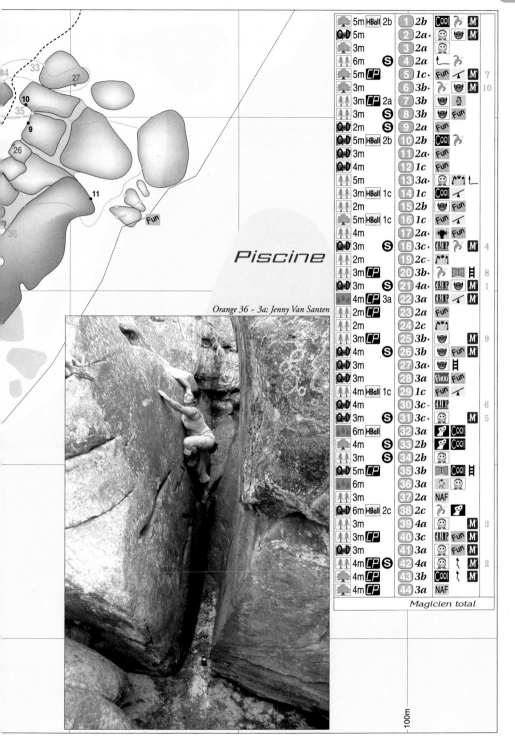

Piscine

Orange 36 – 3a; Jenny Van Santen

N°	Dist.	Grade		Score
1	5m HBall 2b	2b	Cool	
2	Q-D 5m	2a+		
3	3m	2a		
4	6m S	2a		
5	5m CP	1c+	Fun	7
6	3m	3b-		10
7	3m CP 2a	3b		
8	3m S	3b	Fun	
9	Q-D 2m S	2a	Fun	
10	Q-D 5m HBall 2b	2b	Cool	
11	Q-D 3m	2a+	Fun	
12	Q-D 4m	1c	Fun	
13	5m	3a+		
14	3m HBall 1c	1c	Cool	
15	2m	2b	Fun	
16	5m HBall 1c	1c	Fun	
17	4m	2a+	Fun	
18	Q-D 3m S	3c+	CRIMP	4
19	2m	2c-		
20	3m CP	3b+		8
21	Q-D 3m S	4a+	CRIMP	1
22	4m CP 3a	3a	CRIMP	
23	2m CP	2a	Fun	
24	2m	2c		
25	3m CP	3b+		9
26	Q-D 4m S	3b	Fun	
27	Q-D 3m	3a+		
28	Q-D 3m	3a	Flexi Fun	
29	4m HBall 1c	1c	Fun	
30	Q-D 4m	3c-	CRIMP	6
31	Q-D 3m S	3c+		5
32	6m HBall	3a	Cool	
33	4m S	2b	Cool	
34	3m S	2b		
35	Q-D 5m CP	3b	Cool	
36	6m	3a		
37	3m	2a	NAF	
38	Q-D 6m HBall 2c	2c		
39	4m	4a		3
40	3m CP	3c	CRIMP Fun	
41	Q-D 3m	3a	Fun	
42	4m CP S	4a		2
43	4m CP	3b	Cool	
44	4m CP	3a	NAF	

Magicien total

-100m

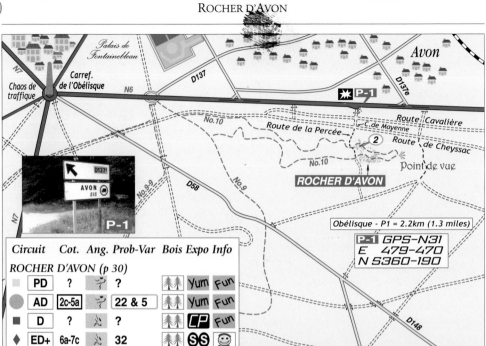

Circuit		Cot.	Ang.	Prob-Var	Bois	Expo	Info
ROCHER D'AVON (p 30)							
▪	PD	?	🧗	?	🌲🌲	Yum	Fun
●	AD	2c-5a	🧗	22 & 5	🌲🌲	Yum	Fun
▪	D	?	🧗	?	🌲🌲	CP	Fun
♦	ED+	6a-7c	🧗	32	🌲🌲	SS	🙂

Obélisque - P1 = 2.2km (1.3 miles)

P-1 GPS–N31
E   479–470
N S360–190

Orange 11b – 3b+; James Bacon

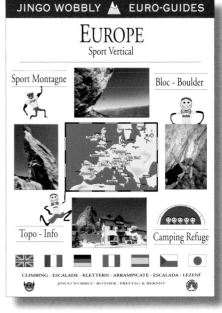

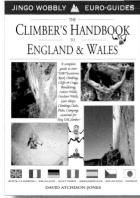

C'est l'un des massifs les plus calmes de la forêt avec un circuit orange plutôt court qui n 'apparaît que dans très peu de topos et un ensemble de passages hors circuit très difficile (7b) qui attirent quelques grimpeurs extrêmes. Le site est cependant pollué par le bruit de la RN-6 toute proche, toutefois assourdi par les arbres. Les blocs contournent une crête qui part du Nord avec une forêt de chênes dense qui peu à peu s'éclaircie pour faire place à une forêt de pins où tout sèche rapidement. Ce circuit offre des passages non balisés aussi intéressant que ceux qui le sont. Bien qu'il n'ait qu'une vingtaine de voies, la réalisation de l'ensemble de ce circuit est épuisante. Le départ est assez bizarre puisqu'il monte et redescend sur le même mètre carré de rocher, mais ne le laissez pas vous décourager. La crête de blocs qui vous emmène vers le (2) est plus représentative du circuit. Il est étrange que la petite dalle entre le (2) et le (3) ne fasse pas partie du circuit - trop facile peut-être ; nous l'avons toutefois ajouté à notre liste du défi du magicien @ 1c - aucune prise n'est permise pour les mains ce qui rend le passage bien plus intéressant. Après les premiers blocs, le circuit suit un sentier sinueux par-dessus des petites bosses et le long de rochers nus. Les problèmes du (6 au 13) sont sympathiques et parfaits pour ceux qui veulent simplement apprécier la beauté du mouvement plutôt que de se soucier de leur force ou de leur technique. Le groupe de blocs au (14) offre les meilleurs passages avec des niveaux de difficulté très variés, de bonnes aires de réception et un séchage rapide. Il se situe tout près du circuit pédestre bleu 10 et reste une zone sympa pour ceux qui ne grimpent pas. Entre le (17) et le (18) la végétation est très dense, mais le (18b) vaut la peine d'être essayé – accès rapide depuis le sentier principal. Pour finir, la montée du Petite Dame d'Avon demande concentration et jugement. Le dernier toit est exposé mais délirant, et les prises sont géniales telles votre exultation si vous le réussissez.

This is one of the quieter areas of the forest and has all the classic ingredients to make it so. It has a small orange circuit that doesn't feature in many other books, and a good collection of super hard desperate (7b) off circuit problems that attract very few punters. You can hear the hum of the main RN-6 not far away, but fortunately it is well dampened by the trees to even make this a pleasant picnic spot. The rocks circumnavigate a ridge, which starts on the northern side in dense oak trees, but then quickly thins out to a lovely pine area that dries out very quickly. This circuit is very much in the 'classical style,' with the climbing between the problems as important and as interesting as the individual marked problems. It may only have 20 individual stopping points, but the complete trip makes for a good work out and is quite tiring. The start is very bizarre as an 'up-down' on the same square metre of rock, don't get put off by this. The ridge of rock leading away down to (2) is more illustrative of the trip: a lot easier than slack rope walking, but still a test of balance and fun for beginners. It is uncanny how the little slab between (2) and (3) escapes being a numbered problem on the circuit – too easy perhaps; we include it on our magician challenge @ 1c – but no hand holds are allowed which makes for great fun. The circuit after the starting boulders takes an excellent winding trail over small humps and along bare rock whenever possible, throwing in a big daunting descent which is actually very pleasant. This central part (6-13), is a lovely wandering trip and is perfect for those just wanting to move over rock without too many technical headaches or power problems. The cluster of boulders at (14) supplies the test piece problems in all grades, plus being quick drying with flat landings. This spot is just off the blue footpath-10, and is an ideal hang out if any of your group are non-climbers (good picnic spot & crash pad drop off area). The circuit is jungleyfied between (17) & (18), but (18b) is a problem worth doing with a wild descent down the nose – just nip back from the main footpath. The finale up the giant Petite Dame d'Avon demands concentration and judgement. The final roof is wild and committing, but the holds are great, as is the elation if you succeed.

Orange 7 ~ 2c; James Bacon

Orange 20 ~ 2c; James Bacon

Orange 9 ~ 4a; James Bacon

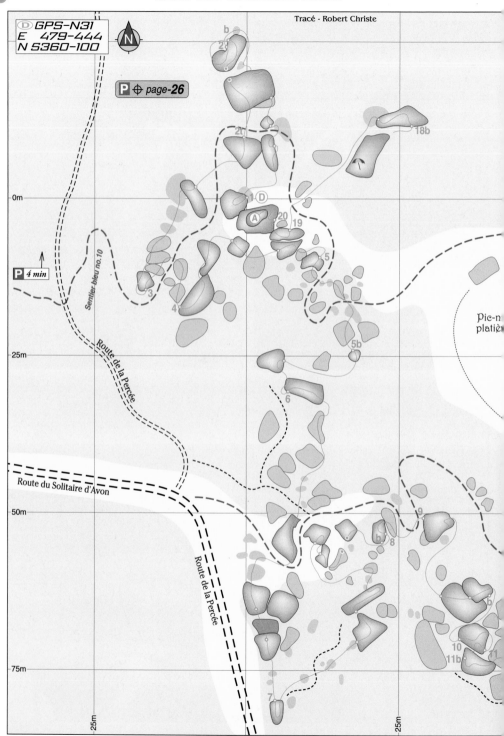

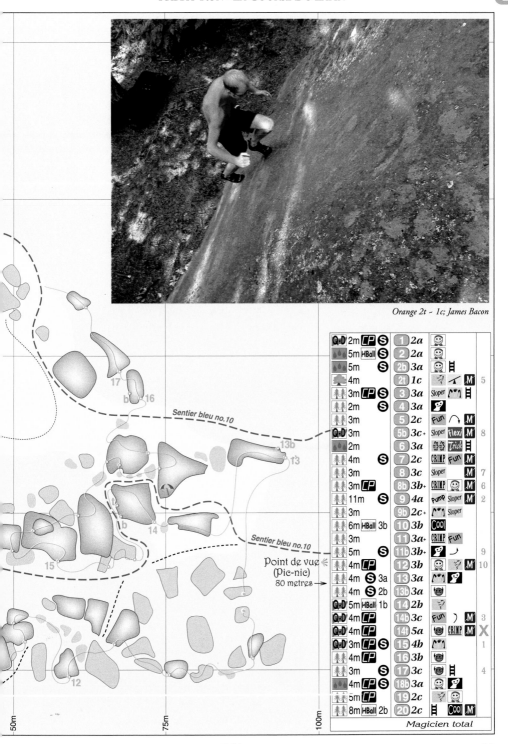

Orange 2t ~ 1c; James Bacon

Q~D	2m	CP S	① 2a	😊			
⛰	5m	HBall S	② 2a	😊			
⛰	5m	S	2b 3a	😊	☷		
♣	4m		2t 1c	🏃 ⤢	.M	5	
🌲	3m	CP S	③ 3a	Sloper ⌢ ☷			
🌲	2m	S	④ 3a	🔲			
🌲	3m		⑤ 2c	Fun ⌢	.M		
Q~D	3m		5b 3c+	Sloper Flexi	.M	8	
🌲	2m		⑥ 3a	✕✕ Trick	☷		
🌲🌲	4m		⑦ 2c	CRIMP Fun		7	
🌲	3m		⑧ 3c	Sloper	.M		
🌲	3m	CP	8b 3b+	CRIMP 😊	.M	6	
🌲	11m	S	⑨ 4a	Pump Sloper	.M	2	
🌲	3m		9b 2c+	⌢ Sloper			
🌲	6m	HBall 3b	⑩ 3b	COOl			
🌲	3m		⑪ 3a	CRIMP Fun			
🌲	5m	S	11b 3b+	🔲 ⌣		9	
🌲	4m	CP	⑫ 3b	😊 🎋	.M	10	
🌲	4m	S 3a	13a 3a	⌢ 🔲			
🌲	4m	S 2b	13b 3a	😊			
Q~D	5m	HBall 1b	⑭ 2b	🎋			
Q~D	4m	CP	14b 3c	Fun ⌣	.M	3	
Q~D	4m	CP	14t 5a	😊 CRIMP	.M	X	
Q~D	3m	CP S	⑮ 4b	⌢		1	
🌲	4m	CP	⑯ 3b	😊			
🌲	3m	S	⑰ 3c	😊 ☷		4	
🌲🌲	4m	CP S	18b 3a	😊			
🌲	5m	CP	⑲ 2c	😊 😊			
🌲	8m	HBall 2b	⑳ 2c	☷ COOl .M			
				Magicien total			

Sentier bleu no.10

Sentier bleu no.10

Point de vue
(Pic-nic)
80 mètres →

17

b 16

13b

13

b 14

15

12

50m 75m 100m

Si vous visitez le site du Rocher Fin, il est en général préférable d'y passer la journée, puisqu'il est assez éloigné du parking . Pendant de nombreuses années, ce fût l'un des plus jolis sites d'escalade de la forêt, notamment grâce à son sable doré et ses grands arbres magnifiques. Malheureusement le massif fût dévasté par la tempête de 1999 et bien que la plupart des arbres furent dégagés, certains furent laissés à une décomposition naturelle, rendant le site peu attrayant. Cependant avec le temps les arbres verts réapparaîtront pour faire revivre la beauté de ce site. Le nom du circuit vient du superbe bloc en forme de cube situé en haut de la colline, offrant une voie très patinée et difficile. Le circuit orange commence en bas de la colline avec tous les autres circuits puis suit les blocs qui sont dispersés sur le versant de cette même colline. Les premiers passages sont simples et permettent de s'échauffer en douceur puisqu'ils ne sont pas très athlétiques – idéal pour l'initiation. Par la suite le circuit demande plus d'efforts donc n'abandonnez pas si au départ vous trouvez les passages trop faciles. Attention au niveau de difficulté du circuit bleu qui est pratiquement de 3 cotations supplémentaires. Assurez-vous donc de rester sur l'orange. Bien que la majorité des passages soit d'un niveau de difficulté tres modéré, il est possible de rehausser cette difficulté selon la technique choisie; le (33) en est un très bon exemple puisqu'une bicyclette peut être utilisée ce qui a 4b rend le passage très intéressant. Les aires de réception sont excellentes, puisqu'en grande partie sableuse, et seulement quelques passages nécessitent une parade. Le site, qui offre au total 4 circuits, est parfait pour les groupes de grimpeurs dont chaque individu a un niveau d'escalade différent. Si vous aimez le Cul de Chien et ses plages de sable fin alors vous apprécierez le Rocher Fin et ses blocs de petite taille.

Orange 40 ~ 3b; Wobbly

ROCHER FIN

Orange 33 ~ 3c+; Phillip Hogan

A trip to Rocher Fin is generally an all day affair 'avec picnic,' since it is about the farthest outcrop from any of the parking areas. For many years it was one of the most beautiful settings in the forest, with lovely golden sand and tall trees, an idyllic picnic spot. Unfortunately, it was massacred by the great storm of 1999 which brought down a great many of the majestic trees. Many of the felled trees were cleared from the actual boulders, but the area has been left to decay naturally and is hardly pleasing to the eye at present. Alas, nature will take its time and in the future, the beautiful bright green trees will return to enhance the areas quiet serenity. The circuit is named after the superb, giant finishing 'Cube' boulder, where the orange circuit climaxes at the top of the hill with a highly slippery and desperado problem. The orange circuit starts at the base of the hill with all the other circuits, and then takes a convenient line following the scattered boulders up the hill, being comfortable and pleasant with technicality throughout. The first couple of problems are straightforward and warm you up gently, and not developing too much angst during the first 10 problems – ideal for the learning climber. The circuit then develops with plenty of character and becomes more demanding, 'doubters' if you are finding it a bit easy at the beginning, stay with it since you will be rewarded. Beware, the blue circuit here is almost 3 grades harder, so you will be well advised to stick to the orange, and you happily don't then end up with pulverised fingertips either. Many problems should be sensibly climbed at a lowish grade, but many also have very good harder ways of doing them, (33) being a fine example where you can do an egyptian at 4b and really make the problem buzz. The landings are mostly sandy and good, with only a few problems really needing a spotter. The whole area has 4 fine circuits and is a good place for any group of mixed ability to enjoy the day. If you like Cul de Chien with with its beachy & sandy feel, you should enjoy it here, especially since most of the problems are on the small side.

"LE CUBE"

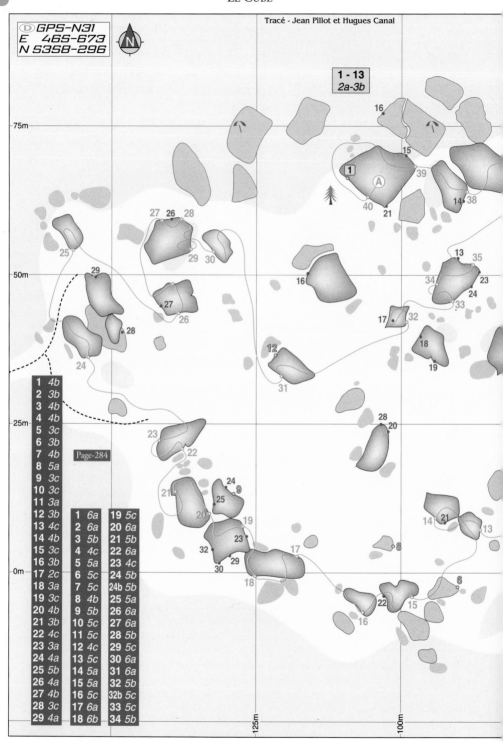

Tracé - Jean Pillot et Hugues Canal

GPS-N31
E 465-673
N 5358-296

1 - 13
2a-3b

1	4b
2	3b
3	4b
4	4b
5	3c
6	3b
7	4b
8	5a
9	3c
10	3c
11	3a
12	3b
13	4c
14	4b
15	3c
16	3b
17	2c
18	3a
19	3c
20	4b
21	3b
22	4c
23	3a
24	4a
25	5b
26	4a
27	4b
28	3c
29	4a

Page-284

1	6a
2	6a
3	5b
4	4c
5	5a
6	5c
7	5c
8	4b
9	5b
10	5c
11	5c
12	4c
13	5c
14	5a
15	5a
16	5c
17	6a
18	6b

19	5c
20	6a
21	5b
22	6a
23	4c
24	5b
24b	5b
25	5a
26	6a
27	6a
28	5b
29	5c
30	6a
31	6a
32	5b
32b	5c
33	5c
34	5b

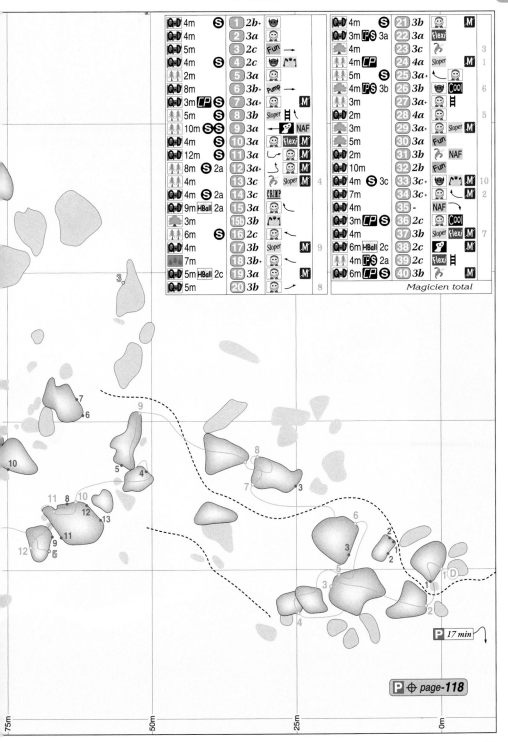

Q-D 4m Ⓢ	① 2b+ 😊
Q-D 4m	② 3a 😊
Q-D 5m	③ 2c Fun →
Q-D 4m Ⓢ	④ 2c 🐒 1
🌲 2m	⑤ 3a 😊
Q-D 8m	⑥ 3b+ Pump →
Q-D 3m CP	⑦ 3a+ 😊 M
🌲 5m Ⓢ	⑧ 3b Sloper 🪜↶
🌲 10m ⓈⓈ	⑨ 3a ← 🐒 NAF
Q-D 4m Ⓢ	⑩ 3a 😊 Flexi M
Q-D 12m Ⓢ	⑪ 3a ↶ 😊 M
🌲 8m Ⓢ 2a	⑫ 3a+ ↷ M
🌲 4m	⑬ 3c 🐒 Sloper M
Q-D 4m Ⓢ 2a	⑭ 3c CRIMP
Q-D 9m HBall 2a	⑮ 3a 😊 ↶
🌲 3m	⑮b 3b 🐒1
🌲 6m Ⓢ	⑯ 2c 😊 ↶
Q-D 4m	⑰ 3b Sloper M
🔺🔺🔺 7m	⑱ 3b+ 😊 ↶
Q-D 5m HBall 2c	⑲ 3a 😊 M
Q-D 5m	⑳ 3b 😊 ↶

Q-D 4m Ⓢ	㉑ 3b 😊 M
Q-D 3m P Ⓢ 3a	㉒ 3a Flexi
🌲 4m	㉓ 3c 🐒
🌲 4m CP	㉔ 4a Sloper M
🌲 5m Ⓢ	㉕ 3a+ 😊
🌲 4m P Ⓢ 3b	㉖ 3b 😊 Cool
🌲 3m	㉗ 3a+ 😊 🎚
Q-D 2m	㉘ 4a 😊
🌲 3m	㉙ 3a+ 😊 Sloper M
🌲 5m	㉚ 3a Fun
Q-D 2m	㉛ 3b 🐒 NAF
Q-D 10m	㉜ 2b Fun
Q-D 4m Ⓢ 3c	㉝ 3c+ 😊 🐒1 M
Q-D 7m	㉞ 3c+ 😊 ↷ M
Q-D 4m	㉟ - NAF ↘
Q-D 3m CP Ⓢ	㊱ 2c 😊 Cool
Q-D 4m	㊲ 3b Sloper Flexi M
Q-D 6m HBall 2c	㊳ 2c 🐒 M
🌲 4m P Ⓢ 2a	㊴ 2c Flexi 🎚 M
Q-D 6m CP Ⓢ	㊵ 3b 😊 M

Magicien total

	3
	1
	6
	5
	4
	9
	8

	10
	2
	7

P ⊕ *page-118*

P *17 min* ↘

75m 50m 25m 0m

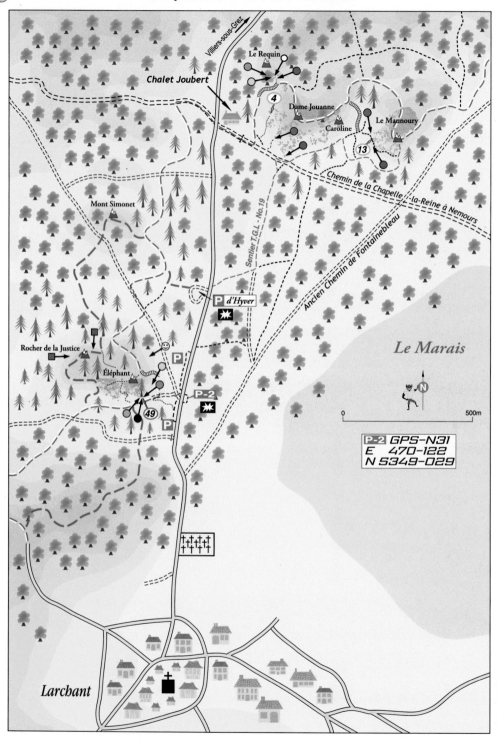

Circuit		Cot.	Ang.	Prob-Var	Bois	Expo	Info
REQUIN - DAME JOUANNE							
	PD	1-3a		50?	🌳	HBall	Fun
	AD+	2b-5a		76	🌳	DBall	👻
	TD	4c-6a		48	🌳	S	😈
○	ED	5b-7b		31	🌳	HBall	👻
DAME JOUANNE - CAROLINE (p 42)							
	AD	1c-4c		79 ?	Q-D	DBall	👻
	D	3-4c		50&(5)	Q-D	HBall	Cool
	TD-	4a-5c		58	Q-D	SS	😈
♦	ABO	6c-8a		10	Q-D	SS	👻
MAUNOURY (p 102)							
	AD-	1c-4b		54 & (6)	Q-D	DBall	Cool
	D-	3a-5b		71	Q-D	DBall	Cool
	TD+	5a-6b		36	Q-D	SS	😈
♦	ABO	7a-7c		16	Q-D	😈	😈
ÉLÉPHANT (p 328)							
☺	ENF	1-2		?	Q-D	Yum	Fun
	AD-	2a-3c		35 +	Q-D	CP	Fun
	AD	2b-4a		44 & (2)	Q-D	DBall	Cool
	D	2b-5c		64&(24)	Q-D	DBall	👻
	TD	3b-6b		30 & (1)	Q-D	HBall	SS
●	ED-	6a-6c		40 & (2)	Q-D	HBall	😈
♦	ABO	7a-8a		40	Q-D	HBall	👻
ROCHER DE LA JUSTICE							
	D	2b-5c		24&(14)	💧	DBall	👻
■	TD	5a-6b		?	💧	👻	BUZZ

BEAL — LA PASSION DANS L'ÂME

Sector REQUIN

Orange 17 - 3b; Libby Graham

DAME JOUANNE - (AD/Orange)

Une visite au sud de Larchant pour y découvrir les sites de la Dame Jouanne, de Maunoury ou de l'Elephant, est toujours fantastique. Lorsque vous quittez la forêt des trois Pignons à Vaudoué, prenez la direction de la Chapelle-La-Reine puis de Larchant. Dans les bois au-dessous de la Dame Jouanne, se situe le Chalet Jobert qui offre d'excellents repas et une bonne bière après une longue journée d'escalade. Il est recommandé de se garer au parking "d'Hyver" car il n'est qu'à quelques minutes des blocs. C'est certainement un site où vous aurez besoin d'être échauffé puisque avec des passages de 12m de hauteur ce n'est pas un crash pad qui vous sortira d'affaire. De nombreux blocs sur ce circuit sont très hauts et attirent surtout et à mon avis les psychotiques ou les fanatiques du suicide ! Cependant le circuit orange est tres intéressant puisqu'il offre divers passages sur des rochers de faible hauteur, toutefois entrecoupés de très hauts blocs. Notre topo vous permettra d'éviter les passages les plus hauts, mais nous vous conseillons cependant de faire la majorité des voies de ce circuit pour apprécier pleinement l'escalade dans ce chaos de blocs. À l'origine il y avait un circuit jaune gigantesque avec plus de 100 passages qui fut par la suite divisé pour donner un circuit jaune plus court à l'ouest du secteur Requin et un second circuit balisé en orange avec environ 80 voies. L'idée qu'un grimpeur puisse apprécier 50 a 60 passages en une seule journée me laisse perplexe, surtout lorsque le circuit est de difficulté moyenne et semble interminable. Pour notre guide, nous avons raccourci le circuit orange afin de finir plus naturellement au (54) qui vous fera grimper les 15 mètres du bloc de la Caroline. C'est l'endroit idéal pour terminer la journée et pour profiter d'une superbe vue sur Maunoury. Pour ceux encore plein d'énergie, il est possible de reprendre le circuit pour retourner à la Dame Jouanne. Pour les autres, il est conseillé de suivre le sentier. Nous avons classifié les blocs Caroline et Dame Jouanne de dangereux, alors soyez prudent.

Orange 23 – 4a; Jingo

A trip down south to Larchant, visiting either Dame Jouanne, Maunoury or Éléphant is always magical. Leaving the forest of Trois Pignons at Vaudoué, you drive up onto the high plains that surround La Chapelle-La-Reine, and immediately experience a feeling of freeness. Here the cloudscapes are majestic (as more rain thunders in from the west!), and you immediately feel that you are going to somewhere quite different. Nipping through the back lanes, you pass through countryside with real farms, instead of cute weekend homes for overpaid city folk. In the woods beneath Dame Jouanne, you will find Chalet Joubert, an old lodge that serves excellent meals and a cool beer at the end of a good day. Parking down the road at the Hyver car park is advised, giving a few minutes walk to the rocks and a chance to warm up the body. It's certainly a place where you want to be warmed up since a crash pad is of academic use from 12 metres up. Many of the circuits here are complete highballs and are of appeal to semi-psychotic, suicidal addicts. The orange however, is a nice compromise and offers a good array of smaller boulders, separated by occasional highballs. Our topo will be of use in working out the higher nasties to bypass, yet still follow the circuit and really enjoy climbing in this superb arena of rock chaos. Originally there was a giant yellow circuit of over 100 problems. This was then divided, leaving a shorter yellow circuit, high up at the western Requin area. The second part was repainted orange, and gives a pretty hefty weight of around 80 problems. The prospect of anyone enjoying over 50-60 problems in a single day somewhat perplexes me, especially when the circuit is of medium difficulty and just seems to keep on going with endless tedium. For our book, we have shortened the orange circuit to a natural conclusion at (54), which ends with an incredible finale on top of the giant 15-metre block of La Caroline. This is a lovely place to finish the day and somewhere to enjoy the fabulous view of Maunoury. For those with extra energy you can follow the circuit back to the top and finish up Dame Jouanne. For those more intelligent, you can walk along the passageways that lead to the top, and finish also by climbing up Dame Jouanne. Both Caroline and Dame Jouanne we classify as deathballs, so go carefully.

This whole area is on a sandy slope and in recent years has seen rockfalls and subsidence, especially up to the NW in the Requin area. The more unstable areas have been wire fenced off. This said, there is still a lot of climbing (big bouldering) to be found. In the central area there are 3 additional historic circuits of Mauve, Blue and Red. There is also an old black/white circuit of around 30 problems in this area - these are excellent and not too hard for a strong climber 5c-6c, but most can be intimidating though, and are well spread out along the hillside.

1 2b	21 3b	41 3a	61 3c	1 4a	19 4c	38 4a	1 4c	21 4b	41 4c	1 6b	21 7a
2 3b	22 3c	42 2b	62 3c	2 4b	20 4a	39 4a	2 4c	22 4c	42 5a	2 6a	22 6a
3 3c	23 3b	43 3b	63 3b	2b 4a	20b 4b	40 4b	3 5b	23 5a	43 4c	3 6b	23 7b
4 4b	24 3b	44 4a	64 3b	3 4a	21 4a	40b 4c	4 4c	24 5a	44 4c	4 6c	24 5c
5 3a	25 4a	45 4a	65 3c	4 4a	22 4b	41 4a	5 4b	25 5b	45 5a	5 5b	25 6a
6 3b	26 4b	46 3a	66 3b	5 4a	23 4b	42 4a	6 5a	26 5b	46 4a	6 6b	26 6c
7 2b	27 3b	47 3c	67 3b	6 4a	24 4a	43 4a	7 5b	27 4c	47 4c	7 6a	27 6a
8 3b	28 3c	48 3c	68 3b	6b 4a	25 4a	44 4a	8 4b	28 4c	48 5b	8 6b	28 6a
9 3c	29 3c	49 3a	69 3b	7 4c	26 3c	44b 3c	9 5b	29 4b	49 5a	9 5b	29 6b
10 3a	30 3c	50 2b	70 3a	8 4b	27 4a	45 4a	10 5a	30 4b	50 5a	10 5b	30 6a
11 3b	31 4a	51 3b	71 3c	9 4b	28 4b	46 4b	11 5a	31 4b	51 5a	11 6a	31 6b
12 3c	32 3b	52 3c	72 3c	10 4b	29 4b	47 4b	12 4a	32 4c	52 5a	12 6b	
13 3a	33 3b	53 3c	73 4b	11 4b	30 4b	48 4b	13 4a	33 5a	53 4c	13 6c	
14 3c	34 3b	54 2b	74 3c	12 4a	31 4a	49 4b	14 4c	34 4a	54 5b	14 6b	
15 2b	35 3b	55 3a	75 3b	13 4a	32 4a	50 4b	15 5a	35 5a	55 4b	15 6c	
16 4a	36 2b	56 3a	76 3c	14 4b	33 4a		16 5a	36 4c	56 4c	16 5c	
17 3a	37 3c	57 3c		15 4a	34 4b		17 4c	37 4c	57 4c	17 5b	
18 3b	38 3a	58 3a		16 4a	35 4b		18 5b	38 5a	58 5a	18 6a	
19 2b	39 2c	59 4a		17 4a	36 4a		19 4c	39 5c		19 6b	
20 4a	40 3a	60 3c		18 4b	37 4b		20 4c	40 4c		20 6b	

Orange. 54 – 2c; Libby Graham

DAME JOUANNE - (AD/Orange)

Point de v[...]
‹‹ (Pic-nic)

Dame
Jouanne
‹‹

0m

50m

75m

125m

Chalet Joubert - 2 min

P ⊕ page-36

P 8 min

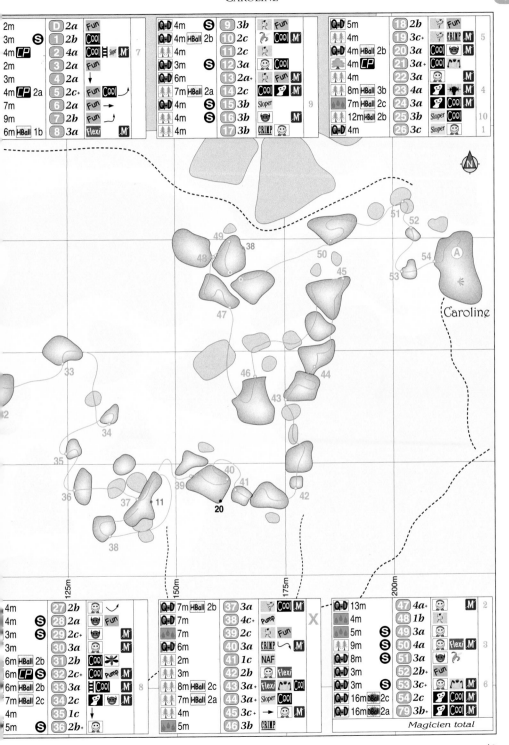

"CAROLINE"

4

Dame Jouanne - (AD/Orange)

43

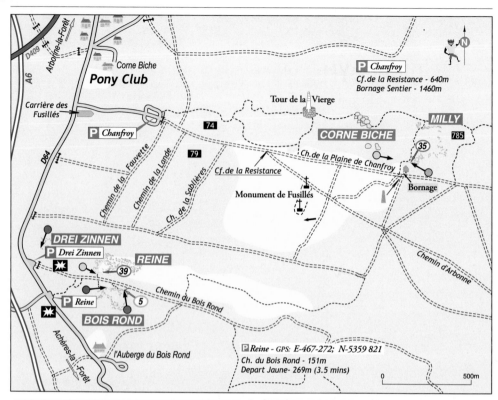

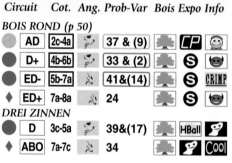

Circuit	Cot.	Ang.	Prob-Var	Bois	Expo	Info
BOIS ROND (p 50)						
AD	2c-4a		37 & (9)		CP	😊
D+	4b-6b		33 & (2)		S	😬
ED-	5b-7a		41&(14)		S	CRIMP
ED+	7a-8a		24		S	😬
DREI ZINNEN						
D	3c-5a		39&(17)		HBall	
ABO	7a-7c		34			Cool

Circuit	Cot.	Ang.	Prob-Var	Bois	Expo	Info
ROCHER DE LA REINE (p 268)						
PD+	1b-4a		59&(14)	Q-D	CP	
D+	3a-6b		57&(14)	Q-D	S	
ED	6b-8a		42	Cool	S	Zzz
ROCHER DE CORNE BICHE						
PD-	1c-4a		31&(16)		CP	Zzz
ROCHER DE MILLY (p 246)						
AD-	1b-4a		48 & (8)		Yum	Zzz
D+	3a-6b		38&(10)		Yum	Zzz

BOREAL

CLIMBING DYNO-MITE
LEARNING to CLIMB on INDOOR WALLS

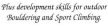
Plus development skills for outdoor Bouldering and Sport Climbing.

Bouldering technique

Alpine safety

Indoor Wall skills

Sport power and endurance

DAVID ATCHISON-JONES

CLIMBING DYNOMITE

If you are new to any sort of climbing or bouldering, this is the perfect book to accelerate your learning progress. All the tips and tricks for sandstone and granite bouldering are explained.

This book shows you all of the different techniques for both indoor and outdoor bouldering. All examples are illustrated by some of the greatest names in bouldering.

You will instantly improve by reading and understanding all the tips and tricks.

All the ropework that you need for holiday sport climbing is covered in detail, from starting out - up to multi pitch techniques. All essential when visiting the European super climbing spots.

Si vous trouvez les circuits jaunes plutôt faciles à faire et que vous êtes à la recherche de problèmes un peu plus difficiles, alors visitez le Bois Rond. Situé seulement à 400m du parking, l'accès y est facile en suivant un chemin bien tracé. Le circuit se déroule dans une pente très boisée d'arbres à feuilles caduques, et bénéficie d'un superbe ensoleillement lors des journées chaudes d'été. Le circuit va dans le sens des aiguilles d'une montre ce qui est facile à suivre pour les grimpeurs qui ne connaissent pas encore très bien les circuits de Fontainebleau. Les blocs sont bien dispersés pour permettre de grimper en toute intimité mais suffisamment rapprochés pour accéder sans difficulté aux problèmes suivants (et déplacer son crash pad aisément). Il y a 3 circuits : orange, bleu et rouge. Le rouge et l'orange sont excellents et sont des classiques de la forêt (attention – le rouge avec ses problèmes courts et raides est un circuit difficile) Malheureusement les blocs du Bois Rond n'ont pas suffisamment de prises de taille moyenne dans les parties les plus raides pour offrir dans le bleu de bons problèmes. C'est donc un circuit qui offre des prises difficiles à atteindre, et des problèmes d'un mouvement ou deux seulement. Dans l'orange (cotation de 3a-4a), les problèmes sont excellents et très plaisants. Le départ se fait sur un problème supplémentaire (D-depart) qui vaut vraiment la peine d'être grimpé, cependant préparez-vous à un début difficile avec une dalle délicate en (2), puis un dièdre tres dur en (5). Il y a de nombreuses variations sur ce circuit puisque toutes les lignes sont indépendantes les unes des autres et toutes excellentes, ainsi nous les avons ajoutées à notre défi du magicien. Cela hausse le nombre total de problèmes pour ce circuit à 46. Les points forts du circuit sont les sorties difficiles (mais faciles à repérer) sur le (28a) et le (32), nous ne vous donnons pas d'indice, mais nous vous conseillons de conserver votre énergie. Ces problèmes sont des classiques ce qui signifie que si vous ne les faites pas lors de vos premiers essais, vous finirez par être si fatigués qu'ils deviendront impossibles à faire. Le circuit se termine en triomphe, très haut sur un grand bloc et vous ramène presque au point de départ.

Orange 30 - 3c; Dave Brown

BOIS ROND - (AD/Orange)

Orange 9 - 3b; Wobbly

If you are happily climbing around the forest on yellow graded circuits but are eager to try something more challenging, then a trip to Le Bois Rond should be just the ticket. It's only 400m from the parking spot and is easily approachable by a good footpath then track. The circuit traces around a small hill that is very well wooded with deciduous trees, but still enjoys wonderful dappled sunshine on those hot, blue skied, summer days. It is an easy circuit to follow and naturally goes round the hill in a clockwise manner, ideal for those climbers unfamiliar with Fontainebleau circuits. The boulders are scattered far enough apart in this small area to give you privacy on your own problems, but close enough to make the next problem only a few metres away (easy to carry a crash pad around too). There are three circuits here; orange, blue and red. Both the orange and the red are excellent (warning – the red is a hard red with short, stiff problems) – but indeed, both are classics of the forest. Unfortunately the boulders at Bois Rond, don't seem to give enough medium sized holds in the steeper parts for good blue problems, hence the blue circuit has quite a few long reaches, bad landings and one move wonders.

At the level of orange however (3a-4a), the problems here are excellent and really enjoyable. You start at an extra problem (D-depart) which is well worth doing, however, be prepared for an early wake up call with a very tricky slab at (2), and then a highly awkward corner at (5); these two problems together can award you the old dog status - even before the sixth problem. A lot of the variations on this circuit are completely different, being independent natural lines and excellent in their own way, so we include them on our magician challenge. This also boosts the circuit up to a comfortable days entertainment at 46 problems. The highlights of the circuit are the awkward top outs (easily spotted) on (28a) and (32), we don't give you any clues but warn you to conserve energy. These are classics whereby that if you don't get them in the first few goes, then you start getting so tired that they become impossible. The circuit finishes triumphantly, high up on a big block and almost back at the start point.

Orange 23- 3c; Dave Brown

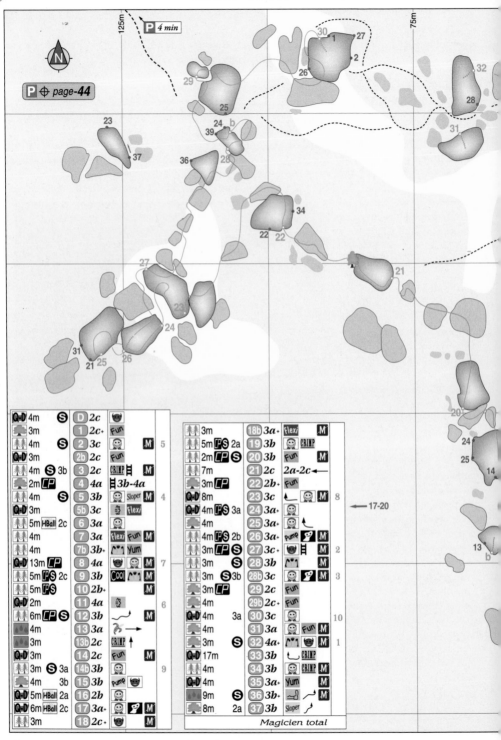

Tracé - André Schwartz

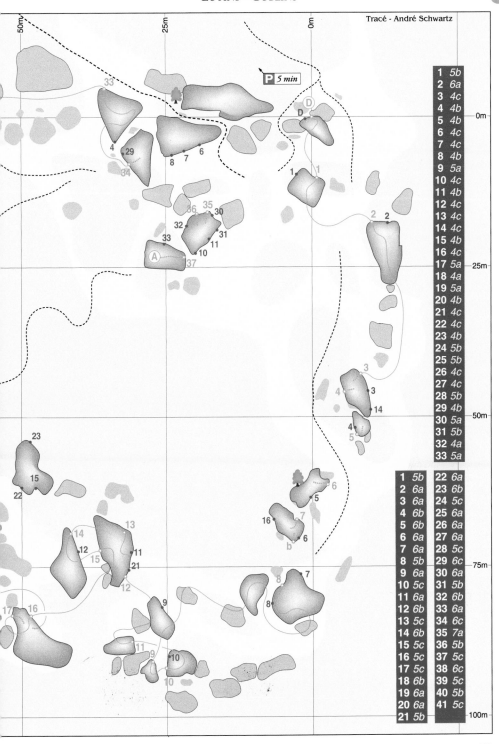

P 5 min

1	5b
2	6a
3	4c
4	4b
5	4b
6	4c
7	4c
8	4b
9	5a
10	4c
11	4b
12	4c
13	4c
14	4c
15	4b
16	4c
17	5a
18	4a
19	5a
20	4b
21	4c
22	4c
23	4b
24	5b
25	5b
26	4c
27	4c
28	5b
29	4b
30	5a
31	5b
32	4a
33	5a

1	5b	22	6a
2	6a	23	6b
3	6a	24	5c
4	6b	25	6a
5	6b	26	6a
6	6a	27	6a
7	6a	28	5c
8	5b	29	6c
9	6a	30	6a
10	5c	31	5b
11	6a	32	6b
12	6b	33	6a
13	5c	34	6c
14	6b	35	7a
15	5c	36	5b
16	5c	37	5c
17	5c	38	6c
18	6b	39	5c
19	6a	40	5b
20	6a	41	5c
21	5b		

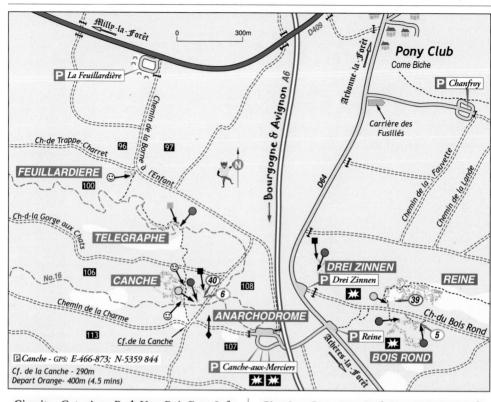

Circuit	Cot.	Ang.	Prob-Var	Bois	Expo	Info
FEUILLARDIÈRE						
😊 ENF	1a-2a	🏃	30	🌳	Yum	Fun
ROCHER DU TÉLÉGRAPHE						
◻ AD+	2c-5c	🏃	18		Ⓢ	CRIMP
⬤ D+	3b-6a	🏃	34		Ⓢ	CRIMP
CANCHE AUX MERCIERS (p58 & 274)						
😊 E-	1a-1c	🏃	36	🌳	Yum	Fun
😊 ENF	1a-2a	🏃	33	🌳	Yum	Fun
⬤ PD-	1a-4a	🏃	44 & (4)	🌳	Yum	🐍
⬤ AD	1b-4a	🏃	41 & (5)	🌳	Yum	Trick
⬤ D+	3b-6b	🏃	44 & (9)	Q-D	CP	Trick
⬤ TD+	4c-7a	🏃	33 & (5)	Q-D	Ⓢ CP	😊
◼ ED	6a-7a	🏃	20	Q-D	CP	Pump
♦ ABO	7b-8a	🏃	26	Q-D	CP	Pump
L'ANARCHODROME						
♦ ABO	6a-8b	🏃	34	🌳	Ⓢ CP	Pump

Circuit	Cot.	Ang.	Prob-Var	Bois	Expo	Info
BOIS ROND (p 50)						
⬤ AD	2c-4a	🏃	37 & (9)	🌳	CP	😊
⬤ D+	4b-6b	🏃	33 & (2)	🌳	Ⓢ	😊
⬤ ED-	5b-7a	🏃	41&(14)	🌳	Ⓢ	CRIMP
♦ ED+	6a-8a	🏃	24	🌳	Ⓢ	😊
DREI ZINNEN						
⬤ D	3c-5a	🏃	39&(17)	🌳	HBall	🤸
♦ ABO	7a-7c	🏃	34	🌳	🤸	Cool
ROCHER DE LA REINE (p 268)						
⬤ PD+	1b-4a	🏃	59&(14)	Q-D	CP	❄
⬤ D+	3a-6b	🏃	57&(14)	Q-D	Ⓢ	❄
♦ ED	6b-8a	🏃	42	Cool	Ⓢ	Zzz

Le site de la Canche aux Merciers a la réputation d'être très fréquenté, mais aussi d'être pollué par le bruit de l'autoroute toute proche. Cette réputation est tout à fait fondée, cependant si vous planifiez bien votre visite, vous pouvez minimiser ces deux inconvénients. Sa popularité est tout à fait méritée grâce à sa bonne sélection de blocs qui sèchent rapidement et aux aires de réception qui sont excellentes. En semaine, il n'est pas impossible de voir jusqu'à 10 autocars sur le parking et de nombreuses voitures, ayant tous déchargé de nombreux bambins. Leurs cris et leurs rires indiquent où se trouvent les rochers. La majorité des blocs sont de 3m de haut environ ce qui est idéal pour les grimpeurs qui ne souhaitent pas faire de passages trop engagés. Il y a un excellent circuit enfants et un superbe circuit jaune dont les prises sont difficiles à atteindre ce qui le rend marginalement plus dur. Les blocs sont bien répartis sur un terrain plat laissant passer la brise qui sèche les voies rapidement. Il y a de nombreux chênes et des hêtres au milieu de ce labyrinthe de blocs apportant de l'ombre et permettant aux enfants de jouer à cache-cache. Les blocs ont des parois verticales et offrent des passages qui sont soit au soleil, soit à l'ombre. En général et vers 16h00 les enfants disparaissent et le site devient l'un des endroits les plus calmes de la forêt. Bien sûr les bruits de l'autoroute persistent, mais comparés aux cris des enfants, ils sont à peine perceptibles. Le circuit orange AD est très varié avec 41 voies. C'est un mélange de traversées et de rétablissements qui testeront votre habilité de grimpeur. Les rochers sont ronds et offrent des prises arrondies plutôt que des réglettes - l'endroit idéal si vous souhaitez reposez vos doigts fatigués. Si vous n'avez pas l'habitude de grimper à Fontainebleau, ce circuit offre une initiation sympathique en particulier pour ceux qui font des voies en 5a ou 6a. C'est un circuit qui récompense les grimpeurs dotés d'une bonne technique et avec un peu d'intelligence et de finesse il est assez facile de trouver la solution à tous les passages. C'est l'endroit idéal pour grimper à vu un circuit complet en une après-midi.

Orange 39 - 3c+; Enrico Schnerr

Orange 15 – 5c; Kristina Wiessner

Orange 20 – 4a; Jean-Alain Jolivet

Orange 18 – 3b; Moritz Regnier

Canche aux Merciers has a reputation of being busy-busy, and hounded by loud motorway noise. Alas this is true, but then again, with a bit of skilful planning you can alleviate both of these detriments. Its popularity is fully deserved since there's a good selection of boulders that dry quickly, and mostly with good landings. Even on weekdays you can find up to 10 coaches parked in the car park, plus a stack of cars having unloaded tiny tots by their thousands. Shouts and screams from kids having a fun time will give you a pretty good idea where the climbing is - opposite the giant sand bowl. Most of the boulders are only 3m high, which makes it a great place for all levels of climbers wanting freak-free bouldering. There is a good children's white circuit here, plus a wonderful yellow circuit with only long reaches to make it marginally harder. The boulders are set nicely apart on a flat, compact area – with around 4 metre gaps that allows the breeze to quickly dry every problem. There is a nice scattered canopy of mixed oak and beech trees to help the kids dodge each other as they run around and play hide and seek in this scattered maze of fabulously shaped rocks. As the blocks have vertical sides all round, you can always find sunny or shady problems here. Suddenly, around four in the afternoon, you notice that the kids have left and it seems one of the quietest places in the whole of Fontainebleau. You do get the hum of constant motorway traffic, but compared to the kids – it seems ever so tranquil. The orange AD circuit has 41 problems with a couple of variations and is a lovely length with lots of diversity. It is a mixture of some fine traverses, and with plenty of good mantelshelf test pieces. The rock is rounded in texture, lending itself to slopers rather than crimps - an excellent place to come if you want to relive throbbing fingertips. If you aren't used to font style climbing, it offers a lovely introduction for any sport climber operating in the s-5a/6a grades. It's a circuit which rewards any boulderer using fine technique; sure you power up many of the problems at a high standard, but with some intelligence and finesse, you can unlock most problems down to the lower font - 3 grades. It's a nice place to on-sight a whole circuit in an afternoon.

Le tranquil Canche aux Merciers - C'est le week-end - err non!   *Orange 26 – 4a; Cyril Hanus*

"Le Magie De Monique - Monique's Magique"

Tracé - Monique et Wladimir Fédoroff, Alain Laloup, Pierre Nédelec et André Schwartz

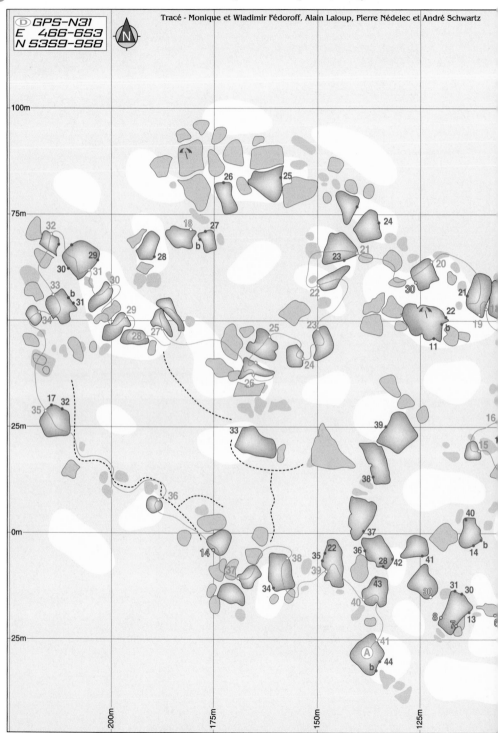

La Canche Aux Merciers - (AD/Orange)

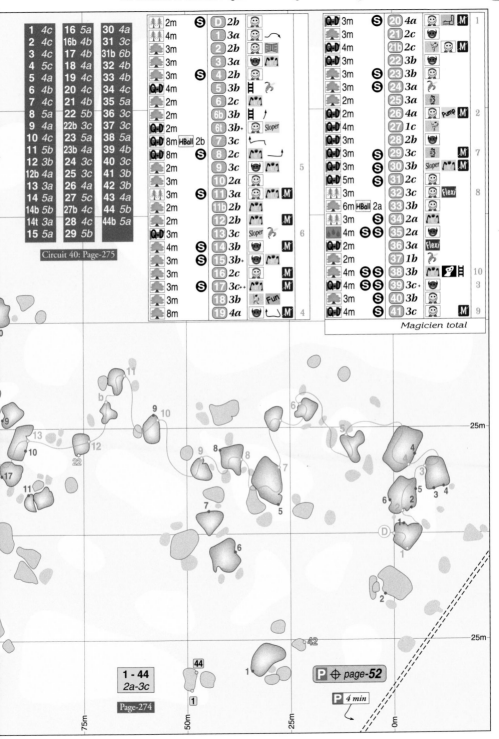

1 4c	**16** 5a	**30** 4a								
2 4c	**16b** 4b	**31** 3c								
3 4c	**17** 4b	**31b** 6b								
4 5c	**18** 4a	**32** 4b								
5 4a	**19** 4c	**33** 4b								
6 4b	**20** 4c	**34** 4c								
7 4c	**21** 4b	**35** 5a								
8 5a	**22** 5b	**36** 3c								
9 4a	**22b** 3c	**37** 3c								
10 4c	**23** 5a	**38** 5a								
11 5b	**23b** 4a	**39** 4b								
12 3b	**24** 3c	**40** 3c								
12b 4a	**25** 3c	**41** 3b								
13 3a	**26** 4a	**42** 3b								
14 5a	**27** 5c	**43** 4a								
14b 5b	**27b** 4c	**44** 5b								
14t 3a	**28** 4c	**44b** 5a								
15 5a	**29** 5b									

Circuit 40: Page-275

Magicien total

1 - 44
2a-3c

Page-274

P ⊕ page-52

P 4 min

TROIS PIGNONS SUD - DIPLODOCUS - (AD/Orange)

Le mot Diplodocus évoque les monstres préhistoriques géants qui, il y a quelques millions d'années, parcouraient la forêt de Fontainebleau à la recherche de leur prochain repas. Heureusement les Diplodocus etaient végétariens ainsi même a cette époque, les grimpeurs auraient pu pratiquer leur sport favori en toute sécurité. Ce site a pris son nom du grand bloc de grès qui domine à 9m de haut et qui - en utilisant un peu son imagination - ressemble à un diplodocus endormi. Les blocs qui entourent ce monstre sympathique ont des formes très particulières et ressemblent presque à des vertèbres géants endormis dans le sable. Les blocs ne sont en général pas très hauts et les sorties de voies sont dans l'ensemble plutôt faciles grâce aux réglettes situées en haut des rochers. Les aires de réception excellentes sont un atout supplémentaire pour faire de ce lieu un site d'escalade très attrayant. Sa popularité a cependant des inconvénients puisque de nombreuses prises ont beaucoup souffert et sont devenues très polies telles de la glace. Bien que ces prises soient agréables au toucher et n'abîment pas les mains, elles n'offrent aucune adhérence. De nombreux passages ont des dévers et demandent donc beaucoup de la puissance. Vos abdominaux vous seront très utiles surtout pour éviter que vos pieds glissent sur les prises marbrées. Il y a 3 circuits : jaune, orange et bleu tous très divertissants - le jaune étant très facile à suivre même sans topo. Ce circuit ''Jurassique'' est un peu trop court pour être très bon. Il a des passages tellement glissants que, même à des niveaux de difficulté inférieure à 5b, il faut souvent utiliser des lancés pour s'assurer une chance de les faire. Nous l'avons cependant pris en compte car il est parfait pour notre défi de magicien, et idéal lorsque les autres sites de la forêt sont humides. C'est un circuit qui sèche rapidement et qu'il vaut mieux conserver pour une journée avec des prévisions d'averses.

The name Diplodocus surely conjures up prehistoric giant monsters roaming about the Fontainebleau forest with rumbling tummies and looking for a good munch. Fortunately the Diplodocus were vegetarians, so us being happy chirpy climbers, would have been safe here all those millions of years ago. This area gets its name from the giant central sandstone block that towers some 9m high, and which resembles a sleeping Diplodocus – abeit with a slight touch of imagination. The blocks that surround this friendly monster are mostly square cut with smooth undercut sides, weird in shape and resembling perhaps giant vertebrae resting in the sand. The blocks are generally low and have square cut edges at the top, to give straightforward and relatively easy finishes. This combined with nice flat sandy landings makes this a very friendly spot. Popularity though does come with disadvantages however, since many of the footholds and handholds have suffered a lot of wear, and given away their sandy surface - consequently you are left with smooth quartzy holds that are like glass. Whilst these smooth holds are kind to worn out skin, they offer no friction at all for finger tape and it is best stick to sweaty skin here. Many problems have undercut and overhanging faces, and this makes for considerably powerful climbing. You need to tense your stomach muscles completely in order to stop your feet from sliding on the glassy footholds. There are 3 circuits here – Yellow, Orange and Blue; all of which are fun and intermixed with each other - with the yellow being very easy to follow, even without a topo diagram. This 'Jurassic' circuit is too short to be great, and has some problems that are so slippery that you must dyno them to stand any chance of doing them at less than 5b. We include it because it does make a good magicien challenge that should be perfect for a morning or afternoon, and ideal when the rocks in other parts of the forest are still damp. It's a very quick drying circuit, and definitely one to save for a day that is likely to give a shower or two.

Arrivé - Orange 23 - 4b; Bertrand Karpinski

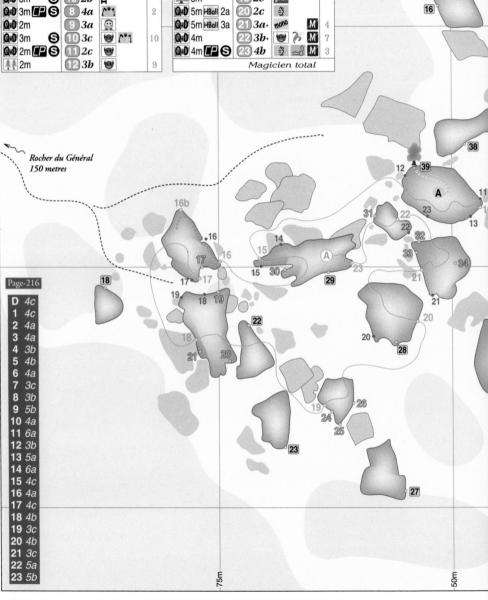

Left table:

Approach		Route		Symbols	
Q•D 4m	SS	1	3b+		
Q•D 4m		1b	2c	Fun	
Q•D 3m		2	4a		5
Q•D 3m		2b	3a		
Q•D 4m	S	3	3c	M	6
Q•D 4m	S 2c	4	2c	Fun	
Q•D 3m	2c	5	5b		
4m	3a	6	3c		X
3m	S	7	3c		
Q•D 3m	S	7b	2b		
Q•D 3m	CP	8	4a		2
Q•D 2m		9	3a		
Q•D 3m	S	10	3c		10
Q•D 2m	CP S	11	2c		
2m		12	3b		9

Right table:

Approach		Route		Symbols	
Q•D 2m		13	4c+		1
Q•D 4m	CP S	14	4a		
Q•D 3m	CP S	14b	3c		X
Q•D 3m		15	3a+	M	
Q•D 4m	CP	15b	3a	M	
Q•D 8m	CP S	16	3c	Pump →	
2m	CP	16b	3b		
3m	CP S	17	3b		8
2m	CP	18	3a		
3m		19	2c	Trick	
Q•D 5m	HBall 2a	20	2c		
Q•D 5m	HBall 3a	21	3a+	mono M	4
Q•D 4m		22	3b+	M	7
Q•D 4m	CP	23	4b	M	3

Magicien total

Rocher du Général
150 metres

75m

50m

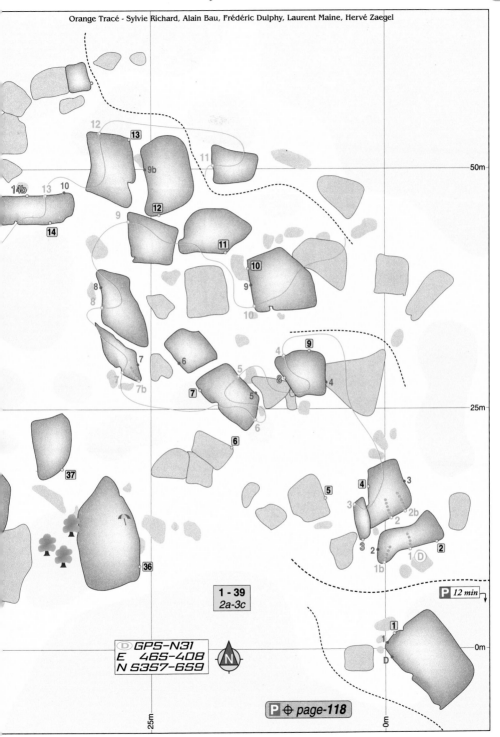

Orange Tracé - Sylvie Richard, Alain Bau, Frédéric Dulphy, Laurent Maine, Hervé Zaegel

1 - 39
2a-3c

Ⓓ GPS-N31
E 46S-40B
N 5357-6S9

P ⊕ page-118

P 12 min

Orange 18 - 2b+; Jingo

Le massif canard à Buthiers est si proche du parking que vous pourriez presque brosser les prises situées en haut du bloc de départ du circuit bleu depuis le haut de votre camping -car. C'est un des rares massif qui offre également 2 café-restaurant à seulement quelques mètres des circuits. C'est un site excellent d'une part pour les grimpeurs passionnés, d'autre part pour ceux qui souhaitent grimper tranquillement et enfin pour ceux qui préfèrent se rassasier et se désaltérer. Un regard rapide sur la taille de certains blocs et de nombreux passionnés se laisseront certainement persuader de quitter leur chausson d'escalade pour un verre au café. En effet, certains rochers sont vraiment très hauts avec malheureusement des aires de réception déplorables. Curieusement, cependant, grimper sur ce circuit demande essentiellement beaucoup d'attention, de prudence et de calme pour éviter de faire des mouvements non contrôlés en haut des blocs sous le regard de spectateurs terrorisés. Le circuit orange situé derrière l'auberge du canard offre une balade sympathique au milieu d'un labyrinthe de rochers. Les passages sont en majorité sur des rochers de faible hauteur avec les mouvements importants situés près du sol. Le premier test des nerfs est dans le (7) avec un dévers exposé, mais qui heureusement a un bon rétablissement ; nous vous recommandons cependant de ne pas tomber (cotation 3c). Les grimpeurs nerveux auront la frousse lorsqu'ils verront les 6 mètres de hauteur du (11) ! La voie n'est pas plus difficile que 2c, il faut seulement utiliser son équilibre et rester complètement calme. Au (29) il y a un petit arbre qui bloque la cannelure située en haut du bloc. La dalle de droite est une bonne alternative à 2a, mais elle n'offre aucune marge d'erreur. Nous avons ajouté un passage supplémentaire (29b) à l'arrière du grand bloc, car c'est selon nous une bonne ligne. La présence du (31) à 5a sur le circuit orange semble bizarre, à moins que vous soyez une girafe. Le circuit finit en beauté avec deux problèmes excellents le (32) et le (34). Ce circuit n'est certes pas idéal pour l'initiation, mais il offre une bonne diversité de passages pour ceux qui souhaitent consolider leur technique. De plus il offre un bon entraînement à tous ceux qui souhaitent tenter par la suite les circuits qui ont des passages plus difficiles et très exposés.

Melun - La Rochette

 Hire

La Belle Etoile Camping (www)
Quai Joffre, 77000 Melun
Tel: 01 64 39 48 12
Open: 01-04 / 31-10
*English & Dutch spoken, nice open site
with grass, small pool for kids and just to
the west of the river Seine, 1km SSE of
Melun. Shop and 'good facilities' on site,
ping pong, volleyball court, swings.*

 *Samoreau*

Samoreau Municipal Camping
Tel: ?
Open: ?
*A small municipal site near the river on the
east side of the Seine. Not expensive, but
limited facilities. There is a vehicle height
barrier, so quite a bore with big vans etc.
Popular in June with the Samois-s-Seine
gypsy music festival.*

 *Milly-la-Forêt*

   **Hire**

La Musardière Camping (www)
Routes des Grandes Vallées
91490 Milly la Forêt
Tel: 01 64 98 91 91
Open: 16-02 / 01-12
*Some English spoken. Half of the site is static
homes, the lower half is trees and a few open
spaces. Basic campsite, no shop, but bread
van in summer. In the major spring holidays,
the site is incredibly busy and the facilities
are overwhelmed. Star attraction is the 4
swimming pools - wonderful in summer.*

Boulancourt - peace and quiet

  Malesherbes

 Hire

Ile de Boulancourt, (www)
6, allée des Marronniers, 77760
Boulancourt
Tel: 01 64 24 13 38
Open: 01-01 / 31-12
*A large site with plenty of soft grass and is
incredibly tranquil. Local shop and bar in
very queiet village, nice facilities.*

 Grez sur Loing

 Hire

Chemin des Prés, (www)
77880 Grez sur Loing
Tel: 01 64 45 72 75
Open: 3rd week in March - 11/11
*A large site with very good English
spoken. A spare field for those wanting
space and camp fires. Well stocked shop
on site, & bar in the local village. Good
facilities with hot water.*

*Musardière - the
pools close at
lunchtime, and
you must wear
proper swimming
trunks; incredibly
well looked after
and impeccably
clean.*

Massif Canard at Buthiers is virtually a drive-in bouldering area, you can almost brush the top holds on the start of the blue circuit from the top of your camper van. There aren't many bouldering areas either that offer two restaurant-café's only yards away, and with the parking perfectly placed in between. It's a great spot for a mixed group of people; keen climbers - and those who are not so keen and just want to increase their waistline whilst getting sozzled - how sensible. A quick glimpse at the size of the larger boulders here will often sway many enthusiastic climbers 'café bound,' for an alcoholic rotunding session and retiring their climbing shoes for the day. Yes, some of the boulders here are on the large size and have landing zones which are decidedly unhealthy. Oddly though, the climbing on the circuits here generally involves an exercise of caution and level headedness, rather than having to do the crux moves high up in a terrorising frenzy of skidding feet, flapping hands and onlookers shrieking in terror. This orange circuit is a lovely trip through a maze of rocks set behind the Auberge de Canard. It operates mostly on the smaller blocks, throwing any desperate problems at you only a few feet off the ground. Your first test of nerve comes at (7), which is an overhanging groove that forces you to lean back and commit yourself, fortunately, the top out is nice and friendly; however - you are highly advised not to fall off this one (3c). Any nervous climber will succumb to a dose of the heebeegeebies with the sight of problem (11), a mere 20 feet! There is nothing harder than 2c on this 'route,' you simply need good balance and have to stay completely calm. The central part of the circuit retraces back through the gorge, with the descents being as hazardous as the ascents. At (29), there is a small tree blocking the top groove. The slab to the right is a lovely alternative, again quite easy at 2a, but with no room for error – a deathball! We've added a nice fun extra (29b), behind the big block, which seemed another appropriate way up. Why problem (31) is on the orange circuit at 5a seems bizarre – unless you are a giraffe. The circuit finishes very nicely with excellent problems at (32) and (34). It certainly isn't a circuit for a beginner, or for those working up their max grade. It offers a fine trip for those wanting to consolidate there all round climbing, and works as a good apprenticeship before attempting some of the harder highball circuits.

"CANARD À L'ORANGE"

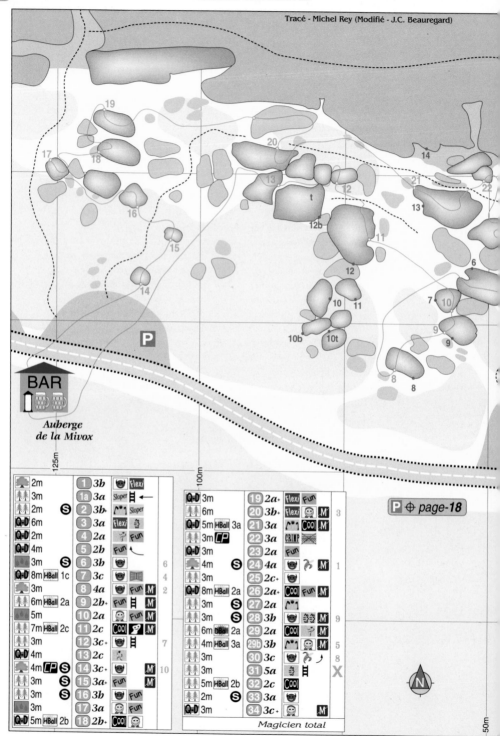

BUTHIERS - MASSIF CANARD - (AD/Orange)

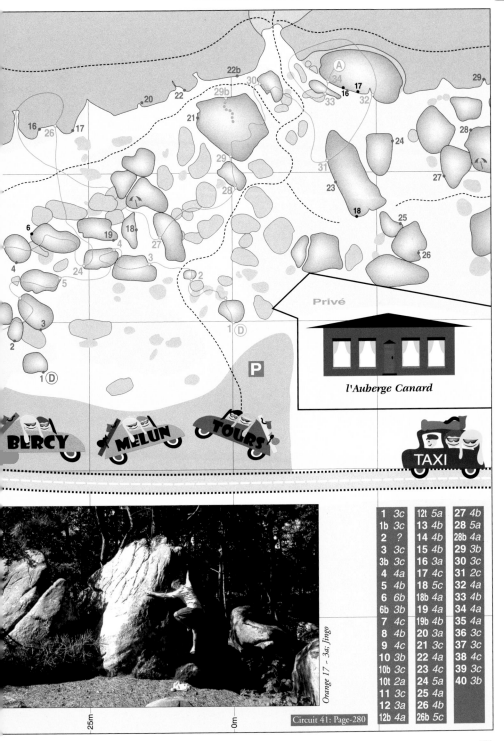

Privé

l'Auberge Canard

BERCY   MELUN   TOURS   TAXI

1	*3c*	**12t**	*5a*	**27**	*4b*
1b	*3c*	**13**	*4b*	**28**	*5a*
2	*?*	**14**	*4b*	**28b**	*4a*
3	*3c*	**15**	*4b*	**29**	*3b*
3b	*3c*	**16**	*3a*	**30**	*3c*
4	*4a*	**17**	*4c*	**31**	*2c*
5	*4b*	**18**	*5c*	**32**	*4a*
6	*6b*	**18b**	*4a*	**33**	*4b*
6b	*3b*	**19**	*4a*	**34**	*4a*
7	*4c*	**19b**	*4b*	**35**	*4a*
8	*4b*	**20**	*3a*	**36**	*3c*
9	*4c*	**21**	*3c*	**37**	*3c*
10	*3b*	**22**	*4a*	**38**	*4c*
10b	*3c*	**23**	*4c*	**39**	*3c*
10t	*2a*	**24**	*5a*	**40**	*3b*
11	*3c*	**25**	*4a*		
12	*3a*	**26**	*4b*		
12b	*4a*	**26b**	*5c*		

Orange 17 – 3a; Jingo

Circuit 41: Page-280

25m   0m

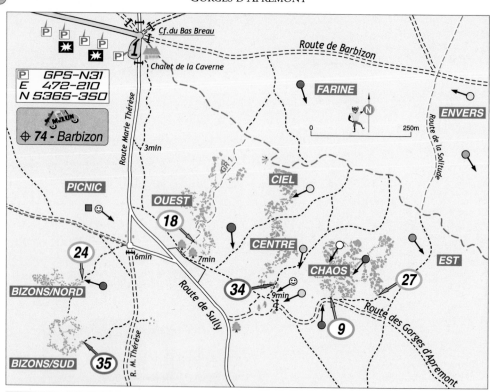

Circuit	Cot.	Ang.	Prob-Var	Bois	Expo	Info
BIZONS - PIQUE NIQUE						
☺ ENF	1-2		37 & 3	Q-D	Yum	Fun
■ TD	4a-6a		9	Q-D	S	☺
BIZONS - NORD (p 170)						
AD+	3-4b		48 & 15		Yum	Sloper
TD-	4a-6b		42 & 15		Yum	☺
♦ ABO	6a-8a		22		S	☺
BIZONS - SUD (p 242)						
D	3-5c		36 & 8		Cool	☺
GORGES - OUEST (p 134)						
AD	2c-4b		46 & (8)		🐒	☺
TD+	5a-6b		46 & (4)		HBall	☺
GORGES - CIEL						
ED-	4c-7a		35 & (7)		🐒	☺
♦ ABO	6b-8a		46		SS	☺
GORGES - CENTRE (p 236)						
☺ ENF	1-2		46 & (5)		Yum	Fun
PD-	2-3		43 & (0)		Cool	🐍
D	3-6a		44 & (6)		Cool	☺

Circuit	Cot.	Ang.	Prob-Var	Bois	Expo	Info
GORGES - CHAOS (p 78 & 192)						
AD-	2-4		42 & (6)	Q-D	Cool	🐍
AD+	3-4		28 & (3)	Q-D	🐒	🐍
D+	4-6a		39 & (2)	Q-D	SS	☺
TD-	4-6b		74 & (2)	Q-D	HBall	🐍
TD+	5b-6c		40 & (0)		Cool	☺
○ ED+	6b-7b		14 & (2)	Q-D	SS	☺
♦ ABO	6a-7c		16	Q-D	SS	☺
GORGES - EST						
D+	4-6a		32 & (7)	Q-D	S	☺
□ ED+	6c-7b		10	Q-D	SS	☺
♦ ABO	6a-7c		23		SS	☺
FARINE						
TD-	4a-6a		50 & (20)		🐒	☺
ENVERS						
PD+	1c-3a		50 & 2		Yum	Fun
AD	2a-4b		45 & 3		Yum	☺
♦ ABO	6a-8b		43		S	☺

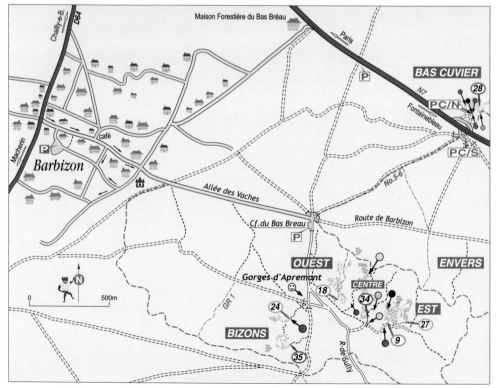

Les célèbres Gorges d'Apremont n'ont en dépit de leur nom aucune gorge. Ce site fut nommé par un individu souhaitant le promouvoir aux touristes. Très proche du pittoresque village de Barbizon, ce massif est une Mecque de l'escalade avec 12 circuits allants du jaune-facile au blanc-tres difficile. À Apremont cependant jaune et facile ne s'associent pas très bien et ce n'est certainement pas un massif pour l'initiation car les débutants n'y apprendront rien sinon la route des urgences de l'hôpital de Fontainebleau. Les collines sont couvertes de blocs et certaines aires de réception sont sinueuses ! Cependant avec un crash pad ou deux et un minimum d'aptitude c'est un excellent site. Le circuit jaune, qui a 42 passages pour la plupart bien balisés, navigue près du picnique zone et peut se suivre sans topo. Cependant soyez prêts pour quelques voies engagées. Nous avons choisi un circuit situé un peu plus haut sur la colline pour les plus adroits et perspicaces. Nous l'avons appelée 'L'école de verre,' ce qui vous donne un indice sur l'état de certaines prises. Curieusement ce circuit s'est pourtant amélioré par sa perte d'adhérence. En général un rocher glissant peut-être très dangereux surtout si vous essayez de mousquetonner votre premier relais à 6 mètres de haut. Cependant en bloc à seulement quelques mètres du sol et avec un crash pad en dessous de vous, cela peut ajouter un peu de tension et oblige à utiliser une bonne technique pour réussir la voie. Sur ce circuit, les prises les plus polies sont en général situées en bas des blocs, indiquant clairement que le sable sur les semelles des chaussons abîme la roche. Si ce n'etait pas pour les prises en forme de banane, ce circuit serait un peu trop monotone et probablement trop facile pour apparaître dans ce topo. Tel qu'il est, il est excellent car les techniques sont variées. Tous les passages figurent sur la liste du défi du magicien puisque seuls les grimpeurs d'un niveau assez élevé seront capables de tous les faire. À ceux un peu nerveux a l'idée de grimper des voies exposées, nous recommandons de laisser les (6), (25) et (42).

Vert/Green 22 - 4b- ; Laura Beaujean

Vert/Green 25 - 4a: Harry Goldner

The famous Gorges d'Apremont; yet no sign of a Gorge in sight? It must have been named by an over enthusiastic real-estate agent or someone trying to sell the area to tourists (which it actually was), and is just a short walk from the picturesque and nouveau chic, Barbizon. The area is a climbing mecca with 12 circuits ranging from the easiest-yellow to the extreme-white. At Apremont however, easy and yellow don't mean the same thing; it's certainly not a place for beginners to learn anything other than the way to the 'Urgence' department of Fontainebleau hospital. These hills are covered in a massive chaos of rocks that runs down the side of the 'Gorge,' some 5-6 metres high and often resting awkwardly close together. Some of the landings are quite undulating! However, with a crash pad or two - and a modicum of skill at landing, the area doesn't seem that bad after you get used to it. The yellow circuit has 42 problems that are usually well marked. It navigates the area close to the picnic area and is possible to follow without a topo, just be prepared for some high problems. A little further up the hill is our choice of entertainment for the more skilled and discerning. We've given it the name 'L'Ecole de Verre' – School of Glass, which is a give away clue to the dazzling shine on many of the holds on this circuit. Surprisingly, this circuit has 'actually improved' by becoming polished to hell. There are times in climbing when slippery rock is nasty and horrible, especially when you are trying to clip your first bolt at 6 metres on a sport route. However, when you are only a few feet off the ground and are traversing above a bouldering mat, then having a few slippery footholds really adds tension and demands skill to solve the problem. With this green circuit, nearly all the polished holds are low down, highlighting that sand on the soles of your feet does grind away the rock to a polished sheen. If it weren't for the banana style footholds, this circuit would be a touch on the dull side and far too easy for the inclusion in this book. As it stands today, it presents an excellent all round challenge of climbing technique with problems that demand a steady head. We include every problem here on the magician challenge since only climbers of reasonable standard will be getting up them all anyway. For anyone of nervous disposition (sain), leaving out (6), (25) & (42), is a sound recommendation, reducing the overall grade from frightening to airy.

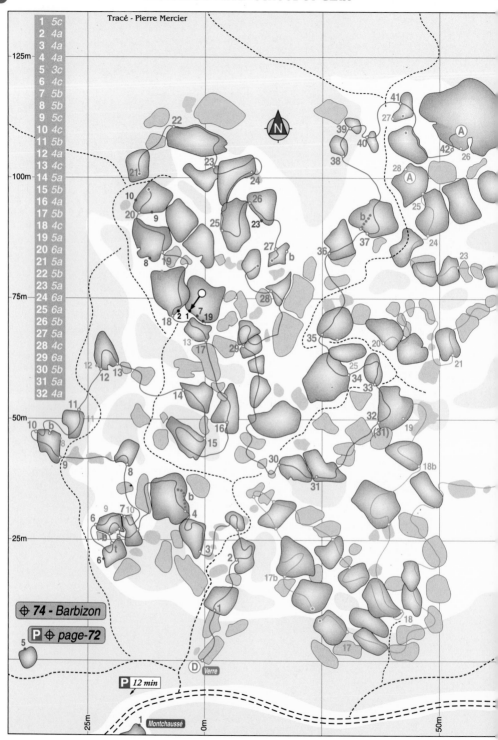

1	5c
2	4a
3	4a
4	4a
5	3c
6	4c
7	5b
8	5b
9	5c
10	4c
11	5b
12	4a
13	4c
14	5a
15	5b
16	4a
17	5b
18	4c
19	5a
20	6a
21	5a
22	5b
23	5a
24	6a
25	6a
26	5b
27	5a
28	4c
29	6a
30	5b
31	5a
32	4a

Tracé - Pierre Mercier

⊕ **74 - Barbizon**

P ⊕ *page-72*

P *12 min*

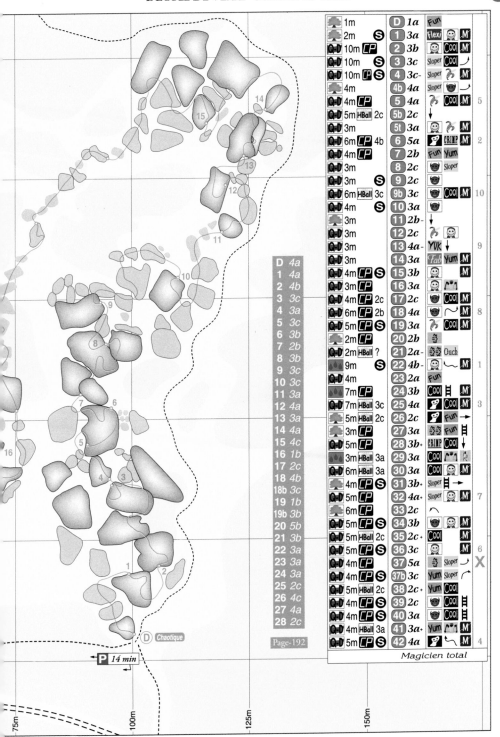

	1m		D 1a	Fun	
	2m	S	1 3a	Flexi	M
Q-D	10m CP		2 3b	COOL	M
Q-D	10m	S	3 3c	Sloper COOL	
Q-D	10m CP		4 3c-	Sloper	
	4m		4b 4a	Sloper	
Q-D	4m CP		5 4a	COOL	
Q-D	5m HBall 2c		5b 2c		
Q-D	3m		5t 3a		M
Q-D	6m CP 4b		6 5a	CRIMP	M
Q-D	4m CP		7 2b	Fun Yum	
Q-D	3m		8 2c	Sloper	
Q-D	3m	S	9 2c		
Q-D	6m HBall 3c		9b 3c	COOL M	
Q-D	4m	S	10 3a		
	3m		11 2b-		
Q-D	3m		12 2c		
Q-D	3m		13 4a-	YUK	
Q-D	3m		14 3a	Fab Yum M	
Q-D	4m CP S		15 3b		M
Q-D	3m CP		16 3a		
Q-D	4m CP 2c		17 2c	COOL M	
Q-D	6m CP 2b		18 4a		
Q-D	5m CP S		19 3a	COOL M	
	2m CP		20 2b		
	2m HBall ?		21 2a-	Ouch	
	9m	S	22 4b-		
Q-D	4m		23 2a		
	7m CP		24 3b	COOL	M
Q-D	7m HBall 3c		25 4a	COOL	M
	5m HBall 2c		26 2c	Fun	
	3m CP		27 3a	Fun	
Q-D	5m CP		28 3b+	CRIMP COOL	
	3m HBall 3a		29 3a	COOL	
Q-D	6m HBall 3a		30 3a	COOL M	
	4m CP S		31 3b+	Sloper	
Q-D	5m CP		32 4a+	Sloper M	
	6m CP		33 2c		
Q-D	5m CP S		34 3b		
Q-D	5m HBall 2c		35 2c+	COOL	
Q-D	5m CP S		36 3c		
	4m CP		37 5a	Sloper	X
Q-D	4m CP		37b 3c	Yum Sloper	
	5m HBall 2c		38 2c+	Yum COOL	
Q-D	4m CP S		39 2c	COOL	
Q-D	4m CP S		40 3a	COOL	
Q-D	4m HBall 3a		41 3a+	Yum M	
Q-D	5m CP S		42 4a	M	

D	4a
1	4a
2	4b
3	3c
4	3a
5	3c
6	3b
7	2b
8	3b
9	3c
10	3c
11	3a
12	4a
13	3a
14	4a
15	4c
16	1b
17	2c
18	4b
18b	3c
19	1b
19b	3b
20	5b
21	3b
22	3a
23	3a
24	3a
25	2c
26	4c
27	4a
28	2c

Page-192

5

2

10

9

8

1

3

7

6

4

Magicien total

D Chaotique

P 14 min

75m   100m   125m   150m

Orange 16 - 2c; Wobbly

Gros sablons est le nom donné à la longue crête au nord-ouest des deux collines du 95.2. Les sections centrales et du sud-est sont renommées pour leurs circuits dont les passages sont effrayants de hauteur. Il y a cependant un petit circuit sympathique sur le nord-ouest de la crête situé dans une très jolie forêt de pins. Il est parfait pour apprendre les caprices de l'escalade sur le grès de Fontainebleau et offre de très bonnes aires de réception. Il ne sera jamais classé comme l'un des circuits classiques de la forêt mais offre néanmoins la possibilité de compléter chaque passage en une seule journée sans pour autant être exténué. Il est un peu plus éloigné que le très populaire 95.2 mais si vous suivez le bon chemin, il est facile à trouver et les 5 minutes de marche supplémentaire valent la peine si vous recherchez le calme et là tranquillité. Le circuit est situé sous des arbres qui ont la fâcheuse tendance de goutter après la pluie, mais en général les prises sèchent rapidement. La forêt, constituée en majorité de larges pins, donne beaucoup d'ombre durant les chaudes journées, mais est assez éclaircie pour permettre au vent de s'engouffrer et de sécher les rochers. Les 15 premiers passages sont sur des blocs de faible hauteur et permettent d'utiliser des techniques très variées. Le circuit est fait de telle manière qu'il est possible de sauter de rocher en rocher mais également de déplacer son crash pad aisément. La première difficulté se trouve au (20), un véritable casse-tête pour les grimpeurs moins expérimentés. Heureusement une fois la technique acquise il est relativement facile à faire. Le circuit suit un tracé latéral à travers la colline, puis descend par le sentier principal vers un très grand bloc offrant deux passages sympas mais hauts. Il remonte ensuite la colline pour arriver sur les hauteurs de la crête au (36) offrant beaucoup d'air et une très belle vue. Il y a là quelques passages assez effrayants qui nécessitent sans aucun doute une bonne parade. Un circuit excellent par sa variété et sa longueur.

Orange 31 – 3c+; Jingo

Orange 38 – 4a; Wobbly

   Gros Sablons - Nord-Ouest - (AD/Orange)

Gros Sablons is the name given to the long ridge to the NW of the twin hills of 95.2. The central and SE sections are famous for big highball circuits and pretty scary days, but there is this very good little circuit on the NW part of this ridge tucked away and set in a lovely thinned out pine forest. It is a good circuit to learn the vagaries of climbing on the Fontainebleau sandstone, and especially whilst offering easy spotting positions and pretty good landings. It will never rank as one of the great classic circuits, but that in turn, means it is very accommodating for most mid grade climbers and offers a challenge where you are highly likely to complete every problem in a day, and without ripping your body to shreds. It is further to walk than the highly populated 95.2, but as long as you take the correct footpath it is relatively easy to find and worth the simple extra five minute stroll for sublime peace and tranquillity. The circuit is mostly set in the trees that do drip a bit after rain, but the holds are well worn and usually dry out nice and quickly. The forest is quite thinned out, and is mainly of large pine, allowing the wind to get in and dry, plus giving welcome shade on a hot day. The first 15 problems are contained in a lovely mixture of small little blocks that are nicely set apart and offer interesting technicality. The circuit works as a continuous set of problems, jumping from one boulder to another; but still very easy to wield your large crash pad around too. (20) Is sure to be the first major problem and present a headache to the less experienced, fortunately it's not that hard when you work out how to do it. The circuit follows a lateral trace across the hill, then down to a giant boulder by the main track that gives a couple of challenging but nice, highball problems. It then traces up the hill to eventually end up on top of the ridge at (36) with some lovely views and a nice airy atmosphere. Up here there are a couple of scary problems that definitely merit the close accompaniment of a good spotter. The circuit gives you a wide range of sandstone textures, grainy slopers low down, then some highly smooth quartzy rock on the top of the ridge. A great intro circuit of variety and a good length.

Orange 36 – 4b; Jingo

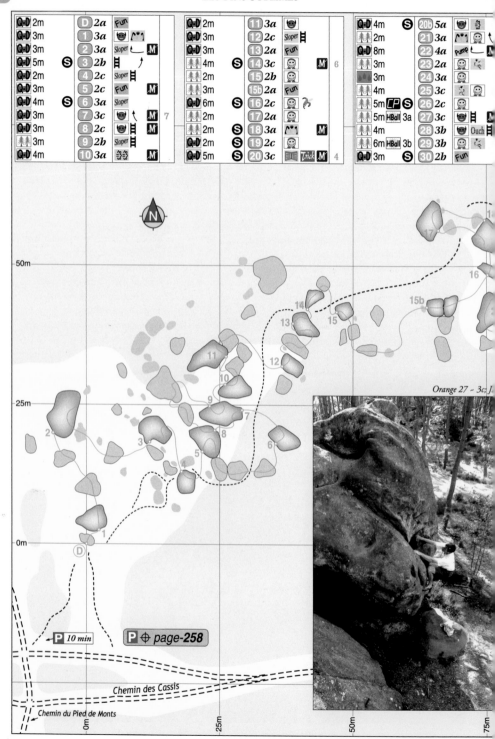

Q=D 2m	D 2a	Fun			
Q=D 3m	1 3a	^^1			
Q=D 3m	2 3a	Sloper ↲ M			
Q=D 5m S	3 2b	‖ ↑			
Q=D 2m	4 2c	Sloper			
Q=D 3m	5 2c	Fun M			
Q=D 4m S	6 3a	Sloper			
Q=D 3m	7 3c	M 7			
Q=D 3m	8 2c	M			
🌲 3m	9 2b	Sloper			
Q=D 4m	10 3a	M			
Q=D 2m	11 3a				
Q=D 3m	12 2c	Sloper			
Q=D 3m	13 2a	Fun			
🌲 4m S	14 3c	M 6			
🌲 2m	15 2b				
🌲 3m	15b 2a	Fun			
Q=D 6m S	16 2c	?			
Q=D 2m	17 2a				
Q=D 2m S	18 3a	^^ M			
Q=D 2m S	19 2c	M			
Q=D 5m S	20 3c	Trick M 4			
Q=D 4m S	20b 5a				
🌲 2m	21 3a	^^1			
Q=D 8m	22 4a	Pump ↲ M			
🌲 3m	23 2a				
▓ 3m	24 3a				
🌲 4m	25 3c				
🌲 5m CP S	26 2c				
🌲 5m HBall 3a	27 3c	‖ M			
🌲 4m	28 3b	Ouch ‖			
🌲 6m HBall 3b	29 3b				
Q=D 3m S	30 2b	Fun			

Orange 27 – 3c; J...

50m

25m

0m

P ⊕ page-258

P 10 min

N

Chemin des Cassis

Chemin du Pied de Monts

0m   25m   50m   75m

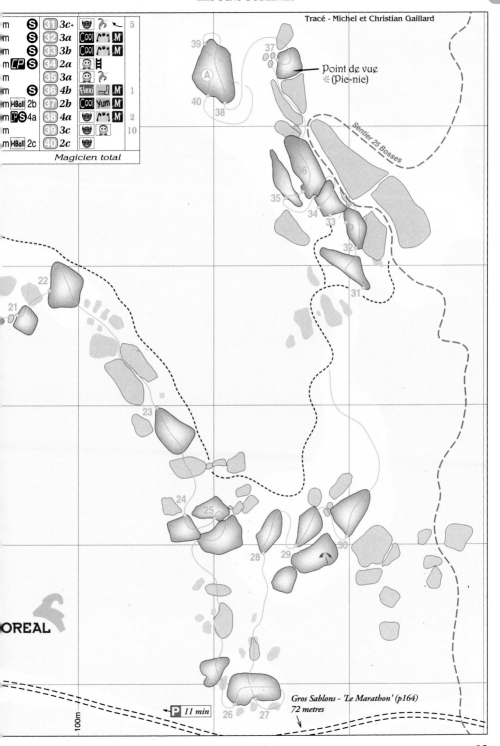

m	S	31	3c+			5
m	S	32	3a	Cool		
m	S	33	3b	Cool		
m CP S		34	2a			
m		35	3a			1
m	S	36	4b	Flexi	M	
m HBall	2b	37	2b	Cool	Yum M	
m PS	4a	38	4a		M	2
m		39	3c			10
m HBall	2c	40	2c			

Magicien total

Tracé - Michel et Christian Gaillard

Point de vue
(Pic-nic)

Sentier 25 Bosses

OREAL

Gros Sablons - 'Le Marathon' (p164)
72 metres

P 11 min

Le site des 'Gorges' de Franchard est assez grand, mais il ne ressemble pas vraiment à une gorge comparé aux canyons géants des Pyrénées et des Alpes. C'est tout simplement un ensemble de grands rochers éparpillés sur deux collines qui sont séparées par une vallée tranquille. Bien que le nom 'hautes plaines' ait été donné à ce site, la partie la plus haute s'élève seulement à 120m. Contrairement à ses voisins célèbres Isatis et Cuisinière, les blocs de ce site ne sont en général pas plus haut que 3 ou 4 mètres et les aires de réception sont parfaites. C'est un bon site pour emmener des débutants puisqu'il y a deux circuits jaune qui offrent des voies d'excellente technicité, pas trop difficiles ou dangereuses et qui valent vraiment la peine d'être essayées. Nous avons appelé ce circuit les arêtes puisqu'il y en a trois exemples excellents et un bon nombre d'autres à essayer si vous souhaitez faire des passages éliminatoires. Les (15) & (40) n'ont pas été retenus pour notre liste du défi de magicien puisqu'ils demandent l'utilisation de prises qui sont vraiment trop horribles. Ils sont également plus difficiles que 4a, niveau de difficulté général donné à ce circuit. C'est un circuit sympa avec de nombreux passages demandant une bonne ténacité pour un niveau de difficulté peu élevé. Certains passages culminent à 4m de haut ! Cependant dans la majorité des cas, les rétablissements sont plutôt faciles grâce aux larges prises situées en haut des blocs – et pour ceux qui sont plus difficiles il est possible de sauter. Sur les pentes les plus basses les rochers sont sous des hêtres qui gouttent souvent longtemps après une averse et ils ne bénéficient pas du vent séchant du sud-ouest. Sur le haut de la crête il y a une jolie forêt de pins où des blocs d'apparence verte sont souvent plus secs qu'ils ne le paraissent. Un endroit super pour grimper par beau temps mais qui peut devenir très humide s'il n'y a pas d'air.

The 'Gorges' des Franchard is a substantially sizeable area, but it's hardly like a gorge when you compare it with the giant canyons of the Alps or the Pyrénées. It is simply a handful of giant stones that are scattered over two baguette shaped hills that run east to west - and separated with an ambling gentle valley running down the middle. It will come as no surprise to find the term 'high plains' means - boulders on both sides of a hilly area – all set in deep trees, and with very little 'plain' to be seen. You won't need oxygen either, since the Hautes-high part is only 120m above sea level. What is comforting though, is that Hautes certainly doesn't apply to the size of the boulders. Unlike its more famous neighbours of Isatis and Cuisinière, you generally only find 3-4m high blocks, and often on their own with ideal landing spots. It's a great place to bring any beginner since there are two yellow circuits that offer excellent technical climbing, and which is both rewarding and not too challenging or dangerous. We've named this tour 'Les Arêtes' because there are three excellent examples on the circuit and many more arêtes to have a go at if you want to try eliminate problems. Problems (15) & (40) have slid out of our magician challenge, because they involve the use of heinous slopers that are grim to hold. They are also harder than 4a which seems a perfect fun level to set this circuit at, and therefore allow a lot of climbers a chance of getting around with only a couple of falls in good style. It is a comfortable circuit that gives you plenty of problems requiring cerebral tenacity for a low grade solution. There are quite a few problems up to 4 metres high! However in most cases, the top outs are friendly and offer good jugs – those without, give you the option to casually jump down if you want. The lower slopes are set in beech trees that can stay dripping for quite a while after rain, and are set in hollows that don't get the SW drying winds. On the top of the ridge you will find a lovely light pine forest where green boulders are often drier than they look, more akin to Cuisinière. A great place to climb on a sunny day, but can get a touch humid if there is no breeze.

NEVER STOP EXPLORING™

Orange 37b - 4a: Jim

Orange 19 – 3b+: James Bacon

Orange 34 - 4c: Jimbo

Orange 15 - 4c: Jimbo

Orange 17 - 3b: James Bacon

"LES ARÊTES"

			No.	Grade	Symbols
Q-D	2m		D	2c	😊
CP	3m		1	3c	Sloper .M'
	3m	S	2	3b	Sloper .M'
Q-D	3m		3	4a	CRIMP
	4m	S	4	3c+	Sloper COOL .M'
Q-D	6m		5	2b	Fun ↶
	5m HBall 3c		5b	4a+	😊 COOL .M'
	8m HBall 2a		6	3a	😊 COOL .M'
	8m		7	3b	↲ Ⅲ
	4m		8	3a+	
	3m		9	2b	😊 ^'1
	3m	S	10	3b	.M'
	3m		11	3b	Sloper ^'1
	4m		12	3a	Fun → Ⅲ
	4m		13	3b	Fun
	4m		14	4b	CRIMP .M'
	3m		15	4c+	Sloper 😊 .M'
	2m		16	3b+	😊
CP	4m		17	3b	😊 .M'
	5m	S	18	3b	Fun .M'
Q-D	7m HBall 3b		19	3b+	^'1 .M'
Q-D	4m	S	19b	3a	COOL Ⅲ
Q-D	4m		19t	2c	😊 ↓
	3m	S	20	4a	Ⅲ 😊 .M'
	4m	S	21	3c	Fun .M'
	4m		21b	4b	😊 .M'
Q-D	5m HBall 2b		21t	2c	Fun COOL
	4m		21q	3c	Ⅲ 😊 .M'
	4m	S	21c	3b	^'1 COOL .M'
	4m	S	22	3b	
	4m	S 2c	23	4a	Sloper Ⅲ
	3m	S	24	3c	Sloper .M'
	4m		25	3b	😊
	3m		26	4a	^'1
Q-D	3m		27	4a	😊
	3m	S	27b	4a+	😊 ^'1 .M'
	3m		27t	3a+	😊 .M'
	3m		28	4a	😊 ↲
	4m		29	3c	😊 ^'1
	4m HBall 3b		30	3b	COOL ^'1
	3m		31	2c+	↓ Fun
	3m		32	4a	😊 CRIMP
	4m HBall 2c		32b	2c	COOL 😊
	3m	S	33	3c	😊 ^'1
	2m		33b	3a	😊
	2m		34	4c	Sloper .M'
	3m		35	3c	😊 ^'1 Ⅲ
	3m		36	3b	😊
	4m		37	3a+	😊 .M'
	4m HBall 2c		37b	4a	😊 COOL .M'

Magicien total

P 2 min

P ⊕ *page-180*

1 - 25
2a-3c

Route du Loup

125m

Orange 14 – 4b; Jim Bacon

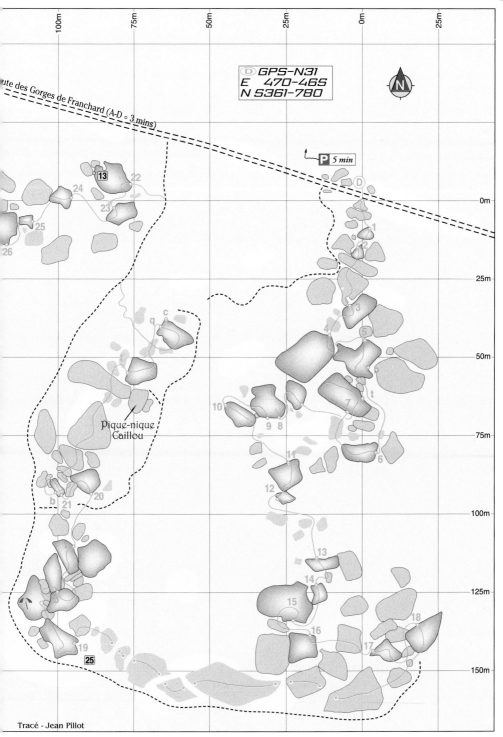

GPS–N31
E 470–465
N 5361–780

Route des Gorges de Franchard (A-D ≈ 3 mins)

P 5 min

Pique-nique
Caillou

Tracé - Jean Pillot

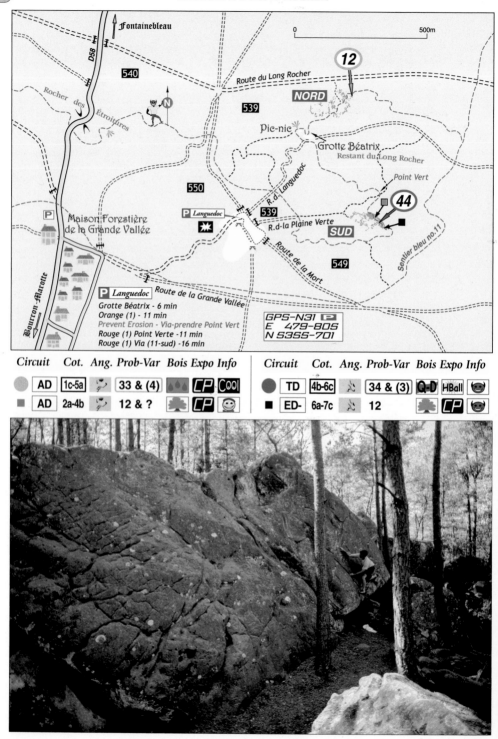

540

Rocher des Étroitures

D58

Fontainebleau

Route du Long Rocher

539

NORD

12

Pic-nic

Grotte Béatrix

Restant du Long Rocher

Point Vert

550

R.d. Languedoc

539

44

SUD

Languedoc

R.d-la Plaine Verte

Sentier bleu no.11

Maison Forestière de la Grande Vallée

Bourron-Marotte

Route de la Mort

549

Route de la Grande Vallée

0   500m

| P Languedoc | Route de la Grande Vallée |

Grotte Béatrix - 6 min
Orange (1) - 11 min
Prevent Erosion - Via-prendre Point Vert
Rouge (1) Point Verte -11 min
Rouge (1) Via (11-sud) -16 min

GPS-N31
E   479-805
N 5355-701

Circuit	Cot.	Ang.	Prob-Var	Bois	Expo	Info
●	AD	1c-5a	🏃	33 & (4)	💧	CP	Cool
■	AD	2a-4b	🏃	12 & ?	🌳	CP	🙂

Circuit	Cot.	Ang.	Prob-Var	Bois	Expo	Info
●	TD	4b-6c	🏃	34 & (3)	Q-D	HBall	👓
■	ED-	6a-7c	🏃	12	🌳	CP	👓

Orange 7 - 4a; Jingo

93

Restant du Long Rocher est une chaîne de collines assez élevée, située à 6km au sud-ouest de Fontainebleau. C'est un site couvert de blocs offrant une grande diversité de passages pour chaque époque de l'année. La face sud sèche rapidement, et c'est là où on peut trouver le circuit rouge. Notre circuit orange est situé sur la face nord de la chaîne. Le site est facile d'accès grâce à de bons sentiers (pratique pour les grands paniers de pique-nique). Nous avons appelé ce circuit le manège puisqu'il offre de nombreux passages verticaux et horizontaux tout autour des blocs. Tous les passages sont mémorables de par la diversité de leur style et de leur technique. La hauteur abrupte du premier bloc en effraiera plus d'un. Heureusement une fois en haut du bloc il y a des prises gigantesques et le passage devient alors plus une affaire de maîtrise de soi plutôt qu'un monstre de technicité. Le temps que vous arriviez au (2) et vous aurez l'impression d'avoir déjà grimpé la moitié du circuit. La grande dalle (3) est rassurante car très plaisante et réalisable. Il est utile

de suivre les flèches orange de bloc en bloc puisqu'il y a d'excellentes lignes entre les passages fléchés de ce circuit. Ce circuit est exposé nord et il est profondément enfoui dans les arbres, ce qui explique que les rochers ne sèchent pas rapidement. Par contre par grosse chaleur, c'est l'un des meilleurs circuits de Fontainebleau puisque la majorité des passages restent à l'ombre toute la journée. Par endroits les voies sont un peu hautes, mais elles offrent un bon apprentissage à tous ceux qui souhaitent grimper les circuits les plus effrayants de la forêt. Un bon circuit à faire avant d'attaquer ''Le Marathon'' au Gros Sablons.

Orange 18 - 2c; Jingo

Orange 19 - 5a; Jingo

Restant du Long Rocher is a long ridge of hills that is 6km south west of Fontainebleau, and forms quite a significant rise with views back to the town over the continuous forest. It is covered with boulders on both sides to give a good variety of climbing for different times of the year. The south side is set in trees and dries quickly, and is covered by our red circuit (note: there are also old markings of yellow, orange & green circuits - fallen victim to decay). To the north side of the ridge is our lovely orange circuit, and is where the hill quietly descends into moss covered jungle! The area is easily accessed with good footpaths (handy for giant picnic hamper access), and the blue footpath sentier-11 cuts through the circuit at several points. Storms in the past have created havoc in this area with fallen trees everywhere, most have now decayed and the circuit has returned to a good outing on rock for most of the way. We have called this circuit the 'Merry-go-round,' since there is so much extra climbing up down and around the blocks. The individual problems are very memorable in their own right, with all styles of problem to test you. The sheer height and bombacity of the first block will strike fear into the hearts of many climbers. Fortunately you can cop out near the top on the gigantic holds, and it is more of a head problem than a technical fiend. You feel like you've climbed half a circuit by the time you reach problem (2). The big slab at (3) reassures you that whilst the problems are an undertaking, they are not suicidal, but quite pleasant and possible. You benefit hugely from following the orange arrows around the boulders, since there is so much excellent in-between climbing on the complete trace of the circuit. There are a couple of parts when you have to walk through the undergrowth to link the three parts of the circuit; look for a small overhanging fang after (23), then drop down to the bottom of the valley to find (26). Because this circuit faces north and is deep in the trees, it won't dry out quickly at all. In a heatwave though, it is one of the most perfect circuits in Font and keeps shade on nearly all of the problems, all day long. It is a bit highball in parts, but offers an excellent apprenticeship for those working up through the more fearful circuits. A good circuit to tick before taking on 'Le Marathon' at Gros Sablons.

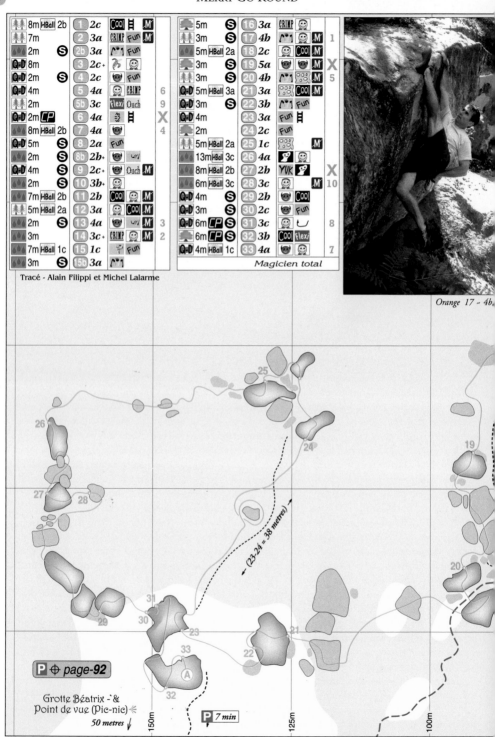

Tracé - Alain Filippi et Michel Lalarme

Magicien total

Orange 17 - 4b

P ⊕ page-92

Grotte Béatrix - &
Point de vue (Pic-nie)
50 metres ↓

P 7 min

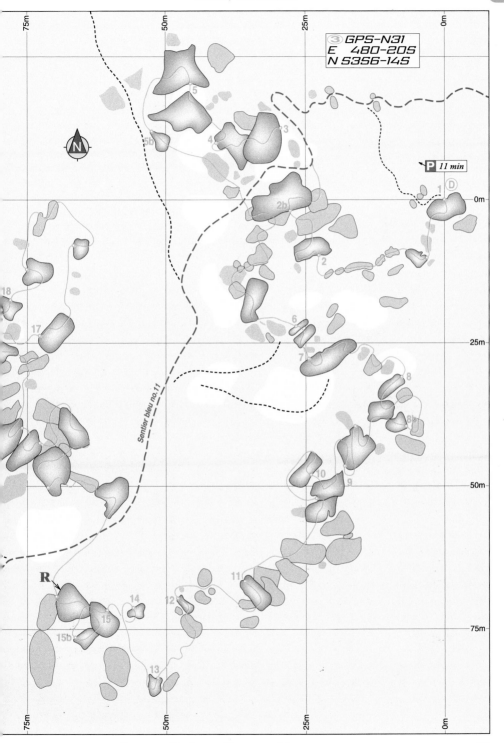

③ GPS-N31
E 480-205
N 5356-145

P 11 min

Sentier bleu no.11

Maunoury est un site magique qui aurait sa place sur la liste des 10 sites d'escalade les plus mémorables. Les rochers sont situés sur le versant sud de la colline et surplombent la forêt de pins qui entoure le charmant village de Larchant. C'est un endroit très tranquille et un peu redouté par les grimpeurs. Les rochers sont très grands presque trop grands pour faire du bloc. Cependant dire que l'escalade sur ce site est effrayante serait une condamnation injuste, les blocs offrent le plus souvent de très bonnes prises donnant des passages superbes. En revanche les aires de réception sont terribles à tel point que même un crash pad ne sert à rien. Il faut en effet exercer la plus grande prudence sur ce site car à une telle hauteur et avec tant de blocs en bas des voies, vous ne survivriez pas à une chute, donc ne tombez pas ! Il y a trois circuits traditionnels : orange, bleu et rouge. Ils offrent tous des voies classiques très typiques de Fontainebleau sur de grands blocs. Le circuit orange a un niveau de difficulté plutôt facile, cependant ce n'est pas un circuit destiné aux débutants. Vous aurez besoin d'adresse, de technique et un esprit calme pour vraiment l'apprécier, si vous possédez ces qualités alors vous passerez un excellent moment au milieu de ces blocs géants. Les 54 passages donnent au total un minimum de 600 mètres de dénivelé à la montée. Le circuit ne vous fait pratiquement jamais mettre le pied au sol donc un tapis ou un pad ne sont pas nécessaires. Le balisage par des points peints sur les rochers est en général plutôt bon sinon nous vous recommandons une photocopie de notre topo pour vous déplacer. Les passages de Maunoury vous feront craquer mentalement, cependant une fois que vous les aurez vus, testés et compris, vous les réussirez tous.

Orange 39 ~ 2a+; Libby Graham

Orange 35 - 2b; Elisa Neuville

Orange 40 – 2b+; Shaun McCance

Orange 54 ~ 3a; Matt Nicholson

Maunoury is a magical place, and would be well placed in anyone's list of 10 memorable climbing spots of all time. The position of the rocks on the south facing hillside is almost perfect, overlooking the pine forest that envelopes the town of the Larchant, alluring the eye with it's magnificent church. There are constantly, extensive 'Ile de France' views eastwards, so often lit up by sunshine and enhanced with puffy white clouds, scattered but uniformly floating at diminishing random. It is a quiet spot and is sensibly feared by most climbers. It is home to a jumbled chaos of highball blocks, fairly described as oversized - not immense however, but just on the giant side. To say that the climbing is fearful would be an unfair condemnation, the rock is often well pocketed and has an abundance of good footholds to make the climbing delightful. The landings on the other hand are dodgy; in fact, so dodgy, that you don't even need a crash pad! From such a height - with such an array of boulders, you wouldn't survive, so you don't fall off, and therefore don't even need a crash pad – logical to the end. The rocks also have a tragic history, years ago a rock fell over during the night onto some sleeping climbers underneath; it is an area that demands tremendous caution. There are three traditional circuits; orange, blue and red; all are classic, full on, and are high ball circuits. This orange circuit may get an easy grade, but it is not a beginner's circuit in any shape or form. You need skill, technique and an astoundingly calm mind to really 'enjoy' this one, if you have those qualities in abundance – then this will be a great day out for you in highball city. It's a full scale undertaking; the 54 problems average at 6 metres, plus the same amount again in link climbing, to give a minimum of 600 metres in your trip. The circuit never really touches the ground, so you don't need a pad or a mat – either would be a headache on this sojourn. Often the circuit is well marked with paint blobs; but if it's not, then a photocopy of our topo in your pocket will be invaluable. Maunoury is uncluttered and best enjoyed in a complete free flowing manner. The look of the problems will psyche you out, they are way impressive; but then again, once seen, once challenged, once captivated - you've just gotta go ticking.

Tracé - Pierre Chambert et Maurice Martin

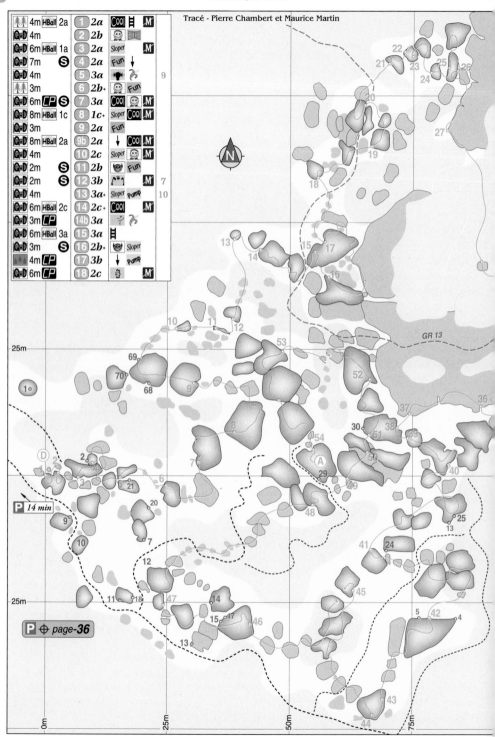

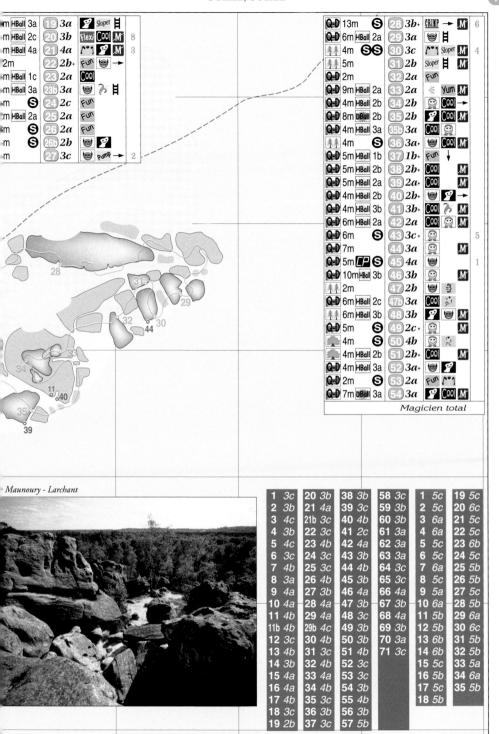

Left column routes:
Route	Grade
m HBall 3a	19 3a
m HBall 2c	20 3b
m HBall 4a	21 4a
2m	22 2b+
m HBall 1c	23 2a
m HBall 3a	23b 3a
m S	24 2c
m HBall 2a	25 2a
m S	26 2a
m S	26b 2b
m	27 3c

Right columns routes:
Q-D 13m S	28 3b+		6
Q-D 6m HBall 2a	29 3a		
4m SS	30 3c		4
5m	31 2b		
Q-D 2m	32 2a		
Q-D 9m HBall 2a	33 2a		
Q-D 4m HBall 2b	34 2b		
Q-D 8m DBall 2b	35 2b		
Q-D 4m HBall 3a	35b 3a		
4m S	36 3a+		
Q-D 5m HBall 1b	37 1b+		
Q-D 5m HBall 2b	38 2b+		
Q-D 5m HBall 2a	39 2a+		
Q-D 4m HBall 2b	40 2b+		
Q-D 4m HBall 3b	41 3b+		
Q-D 6m HBall 2a	42 2a		
Q-D 6m S	43 3c+		5
Q-D 7m S	44 3a		
Q-D 5m S	45 4a		1
Q-D 10m HBall 3b	46 3b		
2m	47 2b		
Q-D 6m HBall 2c	47b 3a		
6m HBall 3b	48 3b		
Q-D 5m S	49 2c+		
4m S	50 4b		
4m HBall 2b	51 2b-		
Q-D 4m HBall 3a	52 3a+		
Q-D 2m S	53 2a		
Q-D 7m DBall 3a	54 3a		

Magicien total

Maunoury - Larchant

#	Gr	#	Gr	#	Gr	#	Gr	#	Gr	#	Gr
1	3c	20	3b	38	3b	58	3c	1	5c	19	5c
2	3b	21	4a	39	3c	59	3b	2	5c	20	6c
3	4c	21b	3c	40	4b	60	3b	3	6a	21	5c
4	3b	22	3c	41	2c	61	3a	4	6a	22	5c
5	4c	23	4b	42	4a	62	3a	5	5c	23	6b
6	3c	24	3c	43	3b	63	3a	6	5c	24	5c
7	4b	25	3c	44	4b	64	3c	7	6a	25	5b
8	3a	26	4b	45	3b	65	3c	8	5c	26	5b
9	4a	27	3b	46	4a	66	4a	9	5a	27	5c
10	4a	28	4a	47	3b	67	3b	10	6a	28	5b
11	4b	29	4a	48	3c	68	4a	11b	5b	29	6a
11b	4b	29b	4c	49	3b	69	3b	12	5b	30	6c
12	3c	30	4b	50	3b	70	3a	13	6b	31	5b
13	4b	31	3c	51	4b	71	3c	14	6b	32	5b
14	3b	32	4b	52	3c			15	5c	33	5a
15	4a	33	4a	53	3c			16	5b	34	6a
16	4a	34	4b	54	3b			17	5c	35	5b
17	4b	35	3c	55	4b			18	5b		
18	3c	36	3b	56	3b						
19	2b	37	3c	57	5b						

Orange 16 – 4b; Karim Benkorba

Vous vivrez une véritable aventure si vous suivez ce circuit. Bien qu'il n'ait que 18 à 19 passages listés, il vous emmène tout en haut de la colline de Franchard Cuisinière, et vous fait balader du haut en bas des plus grands blocs qui sont éparpillés sur son passage, avant de retourner en bas de la colline pour finir juste à côté du très connu Karma 8a. Ces montées et ces descentes ajoutent beaucoup d'escalade à ce circuit et le transforment en une fantastique excursion. Pour votre sécurité, nous vous recommandons d'avoir suffisamment d'expérience en cotation 3a, car ce circuit a de nombreux passages exposés dont il ne vaut mieux pas chuter. Une chute au (10) par exemple serait tout particulièrement désastreuse ! C'est de toute façon un passage à l'aspect tellement horrible et menaçant que beaucoup se sentiront trop effrayés pour avoir envie de l'essayer. Le reste du circuit est très divertissant et offre de bons défis. À première vue les rochers, tranquillement logés derrière une dense forêt de pins, paraissent très verts. Cependant après inspection, vous vous rendrez compte que pratiquement tous les passages ont été nettoyés et qu'ils restent secs. Le circuit orange est situé sur la crête nord et comme le vent y circule très bien, les blocs sèchent très rapidement. La partie centrale du circuit située en haut de la colline est l'endroit idéal pour profiter de vues splendides et pour faire un pique-nique à l'ombre ou au soleil selon votre choix. Il y a également un très long circuit de montagne sur ce site. Il est très poli et se fait en défis de vitesse. Donc ne soyez pas surpris si vous voyez de drôles de gens grimpant à vive allure avec leurs sacs à dos, leurs bandeaux et leurs shorts en lycra – bizarre !

Orange 2 – 4c; Laurent Charlatte

This circuit is more of an adventure trip than a collection of small problems. There are only 18-19 listed problems, which would suggest a mere 80 metres of actual climbing perhaps. However, this circuit takes a long trip up to the top of the hill at Franchard Cuisinière, wandering up and down most of the big boulders scattered in its path - before returning back down the hill to finish just next to the famous Karma 8a. This upping and downing adds a huge amount of climbing and makes it a wonderful excursion, giving around 400 metres of cranking. You need to be a competent climber in the 3a grade for simple safety reasons on this circuit, since many of the boulders are high and falling off is not a viable option. In fact, falling off the crux problem (10) which is a realistic 4b, could be exceptionally unhealthy! An optimistic outcome would be a trip to hospital. At least (10) looks mean and nasty, so you are not likely to even attempt it if you are faint hearted or weak armed. This said, the rest of the circuit 'without this problem,' is still a very good challenge and perfect for a morning or afternoon's entertainment. Franchard Cuisinière is a very large area and covers most of the hills south of the parking area. At first sight, all the rocks appear big and green, murmuring quietly beneath a canopy of pine trees. However, after close inspection, you will find that nearly all the problems are clear of lichen and stay dry for most of the time. The orange circuit is located on the main northern ridge, and because it runs from west to east, the wind funnels around it very well - allowing it to dry out very quickly indeed. The central part of the circuit is high up on top of the hill and is a lovely place to get some good views, perfect for a picnic in the shade or sun. There is also a very long mountain circuit here, painted in red or orange dashes. It is incredibly polished and done as a speed challenge, you may see some odd folk racing around it with rucksacs on, sweat bands, lycra shorts – bizzare!

Orange 10 – 4b; James Bacon

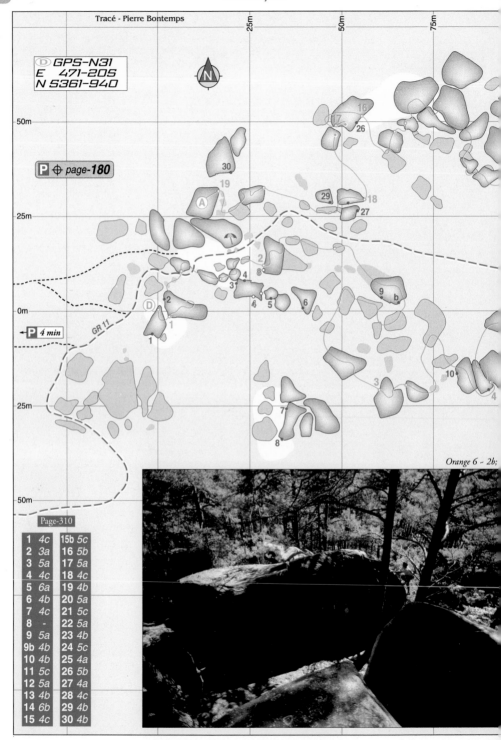

Tracé - Pierre Bontemps

25m   50m   75m

Ⓓ **GPS-N31**
E   471-205
N 5361-940

N

50m

Ⓟ ⊕ page-**180**

16
17   26
30
19
29   18
A   27
25m
2
8
4
3   9   b
2   6
Ⓓ   4
0m   2   5
1
1   3
← Ⓟ 4 min
GR 11   10
4
25m
7

8

Orange 6 - 2b;

50m

Page-310

1	*4c*	**15b**	*5c*
2	*3a*	**16**	*5b*
3	*5a*	**17**	*5a*
4	*4c*	**18**	*4c*
5	*6a*	**19**	*4b*
6	*4b*	**20**	*5a*
7	*4c*	**21**	*5c*
8	*-*	**22**	*5a*
9	*5a*	**23**	*4b*
9b	*4b*	**24**	*5c*
10	*4b*	**25**	*4a*
11	*5c*	**26**	*5b*
12	*5a*	**27**	*4a*
13	*4b*	**28**	*4c*
14	*6b*	**29**	*4b*
15	*4c*	**30**	*4b*

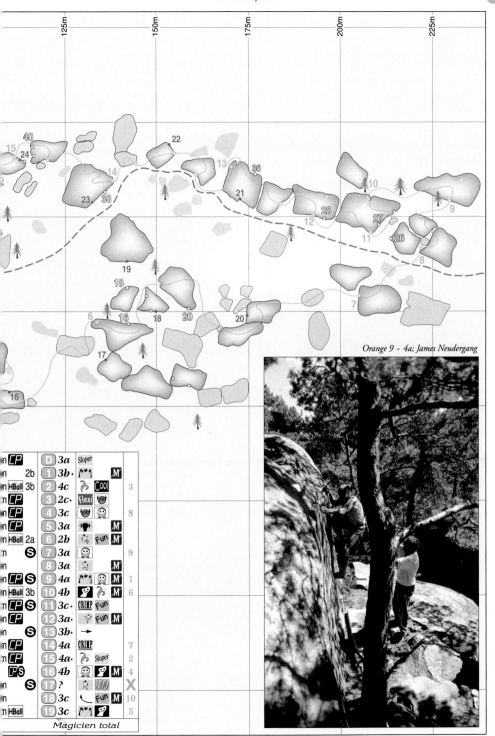

Orange 9 - 4a; James Neudergang

n **CP**	D	*3a*	Sloper
n	1	*3b+*	
n HBall 3b	2	*4c*	COOL
n **CP**	3	*2c+*	Flexi
n **CP**	4	*3c*	
n **CP**	5	*3a*	
n HBall 2a	6	*2b*	Fun
n **S**	7	*3a*	
n	8	*3a*	
n **CP S**	9	*4a*	
n HBall 3b	10	*4b*	
n **CP S**	11	*3c+*	CRIMP Fun
n **CP**	12	*3a+*	Fun
n **S**	13	*3b+*	→
n **CP**	14	*4a*	CRIMP
n **CP**	15	*4a+*	Sloper
CP S	16	*4b*	
n **S**	17	*?*	BW
n	18	*3c*	Fun
n HBall	19	*3c*	

Magicien total

"42 Bosses"

C'est le circuit idéal lors d'une journée de canicule puisque, d'une part, il suit une crête bien ventée et que d'autre part, la plupart des voies sont bien ombragées. C'est donc un site à ne pas oublier durant une vague de chaleur. Les passages longent le ''Sentier des 25 Bosses''. Durant le week-end, le sentier se remplit de coureurs et de randonneurs, mais durant la semaine c'est un endroit très calme et tranquille. Bien que nous ne puissions pas vous promettre que vous serez seul à grimper, nous vous conseillons ce site si vous souhaitez grimper loin des autres. C'est un circuit dont la difficulté est modérée, où vous aurez la possibilité de faire la majorité des passages à vu et où il vous sera aisé de repérer les voies les plus horribles et difficiles. Nous avons décidé de terminer le circuit sur le (42), passage sympa, offrant de belles vues vers le nord-ouest au-delà de la forêt des Trois Pignons. Après le (42) l'escalade change et les voies enfouies dans la végétation sont de moins bonne qualité. La forêt est très humide et nous vous déconseillons donc de visiter ce site en-dehors d'une période ensoleillée. En revanche même humide, la forêt (sans sable) permet une ballade sympathique. Les passages n'ont pour la plupart aucune trace de magnésie et les résoudre devient un véritable défis physique et mental. Il arrive parfois que certaines voies soient couvertes d'aiguilles de pins, mais elles peuvent être nettoyées facilement avec un pof. Les passages ne sont pour la plupart pas très haut, mais nombre d'entre eux sont difficiles et demandent beaucoup d'énergie. Ils offrent également des variantes diaboliques pour les adeptes des grattons. C'est un site paradisiaque avec la senteur des pins, le bruit du vent et le chant des oiseaux, la lumière charismatique et le bois qui craque. Réservez ce circuit pour un jour d'été exceptionnel.

Orange 15 - 3a; Wobbly

Le Grand Canyon de Cathédral (with the wobbly bridge)

This is a perfect circuit for a real scorcher of a day since most of the problems are well shaded and enjoy wonderful dappled sunshine. It also follows a ridge that seems to catch any wind blowing, definitely worth remembering during a heatwave. The problems run alongside the major circular footpath of the Trois Pignons - 'Sentier des 25 Bosses' (footpath of 25 hills). At weekends the sentier is busy with runners and ramblers, alternatively during midweek, the whole area is wonderfully quiet and tranquil. I can't promise that you'll be on your own, but it's one of the best places to pick if you want a whole circuit to yourself (apart from the mean-black frightener at Gros Sabons). This is a circuit of comfortable difficulty, one where you can enjoy on-sighting most problems, and where the harder nasties can be easily spotted. This circuit began life as a very easy tour, but was then expanded up to 52 problems - upping the grade to AD+. During the great storm of 1999, the last 10 problems of the circuit were cataclysimically blitzed with fallen trees, and this part is still enclosed by a jungle of debris. The circuit comfortably ends on a nice high at problem (42), with lovely views to the NW across the Trois Pignons forest. Thereafter, the whole nature of the climbing changes and the buried problems are generally of lower quality and sulk in a depressing passages. The forest here seems to thrive on dampness with mosses growing in abundance, so don't even dream of coming here outside of a good spell of dry weather. On the plus side, a dry rainforest gives a very bouncy and enjoyable stomp through the woods, and is sand free! The problems are usually unchalked, thereby offering both a physical and mental challenge to crack the code. Sometimes entire problems are coated with pine needles, but these can easily be swished off effortlessly with your pof so don't worry. Most problems are low but have a good punch to them, and many are surprisingly tricky with fiendish variations for the crimpers. It's certainly not an area suited to mindless power training, and is completely unsuitable for slappy-thugs. This outcrop is about elegant paradise; the smell of natures pine needles, mystical wind noises and elegant birdsong, charismatic light and creaking bark; it's the forest at its best. Reserve this circuit for a magical summer's day.

Tracé - Jacques Meynieu

GPS-N31
E 465-435
N 5356-041

P ⊕ page-118

P 8 min

Sentier 25 Bosses

GR 1

GR 1

Depart Orange

P 7 min

🌲 3m		1	3c	😊	🪜
🌿 3m		2	2b	😐	
🌿 4m	S	3	3b	Fun	
🌳 4m		4	4a+	😊	🪜
🌲 4m	S	5	3b	😊	🪜
🌲 3m		5b	3c	Flexi	🪜
🌲 3m		6	3a	NAF	←
🌳 5m	S	7	2b	Fun	
🌿 4m	S	7b	4c	🧗	🪜
🌲 5m		8	3c	Fun	
🌲 5m	CP S	8b	6a+	Trick	
🌲 3m		9	3c		
🌳 3m		10	3a+	🧗	
🌲 4m		11	2c+		
🌲 4m	SS	12	3c	😊	🧗
Q-D 2m		13	2b	🧗	🧗1
🌲 7m		14	2a	Fun	↪
🌲 4m		14b	3a	🧗	
🌲 4m		15	3a	📖	
🌿 10m		16	3c	↪	
🌿 5m	CP	16b	4b	😊	🧩
🌲 3m	S	17	2c	🧗1	
🌲 6m		18	1c	∧	
🌲 3m		18b	5a	🧗1	😊
🌲 5m	S	19	3b	∿	Fun

Chemin de
L'Avenir de
Vaudoué

Chemin de la Cathédrale

🌲🌲 3m	Ⓢ	20 3b	😊	Flexi	
🌲🌲 3m		21 2c	🏃		
🌲🌲 5m		22 3c	⌐ Fun	.M'	
🌲🌲 6m		23 2c	L		
🌲🌲 3m	Ⓢ	24 3a	Fun		
🌳 4m		25 1c+	🏃		
Q-D 9m		26 3c+	← 🐍	.M'	
Q-D 2m	Ⓢ	27 2c+	Fun		
🌲🌲 4m	Ⓢ	28 4b	CRIMP	.M'	2
💧💧 4m		29 2c	↓		
💧💧 5m		29b 4a	CRIMP Cool	.M'	6
🌲 4m		30 4a	Flexi	.M'	7
🌲🌲 3m		31 2a	⌁		

Orange 7 - 2b: Wobbly - Ascent ou descent, fun

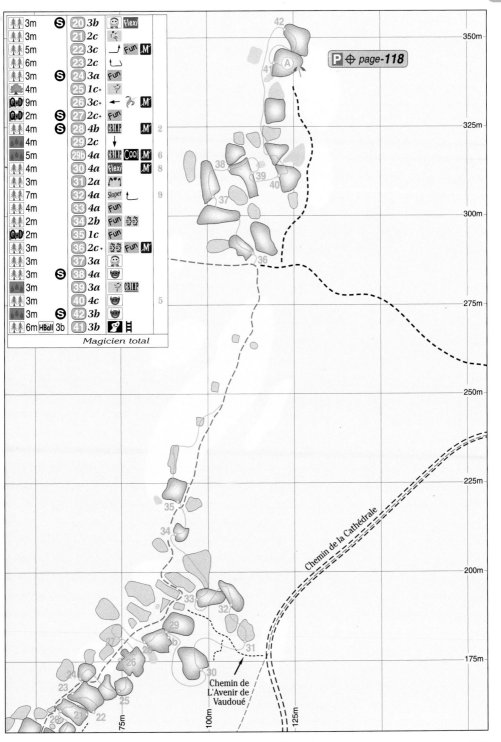

🌲🌲 3m	Ⓢ	20	3b	😊 Flexi	
🌲🌲 3m		21	2c	🏃	
🌲🌲 5m		22	3c	Fun M*	
🌲🌲 6m		23	2c	⌒	
🌲🌲 3m	Ⓢ	24	3a	Fun	
🌳 4m		25	1c+	🏃	
9m		26	3c+	← 🏃 M*	
2m	Ⓢ	27	2c+	Fun	
🌲🌲 4m	Ⓢ	28	4b	CRIMP M*	2
4m		29	2c	↓	
5m		29b	4a	CRIMP COOl M*	6
🌲🌲 4m		30	4a	Flexi M*	8
🌲🌲 3m		31	2a	⌃🔴	
🌲🌲 7m		32	4a	Sloper	9
🌲🌲 4m		33	4a	Fun	
🌲🌲 2m		34	2b	Fun 🤸	
2m		35	1c	Fun	
🌲🌲 3m		36	2c+	🤸 Fun M*	
🌲🌲 3m		37	3a	😊	
🌲🌲 3m	Ⓢ	38	4a	😊	
3m		39	3a	😊 CRIMP	
3m		40	4c	😊	
3m	Ⓢ	42	3b	😊	
🌲🌲 6m	HBall 3b	41	3b	😊 ☰	

Magicien total

P ⊕ *page-118*

page-118

Chemin de la Cathédrale

Chemin de
L'Avenir de
Vaudoué

350m
325m
300m
275m
250m
225m
200m
175m

75m
100m
125m

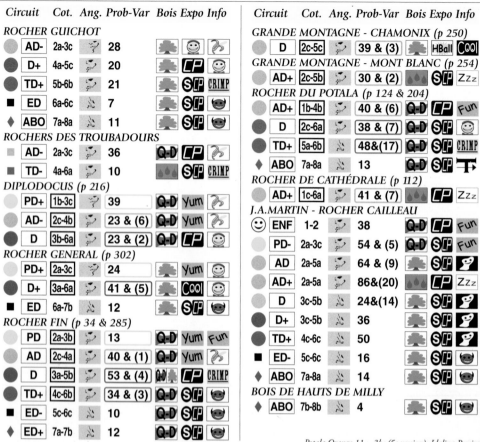

Circuit	Cot.	Ang.	Prob-Var	Bois	Expo	Info
ROCHER GUICHOT						
AD-	2a-3c		28	tree	☺	
D+	4a-5c		20	tree	CP	☺
TD+	5b-6b		21	tree	SCP	CRIMP
ED	6a-6c		7	tree	SCP	☺
ABO	7a-8a		11	tree	SCP	☺
ROCHERS DES TROUBADOURS						
AD-	2a-3c		36	Q-D	CP	
TD-	4a-6a		10		SCP	CRIMP
DIPLODOCUS (p 216)						
PD+	1b-3c		39	Q-D	Yum	
AD-	2c-4b		23 & (6)	Q-D	Yum	
D	3b-6a		23 & (2)	Q-D	CP	☺
ROCHER GENERAL (p 302)						
PD+	2a-3c		24	tree	Yum	☺
D+	3a-6a		41 & (5)	tree	Cool	
ED	6a-7b		12	tree	SCP	☺
ROCHER FIN (p 34 & 285)						
PD	2a-3b		13	Q-D	Yum	Fun
AD	2c-4a		40 & (1)	Q-D	Yum	
D	3a-5b		53 & (4)	Q-D	CP	CRIMP
TD+	4c-6b		34 & (3)	Q-D	SCP	☺
ED-	5c-6c		10	Q-D	SCP	☺
ED+	7a-7b		12	Q-D	SCP	☺
GRANDE MONTAGNE - CHAMONIX (p 250)						
D	2c-5c		39 & (3)	tree	HBall	Cool
GRANDE MONTAGNE - MONT BLANC (p 254)						
AD+	2c-5b		30 & (2)		SCP	Zzz
ROCHER DU POTALA (p 124 & 204)						
AD+	1b-4b		40 & (6)	Q-D	CP	Fun
D	2c-6a		38 & (7)	Q-D	SCP	☺
TD+	5a-6b		48&(17)	Q-D	SCP	CRIMP
ABO	7a-8a		13	Q-D	SCP	T
ROCHER DE CATHÉDRALE (p 112)						
AD+	1c-6a		41 & (7)		CP	Zzz
J.A.MARTIN - ROCHER CAILLEAU						
☺ ENF	1-2		38	Q-D	CP	Fun
PD-	2a-3c		54 & (5)	Q-D	SCP	Fun
AD	2a-5a		64 & (9)	tree	SCP	
AD+	2a-5a		86&(20)		CP	Zzz
D	3c-5b		24&(14)	tree	SCP	
D+	3c-5b		36	tree	SCP	
TD+	4c-6c		50	tree	SCP	
ED-	5c-6c		16	tree	SCP	☺
ABO	7a-8a		14	tree	SCP	☺
BOIS DE HAUTS DE MILLY						
ABO	7b-8b		4	tree	SCP	☺

Potala Orange 11 ~ 3b+(5c version); Idalina Pereira

The Westway Climbing Centre: London's premier climbing wall - for all your training needs.

With over 100 roped lines and 300 routes to choose from, a state of the art bouldering wall that has been hailed as one of the best training walls in the country, and the likes of Steve McClure, Gaz Parry and Neil Gresham regularly setting our boulder problems, you would be crazy not to come down and check us out.

Westway Sports Centre
1 Crowthorne Road
London
W10 6RP
T: 0208 969 0992
www.westwaysportscentre.org.uk

WESTWAY CLIMBING

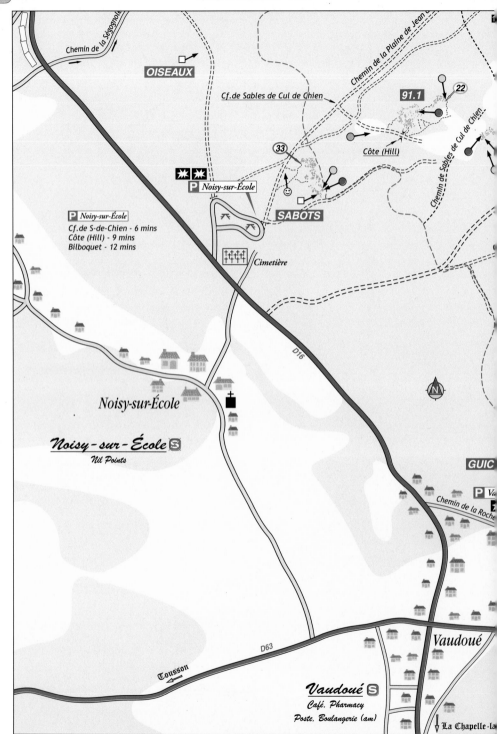

Chemin de la Ségognole

OISEAUX

Chemin de la Plaine de Jean

Cf.de Sables de Cul de Chien

91.1

22

33

Côte (Hill)

Chemin de Sables de Cul de Chien

SABOTS

P Noisy-sur-École

P Noisy-sur-École
Cf.de S-de-Chien - 6 mins
Côte (Hill) - 9 mins
Bilboquet - 12 mins

Cimetière

D16

N

Noisy-sur-École

Noisy-sur-École S
Nil Points

GUIC

P Va

Chemin de la Roche

D63

Tousson

Vaudoué

Vaudoué S
Café, Pharmacy
Poste, Boulangerie (am)

La Chapelle-la

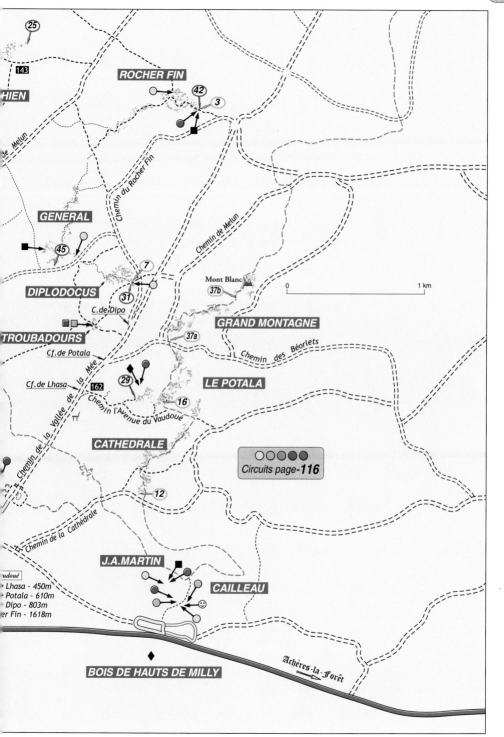

Circuits page-**116**

Rocher du Potala (parfois appelé Rocher de la Mée) est un massif à visiter lors d'une première visite à Fontainebleau. Il y a trois circuits : orange, bleu et rouge – facile, moyen et difficile – et les aires de réception sont pour la plupart excellentes. Le circuit orange offre 40 voies très variées qui plairont à tous les grimpeurs. Nous recommandons un peu d'échauffement avant de débuter puisque le départ du circuit demande beaucoup d'efforts en particulier avec le deuxième passage très exposé. Cependant ne vous laissez pas impressionner par le départ car le reste du circuit offre de très bons passages à bonne hauteur. Certaines voies sont des descentes combinées avec des montées, culminant avec le trou du (9) où, si vous avez des kilos en trop ou êtes rondelet, vous aurez à subir la presse. Le (11) est diabolique et ne devrait pas figurer sur ce circuit. Cependant il peut se faire avec un croche-talon en utilisant les mêmes prises. Peu après le (15) est impossible pour tous ceux qui ne peuvent pas utiliser les aplats. Le second groupe de blocs offre des voies avec très peu de hauteur, de bonnes aires de réception et des passages sympas. Le circuit s'en va ensuite dans les bois pour rejoindre le dernier groupe de blocs dans un site calme et tranquille, situé assez haut et qui bénéficie de beaucoup d'ombre dans l'après-midi. En fin de circuit, de nombreux passages peuvent être fait de différentes manières, compliquant les choses pour ceux qui suivent les cotations de très près. À l'origine, l'idée etait de créer un circuit géant pour relier le circuit Grande Montagne orange – à 100 mètres au nord. C'est pourquoi le tracé original finit en bas de la colline sur un petit rocher au milieu de nulle part, ce qui est bien dommage. Si vous n'êtes là que pour une journée, alors nous vous conseillons de finir au bleu (37), une arête tres plaisante qui vous fait terminer en beauté en haut du plus grand bloc, plutôt que dans les fougères et l'humidité de la mousse.

Orange 10 - 3b; Idalina Pereira

Orange 2 - 4a; Jingo

Orange 38b – 4b; Franck Tortuné

TROIS PIGNONS SUD - LE POTALA - (AD+/Orange)

Orange 25 ~ 3a; Nicolas Auclair

Rocher du Potala is the ideal place to visit on your first trip to Fontainebleau (sometimes referred to as Vallée de la Mée). There are three circuits here Orange-Blue-Red; easy, medium and hard, and the landings are mostly excellent. The orange circuit is a nice length of over 40 problems and with plenty of variety to suit most tastes. You almost need to warm up since the start seems full on, throwing in an almost terrifying second problem as a reasonable highball, or alternatively (2b) a sloper from hell. Don't be put off, since the circuit then settles down to some lovely low level problems with fun traversing. Some problems are descents combined with ascents, culminating with the hole on (9) – decision, belly down or belly up - that's a secret; if you are overweight or rotund – then suffer 'Le Squeeze.' Sense of humour failure will ensue at (11), which is obviously fiendish and on the wrong circuit. However, it can be unlocked with a foot hook, and still staying on the same handholds for the problem. Soon after, (15) will spit off anyone who can't deal with slopers. The second group of boulders is similar with low problems, good landings and some fun ups and downs. The circuit then wanders around the woods in a friendly fashion to the final group of blocs which are set high up, they get excellent afternoon shade, and are often a nice and quiet. A lot of the problems on the circuit in the latter part can be done in many different ways, complicating matters for the grader. Additionally this does give the climber a huge amount of extra climbing. The original traced circuit ends down the hill on a pebble in the middle of nowhere, which is a pity. The idea was to create a monster huge circuit and link up with the Orange circuit of Grand Montagne – about 100 metres to the north. If you are just here for the day, then it is better just to finish up blue 37, a lovely and pleasant arête, therefore finishing triumphantly on top of the highest block, rather than a damp fizzle, squnching hopelessly in the ferns and the moss.

			No.	Grade	Icons	Ref
Q-D	3m		1	3b		
Q-D	3m	HBall 3c	2	4a	M	6
Q-D	3m		2b	4b	Sloper M	4
Q-D	3m		3	4a+	Sloper Flexi M	7
Q-D	7m	S	4	3a	Fun	
Q-D	3m		5	3b		
Q-D	8m		6	3b	Fun Pump	
Q-D	6m	S	7	2c		
Q-D	7m	S	8	3a	↓	
Q-D	6m		9	3b	BW M	
Q-D	6m	S	10	3b	M	
Q-D	3m	CP S	11	3b+	Sloper M	1
✲✲	3m		11b	2a	Fun	
Q-D	4m	S	12	2c+		
✲✲	3m		13	3b		
Q-D	3m		14	4a	Flexi	
✲	4m		15	4b+	Sloper Pump	
✲✲	7m		16	3b		
✲✲	3m		16b	2c	Sloper	5
Q-D	3m		17	3b	CRIMP	
✲✲	2m		18	3a	NAF	
✲	8m		19	1c		
✲	3m		20	2c		
Q-D	8m		21	2c		
Q-D	3m	S	22	3c+		9
✲✲	3m	S	23	3c+	Pump M	10
	5m	CP	24	2c	COOl	
Q-D	5m	CP S	25	3a		
Q-D	4m	S	26	2a		
✲✲	3m		27	4a	COOl	
Q-D	4m	S	28	3b	Fun	
Q-D	5m	CP S	29	2b		
Q-D	7m	HBall 2a	30	2a	↓	
Q-D	3m		31	2b		
Q-D	3m	S	32	4a	↑	
Q-D	3m		33	3a		
✲✲	3m		34	3c+	↑	
✲✲	3m	S	35	3b		
✲✲	3m		35b	1b	Fun	
Q-D	3m		35t	2a+		
✲✲	3m		36	3a	Flexi	
Q-D	4m		37	3a		
✲✲	5m	3a	38	4c		2
Q-D	3m		38b	4b	M	3
Q-D	5m	HBall 2b	39	2b		
Q-D	4m	CP S	40	4a	COOl	8
✿	5m	HBall 2b	37	2c+	M	

Magicien total

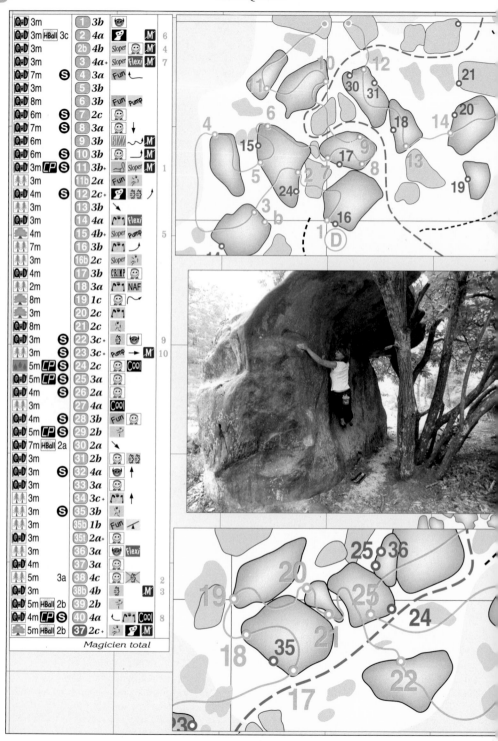

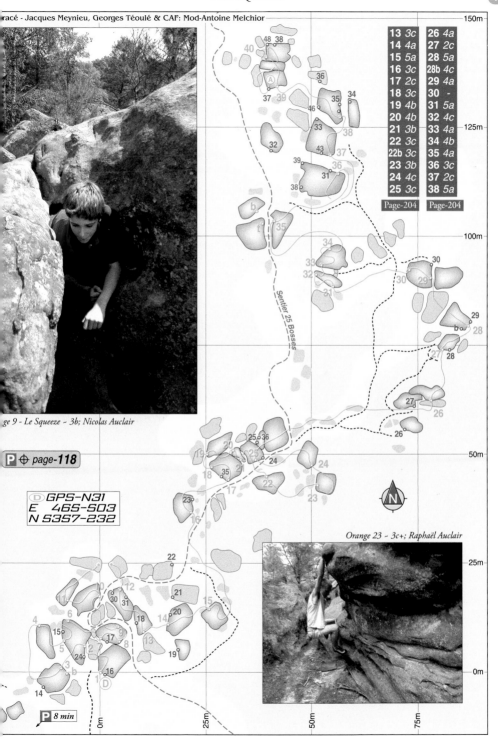

racé - Jacques Meynieu, Georges Téoulé & CAF: Mod-Antoine Melchior

13	3c	26	4a
14	4a	27	2c
15	5a	28	5a
16	3c	28b	4c
17	2c	29	4a
18	3c	30	-
19	4b	31	5a
20	4b	32	4c
21	3b	33	4a
22	3c	34	4b
22b	3c	35	4a
23	3b	36	3c
24	4c	37	2c
25	3c	38	5a
Page-204		Page-204	

ge 9 - Le Squeeze - 3b; Nicolas Auclair

P ⊕ page-118

GPS-N31
E 465-503
N 5357-232

Sentier 25 Bosses

Orange 23 - 3c+; Raphaël Auclair

P 8 min

95.2 est un nom dont vous vous rappellerez facilement puisque c'est tout simplement l'un des meilleurs sites d'escalade de la forêt des Trois Pignons. 95.2 est la hauteur entre les collines de l'ouest et de l'est de ce massif. Ce site est populaire du fait de ses 4 principaux circuits, jaune, bleu, rouge et blanc situés sur le côté est de la colline. Souvent oublié par de nombreux grimpeurs, le côté ouest de la colline reste peu fréquenté et l'escalade y est moins intensive du fait du niveau de difficulté moins élevé. Cette partie de la colline est constituée de sable très doux et l'érosion y est extrême, en particulier avec l'écoulement de l'eau de pluie. Par conséquent, elle a été clôturée afin d'éviter les piétinements et ainsi contrôler l'érosion de manière plus efficace. À l'origine le niveau de difficulté du circuit était de AD+ (vert) avec 50 passages ; mais celui-ci a été modifié à AD, omettant les blocs de l'espace clôturé et supprimant certaines voies sur les rochers trop fragiles. C'est un circuit superbe avec une cotation AD plutôt difficile. Il est possible d'ajouter des variantes et de trouver des passages cachés un peu plus faciles. Les aires de réception sont bonnes pour la plupart, mais notez qu'il est préférable d'avoir un coéquipier pour une bonne parade dans les passages les plus difficiles. C'est un site qui s'apprécie le mieux le matin de bonne heure lorsque les rayons du soleil sont sur les voies et que tout est calme et serein. Aux alentours de 7h du matin, le soleil est bien appréciable et illumine les passages bien différemment de l'après-midi ; c'est le moment magique pour grimper. Même durant la journée et en pleine chaleur, il y a des passages à l'ombre en haut de la colline. C'est l'endroit idéal pour faire du bloc si vous n'êtes pas comme Schwarzeneger et c'est également un site de pique-nique très sympa. Faites attention lorsque vous descendez de la colline pour retourner vers le début du circuit puisqu'il y a toujours un problème d'érosion dans ce secteur.

Orange 11 - 4c; Dorotheé Banvillet

Orange 1 - 4a; Dorotheé Banvillet   *Orange 37 - 3a; Cecile Saloni*

Orange 40 – 4a; Patrick Banvillet

95.2 is a funny name for an area of the forest, but one that you get used to quite quickly, simply because it's one of the best climbing areas in the Trois Pignons forest. The number comes from the spot height found between the western hill and the eastern hill in this part of the forest, and is neither the highest point of either. The area is most famous for the 4 main circuits of yellow, blue, red and white on the Eastern hill. Often forgotten by many, the western hill remains less crowded and a lot less intense due to the lower grade of climbing available. There are many boulders set in sandy soil to the south of the western hill, which is the original direct approach from the car park at La Croix St. Jérôme. This hillside is made of very soft sand and has a tremendous erosion problem from water run off, consequently it has been fenced off to protect and stop any further needless ground slip erosion from walking shoes etc. The original circuit was AD+(green) with some 50 problems; but this has been reduced to AD, omitting any boulders in the protected area and deleting a few problems on obviously soft rock. It is a superb circuit and at the very top end of AD. It is also a continuous circuit that keeps you on rock for most of the way, taking an interesting and twisting route through the wonderful central labyrinth of cool passages. There is plenty of scope to add variations at many points, and also find a lot of easier hidden problems. The landings are mostly good, but please note that the harder problems here mostly benefit from having a good spotter. The hill is at its best in very early morning when the sun warms the problems in the middle of the circuit and the whole area is quiet and serene. At around 7 in the morning, the early sunshine is lovely and illuminates the problems in a way that is so different to the afternoon sun; it's the magical time to come here. Even in the heat of the day, you can still find problems in the shade on the top of this hill. It's a perfect place to enjoy bouldering if you are not an Arnold, and is a lovely picnic area too. Note: Please be careful when descending the hill to the start of the circuit since there is still a problem with ground slip erosion.

Orange 33 ~ 3c+; Rodolphe Brault

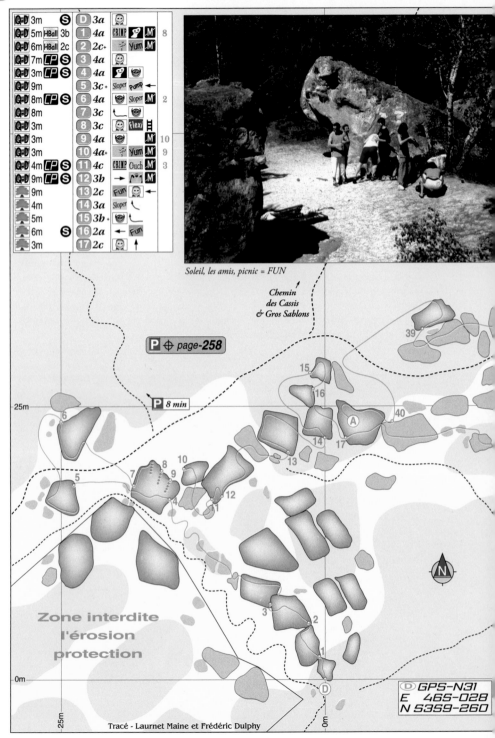

Q-D 3m		D 3a	😐		
Q-D 5m HBall 3b		1 4a	CRIMP 💢 M		8
Q-D 6m HBall 2c		2 2c+	Yum M		
Q-D 7m CP S		3 4a	😐		
Q-D 3m CP S		4 4a	💢 😁		
Q-D 9m		5 3c+	Sloper Pump ←		
Q-D 8m CP S		6 4a	😁 Sloper M		2
Q-D 8m		7 3c	😁		
Q-D 3m		8 3c	😐 Flexi		
Q-D 3m		9 4a	😁 M		10
Q-D 3m		10 4a+	Yum M		9
Q-D 4m CP S		11 4c	CRIMP Ouch M		3
Q-D 9m CP S		12 3b	→ M		
🌲 9m		13 2c	Fun 😁 ←		
🌲 4m		14 3a	Sloper		
🌲 5m		15 3b+			
🌲 6m S		16 2a	← Fun		
🌲 3m		17 2c	😐		

Soleil, les amis, picnic = FUN

Chemin des Cassis & Gros Sablons

P ⊕ page-**258**

P **8 min**

25m

Zone interdite l'érosion protection

0m

25m

D GPS-N3I
E 46S-028
N S3S9-260

Tracé - Laurnet Maine et Frédéric Dulphy

Ce circuit est idéal pour les grimpeurs qui ont de bonnes compétences et qui recherchent une variété de mouvements. C'est un circuit avec peu de grattons, mais qui reste intéressant. De bons nerfs sont un atout majeur pour grimper certaines lignes qui sont très hautes. La Rigole par exemple avec le malchanceux numéro (13) est tout particulièrement bien chiffré si on peut dire ! Il est déconseillé aux superstitieux. Bien que ce circuit soit exposé sud, de nombreux passages en particulier les plus durs, restent ombragés dans l'après-midi ; un choix judicieux pour les journées ensoleillées. La zone de départ a été fermée aux voitures et fait place aux artistes ; massivement ombragée par d'énormes chênes, elles est idéale pour un pique-nique lorsqu'il fait très chaud. Il faut noter qu'il y a seulement une voie pour s'échauffer avant les blocs géants. Au (3) vous devez descendre du haut du bloc de 7m en utilisant une chaîne.

Orange 3 - 3c; Sandy Ogilvie

La Rigole (13) n'est pas le passage le plus difficile, mais c'est celui où il y a le plus d'échecs. Lorsque vous commencez à être fatigué autour des 30e voies, nous vous conseillons de faire une pause puisque le reste du circuit apporte des passages compliqués qui sont difficiles à faire à vu. Les variantes du (41) valent la peine d'être toutes faites puisque les lignes sont toutes indépendantes. (41t) se débarrassera des grimpeurs qui ne souhaitent pas s'engager. Le GRI a été dévié en haut de la colline pour arrêter l'érosion. Les 4 derniers passages sont situés dans la zone de passages interdite donc les grimpeurs doivent seulement accéder à ces blocs s'ils restent sur les rochers – ne touchez pas les clôtures. Ces 4 derniers passages sont excellents, mais la roche est très friable donc ne faites pas plus de 3 essais pour chacun d'entre eux. Vous pouvez passer une journée entière sur ce circuit qui est très polyvalent et qui vaut la peine d'être visité.

Orange 14 & 15 - 2b-2c; Philip Hogan

This circuit is perfect for those climbers who have good all round expertise and are looking for every style of move to entertain the day. Another fine merit, is that there are virtually no crimps on it, so those with sore fingertips can have a soothing time here. It is certainly a circuit with interest, and a steady head is a major asset for some of the highballs; I think 'La Rigole' at unlucky number (13), is particularly well numbered to say the least! Those who are superstitious should give this problem a miss! Even though the circuit faces south, there always seems to be dappled shade on a lot of the problems, especially in the afternoon on the hard test pieces that occupy the latter part of the circuit; a fair choice on a sunny day. The starting area has been closed from cars, and now makes an enchanting artists spot; cool and densely shaded by massive old oak trees and perfect for a picnic during a scorcher. You only get one problem as a warm up before two giant high balls come thumping in. At (3) you have to descend using a long chain down an overhanging wall to even get off the top of the 7 metre block. There is continued interest as the circuit develops with a cute jump at (10). La Rigole (13) is not the hardest problem, but probably sees the most defeats. Finding the middle part of the circuit takes perseverance but is well worth it, and is rewarded by quietness. The circuit slowly works its way up the hill to the side of the GR1-popular footpath. Just when you are starting to get tired around the mid 30's, stop and have a break since it then throws a whole variety of complicated problems that are difficult to on-sight and will easily catch you out. Doing all the variations at (41) is really worthwhile since they are all fine independent problems on their own, (41t) is guaranteed to spit off the uncanny, or those without total commitment. The GR1 footpath at the top of the hill has been redirected to stop ground erosion. The last 4 problems are in this prohibited walking zone, so climbers should only get to the problems by climbing over the rock in a circuit fashion – don't touch the fences. The last 4 problems are excellent, but are on soft rock, so don't work the problems here – 3 tries and move on. It's a full day out on this one, totally versatile and rewarding.

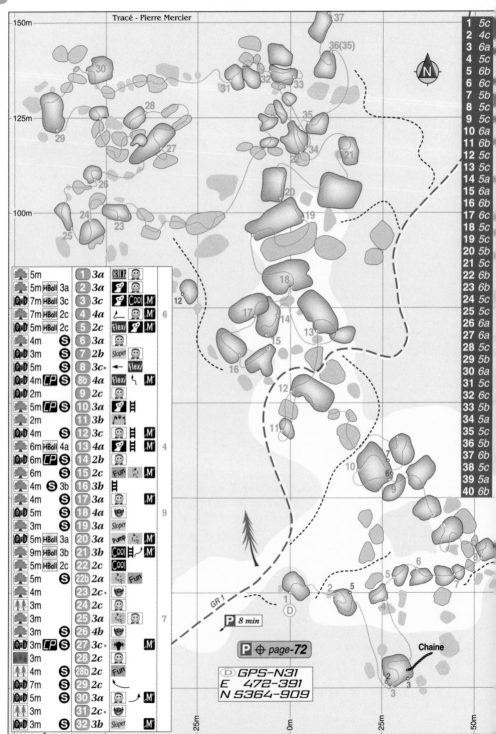

Tracé - Pierre Mercier

1	5c
2	4c
3	6a
4	5c
5	6b
6	6c
7	5b
8	5c
9	5c
10	6a
11	6b
12	5c
13	5c
14	5a
15	6a
16	6b
17	6c
18	5c
19	5c
20	5b
21	5c
22	6b
23	6b
24	5c
25	5c
26	6a
27	6a
28	5c
29	5b
30	6a
31	5c
32	6c
33	5b
34	5a
35	5c
36	5b
37	6b
38	5c
39	5a
40	6b

P ⊕ page-72

Ⓓ GPS-N31
E 472-391
N 5364-909

P 8 min

GR 1

Chaine

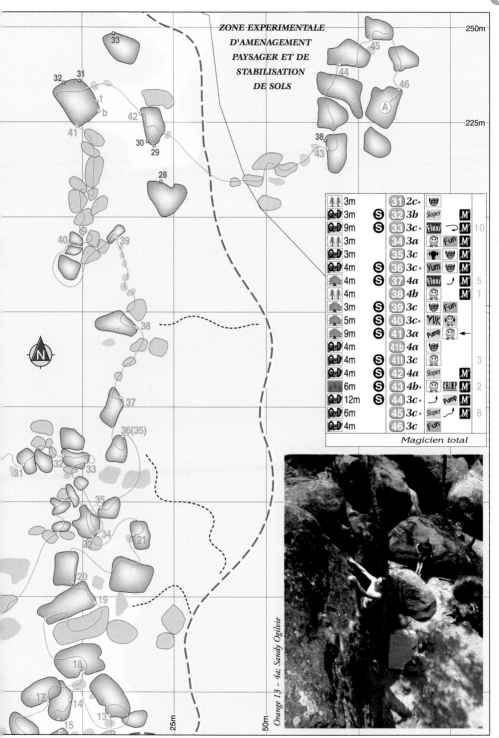

ZONE EXPERIMENTALE
D'AMENAGEMENT
PAYSAGER ET DE
STABILISATION
DE SOLS

250m

225m

🌲🌲 3m		31 2c+		
Q-D 3m	S	32 3b	Sloper	M 10
Q-D 9m	S	33 3c+	Flexi	M
🌲🌲 3m		34 3a	Fun	M
Q-D 3m		35 3c		M
Q-D 4m	S	36 3c+	Yum	M
🌲 4m	S	37 4a	Flexi	M 5
🌲🌲 4m		38 4b		M 1
🌲 3m	S	39 3c	Fun	
🌲 5m	S	40 3c+	YUK	
🌲 9m	S	41 3a	Pump	
Q-D 4m	S	41b 4a		
Q-D 4m	S	41t 3c		3
Q-D 4m	S	42 4a	Sloper	
🌲 6m	S	43 4b+	CRIMP	M 2
Q-D 12m	S	44 3c+	Pump	M
Q-D 6m		45 3c+	Sloper	M 8
Q-D 4m		46 3c	Fun	

Magicien total

Orange 13 – 4a; Sandy Ogilvie

Orange 33 – 3a; Dimanche (Sunday)

Franchard Isatis est l'un des meilleurs sites à visiter. Il offre des blocs superbes de 3 ou 4 mètres donnant des circuits bleu, rouge et blanc et des passages hors circuits désespérés comme l'arête de l'Angle Ben (7a+) et l'impressionnant L'arrache cœur 7c. Si vous n'êtes pas très fort et que vous visitez ces lieux avec un groupe de grimpeurs, ne vous laissez pas décourager puisqu'il y a un circuit orange pittoresque à travers les bois. Il est très divertissant et le niveau d'escalade est accessible à tous. Bien qu'il débute dans un lieu différent, il rejoint les autres circuits. Ce n'est pas le meilleur circuit comparé à ses équivalents locaux, mais il offre un excellent apprentissage dans l'art d'utiliser les grattons sur les dalles et dans la lévitation sur les prises invisibles. Le nom du circuit vient de la dalle (2). C'est une petite dalle avec des prises minuscules. Les grattons sont si fins qu'il est juste possible de poser une pièce de monnaie en équilibre ! C'est une bonne introduction de ce qu'il vous attend sur les autres dalles. Il n'y a rien de bien difficile sur les hauts passages en haut de la colline ; le premier est une dalle magnifique et probablement l'une des lignes les plus agréables à Isatis. Le second suit la voie la plus facile du Dru, similaire en forme à celui de Chamonix mais plus petit et beaucoup plus solide. Ce circuit recherche les passages courts sur petits rochers plutôt que les grands blocs dépourvus de bonnes prises. Le (13) est un classique, typique du divertissement que vous pouvez avoir sur un circuit orange. De nombreux passages vous mettront au défi puisqu'ils offrent différentes variantes. Pour les grimpeurs qui ont peu de temps le mieux est de finir au (40), puisque après ça le circuit a moins d'intérêt et se perd dans les sous-bois. C'est le circuit idéal d'une part pour améliorer votre technique sur dalle, et d'autre part parce qu'il est situé sous une couverture d'arbres qui vous protège du soleil d'été. Il est également une bonne alternative pour ceux qui progressent lentement sur le circuit bleu.

Orange 27 ~ 4b; Olivier Jaskulke & Laurence

Le Prises géant; le dalle no.2 ~ 4a (The hand holds for slab no. 2 - big eh!)

Orange 17 - 3c; Alain Lemeur

Franchard Isatis is one of the great spots to visit in Fontainebleau. It is where superb blocks of sandstone up to 3-4m high, stand proud and give wonderful circuits of Blue, red, white, and off circuit desperates such as the exasperating arête of Angle Ben's (7a+), and the highly impressive L'arrache-Coeur 7c. On the higher probability that you are not so strong and have ended up in a group of climbers visiting here, don't be disheartened since there is this quaint orange circuit that wanders through the woods. It will present you with a lot of fun and amusement at an achievable level, and although it starts in a different area, it later joins together with the other circuits. It's not a great circuit compared to its local counterparts, but certainly offers an excellent apprenticeship in the art of crimping on slabs and levitating on invisible footholds. We have named the circuit after the slab at (2). The slab is small, but, the holds are miniscule. The crimps are so thin that balancing coins on them is only just possible! It is a good taste of things to come on the slabs later on. Fortunately there is nothing too difficult about the early highballs on the giant blocks at the top of the hill; the first being a magnificent slab and probably one of the most enjoyable 'routes' at Isatis. The second takes the easiest way up the Dru, similar in shape to the one in Chamonix, but smaller, and a lot more solid. This circuit is more of a weave through the forest looking for small problems on shorter boulders, rather than tackling the bigger blocks themselves, which are invariably meanly deprived of good holds. (13) is a classic short problem, but typifies the fun you can have on a 'happy-orange' circuit. There is plenty on the circuit to challenge you since many problems have variations and other possibilities locally. Those climbers short on time (and high on intelligence), will most probably finish on the lovely high block of 40, since the circuit has little merit after this and wanders back into the undergrowth. It's a lovely circuit to improve your slab climbing without having to rip your fingertips to pieces, and rests under a canopy of thick trees to protect you from the powerful sun in summer. It is also an ideal alternative for those making slow progress on the blue circuit.

Orange 13- 3b+; Katia Dore

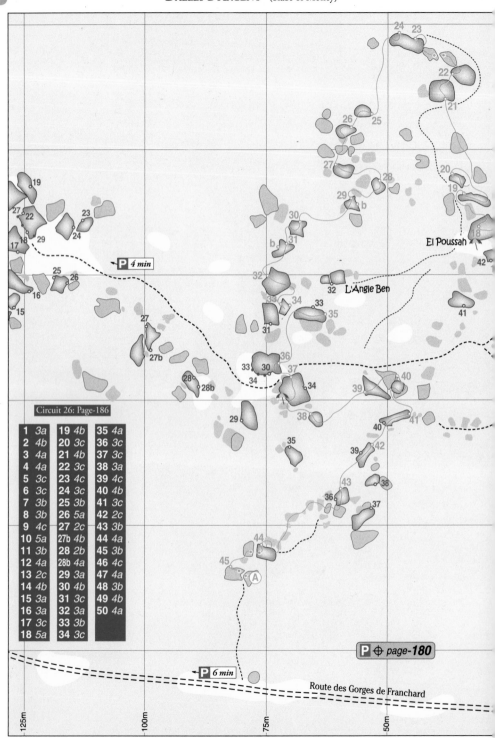

El Poussah

L'Angle Ben

Circuit 26: Page-186

1	3a	19	4b	35	4a
2	4b	20	3c	36	3c
3	4a	21	4b	37	3c
4	4a	22	3c	38	3a
5	3c	23	4c	39	4c
6	3c	24	3c	40	4b
7	3b	25	3b	41	3c
8	3b	26	5a	42	2c
9	4c	27	2c	43	3b
10	5a	27b	4b	44	4a
11	3b	28	2b	45	3b
12	4a	28b	4a	46	4c
13	2c	29	3a	47	4a
14	4b	30	4b	48	3b
15	3a	31	3c	49	4b
16	3a	32	3a	50	4a
17	3c	33	3b		
18	5a	34	3c		

Route des Gorges de Franchard

P ⊕ page-180

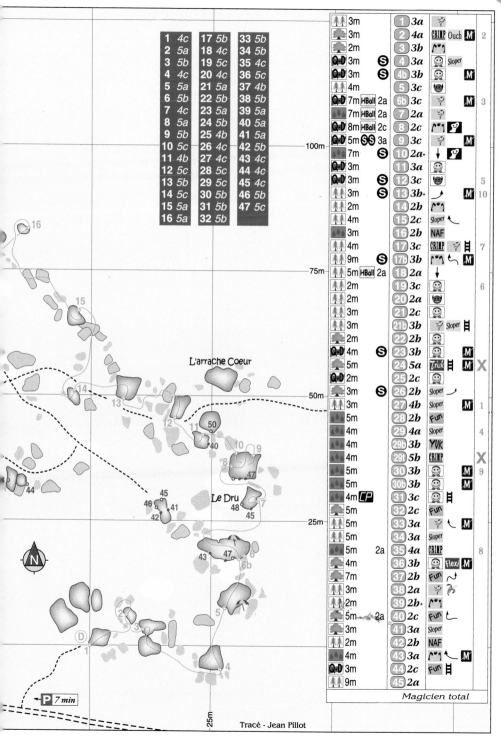

1	4c	17	5b	33 5b
2	5a	18	4c	34 5b
3	5b	19	5c	35 4c
4	4c	20	4c	36 5c
5	5a	21	5a	37 4b
6	5b	22	5b	38 5b
7	4c	23	5b	39 5a
8	5a	24	5b	40 5a
9	5b	25	4b	41 5a
10	5c	26	4c	42 5b
11	4b	27	4c	43 4c
12	5c	28	5c	44 4c
13	5b	29	5c	45 4c
14	5c	30	5b	46 5b
15	5a	31	5b	47 5c
16	5a	32	5b	

L'arrache Coeur

Le Dru

Magicien total

Tracé - Jean Pillot

Fontainebleau Château; impressive pad but closed on tuesdays, scenic gardens and restful ambience

Hotel Le Cygne - Milly-la-Forêt; excellent terrace for an afternoon beer.

Fontainebleau merry-go-round; quaint for the tiny tots

Barbizon; plenty of art to browse, new and old

L'Hotel de l'Aigle Noir; definitely 'the' upmarket place to stay in Bleau

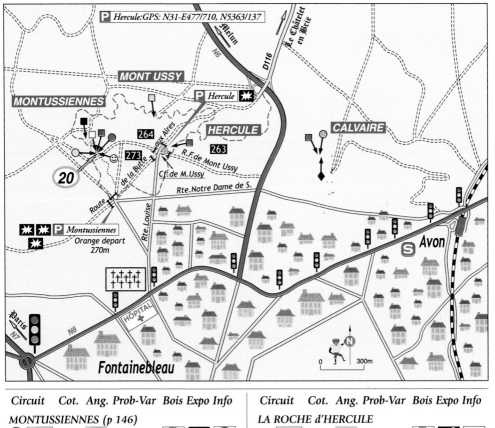

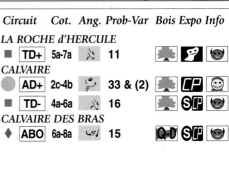

Circuit	Cot.	Ang.	Prob-Var	Bois	Expo	Info
MONTUSSIENNES (p 146)						
☺	ENF	1-3a	36 & (6)		CP	😊
⬤	PD-	1c-3c	28 & (8)		Cool	Fun
⬤	AD	2c-5a	31 & (4)		CP	😈
■	D+	4a-6a	38		SP	😈
⬤	ED-	5b-6c	33 & (2)		SP	😈
♦	ED+	7a-7c	16		SS	😈
MONT USSY						
⬜	PD	1c-3c	?		CP	🌵
■	D	4a-5b	?		CP	🌵
■	ED+	4c-7c	25 & (2)		CP	😈

Circuit	Cot.	Ang.	Prob-Var	Bois	Expo	Info
LA ROCHE d'HERCULE						
■	TD+	5a-7a	11		👻	😈
CALVAIRE						
⬤	AD+	2c-4b	33 & (2)		CP	😊
■	TD-	4a-6a	16		SP	😈
CALVAIRE DES BRAS						
♦	ABO	6a-8a	15		Q-D SP	😈

BOREAL

Montussiennes est l'un des rares sites d'escalade accessible à pied depuis le centre-ville de Fontainebleau. On y trouve souvent des enfants qui grimpent après l'école. Situé dans une forêt de chênes dense (qui sèche lentement) il fait partie des 3 sites d'escalade du Mont d'Ussy. À l'est du circuit au Carrefour du Mont d'Ussy, il y a 2 grands obélisques (Rocher d'Hercule) avec 16 passages spectaculaires, 3 faciles, 2 difficiles et les autres cotées à 5 et 6a. De nombreux blocs sont éparpillés au milieu des fougères avec un circuit TD non marqué qui est très populaire du fait qu'il soit si près de Fontainebleau. Le circuit orange débute à 500m à l'ouest, juste derrière la grotte de Montussiennes avec son toit spectaculaire tout noir du fait des nombreux feux de camp. Autour de cette cave géante il y a de superbes dévers qui semblent avoir des prises parfaitement placées. Il y a également une bonne concentration de plus petits blocs qui offrent un circuit rouge très dur mais excellent, ainsi qu'un circuit de passages rouge et blanc aux cotations de 7a ou plus. Étonnamment, les rochers offrent un excellent circuit orange ainsi qu'un circuit jaune plus facile. Il y a un circuit bleu qui n'est pas marqué mais qu'il est préférable de laisser de côté. Les rochers semblent parfaits pour un niveau de difficulté à 3b-4b. Le circuit est court avec seulement 31 passages. Il est ombragé durant la plus grande partie de la journée et donc il est idéal durant l'été. Le jaune est sympa et facile à suivre (les numéros ont récemment changé). L'orange est agréable et varié et assez marrant en particulier avec le (9), où il faut sauter et diriger votre postérieure dans un trou vous permettant de démarrer le passage assis. Si vous ne connaissez pas cette astuce le passage est infaisable. Le (5b) est un bijou, nous l'avons inclus, mais avons réalisé qu'il est un peu difficile pour la majorité des grimpeurs qui suivent les circuits orange. Certaines prises sur le circuit manquent d'adhérence, mais le plastique des chaussons permet de remédier à ce problème. Dans l'ensemble c'est un site merveilleux.

Montussiennes is one of the few climbing areas within walking distance from Fontainebleau town centre, and there's often plenty of enthusiastic kids here climbing after school. It's an area set in a heavily wooded Oak Forest (slow drying), and forms part of the three Mont Ussy climbing areas. To the east of our circuit at the Carrefour Mont Ussy, there are two big obelisks (Roche d'Hercule) with 16 problems taking good spectacular lines, 3 easy, 2 hard, and the others being in the 5-6a grade. There are also many scattered boulders amongst the ferns in the forest here, with an unmarked TD circuit that enjoys constant traffic due to the close proximity of Fontainebleau. Our orange circuit starts 500m to the west of here, just beneath the grotto de Montussiennes with its spectacular roof on one side, and scene of a few too many camp fires with its blackened roof. Around this giant cave are superb overhanging walls that seem to have perfectly placed pockets at reasonable intervals for the urban gorilla. In this area are also a good concentration of smaller boulders that are invariably mushroom shaped, offering an excellent thuggy red circuit, plus a whole circuit of red and white delicacies, all at reasonable 7a and above. Quite amazingly, the rocks here offer an excellent orange circuit with an easier yellow companion too. There is an unmarked blue circuit but it is perhaps best left to rest, since nearly all the problems are eliminates and are not very satisfying. The rock here seems to suit 3b-4b problems, and gives some really excellent examples of low and friendly bouldering. The circuit is small at only 31 problems, and is shaded for most of the day, making it a perfect choice in a hot summer with time left for a visit to the swimming pool. The yellow is fun and quite easy to follow (Numbers recently changed). The orange circuit is nice and varied, and somewhat comical at (9), you can literally jump off the ground to steer your bum into a scoop and make a perfect sitting start to the problem; and if you don't – wow, it's desperate. (5b) is such a gem of a problem that we have included it, but realise that it is a wee bit too hard for the average orange fun climber. Some of the holds on the circuit are slippy, but nothing that good clean rubber can't handle. Overall, it's a lovely venue.

Orange 5b - 5a+; Matt Nicholson

Tracé - Olivier Leray

4m CP	1 4a+			9
6m CP	2 3c			
3m CP	3 3b+			
4m CP	4 4b			4
4m CP	5 4a			
4m CP S 5a	5b 5a-	Sloper	M	X
5m HBall 3b	6 3b	Cool Fun		
4m S	6b 3b	Fun		
3m	7 4a	Fun M		10
4m CP	8 3b	Cool		
4m	9 3c+	Trick M		7
3m CP S	10 3b	Flexi		
3m CP	11 3c			
3m CP	12 4a+	Sloper M		5
3m	12b 3a	Fun		
3m	13 3a-	Flexi Fun		
3m	14 3b-	M		
3m CP	15 4a+	M		1
6m S 3b	16 3b-	Fun		
4m CP 3a	17 3c-	Cool M		
3m CP	18 3b	Fun		
7m CP S	19 3c+	Cool		3
4m S 4b	20 4b			
3m CP	21 3a+	Fun		
3m CP	22 3c-	Sloper		
2m	23 4b-	CRIMP M		2
8m CP S	24 4a+	Pump M		8
3m CP	25 4a-	Fun		
4m CP S	26 3b	Cool		
3m S	27 2c			
11m S	28 3b	M		
3m S	29 4b	M		6
3m CP	30 3a	Fun		
4m CP 3b	31 4a	Fun Cool M		
4m CP	31b 4c+	Sloper M		X

Magicien total

1	5b	18	5b
2	5c	19	5c
3	6b	20	6a
4	6b	21	5b
5	6a	22	5c
6	6a	23	5c
7	5c	24	6c
8	6b	25	6b
9	5c	26	6b
10	6b	27	6a
11	6b	28	6b
12	6a	29	6c
13	6a	30	5c
14	5c	31	5c
15	5c	32	6b
16	6b	33	6b
17	5b		

75m

50m

25m

0m

Sentier bleu

Secteur 25-28

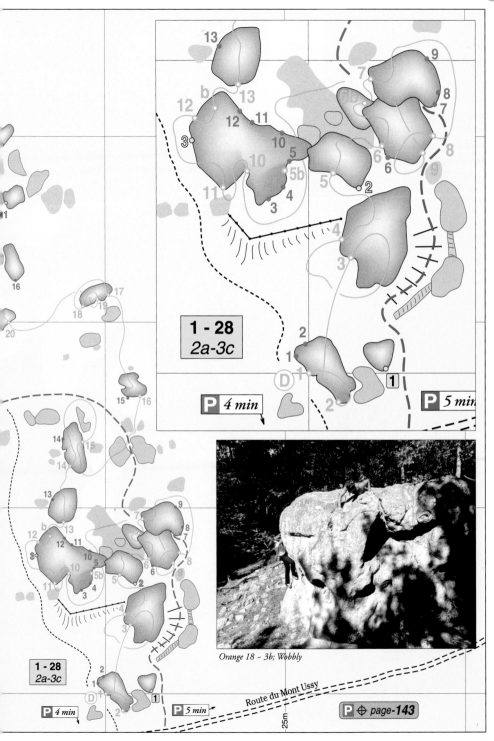

1 - 28
2a-3c

P 4 min

P 5 min

1 - 28
2a-3c

P 4 min

P 5 min

Orange 18 – 3b; Wobbly

Route du Mont Ussy

25m

P ⊕ page-143

"L'Automne"

Rocher Canon - (AD/Orange)

Orange 43 - 4a; Mark Sims

C'est un excellent circuit pour les grimpeurs confirmés visitant Fontainebleau pour la première fois, mais il est peu adapté aux débutants. Les passages sont variés et offrent peu de mauvaises surprises. C'est un circuit facile à localiser situé à seulement une minute du parking. Rocher Canon est un des plus importants massifs d'escalade de la forêt avec 8 circuits. Il y a même deux circuits bleu, qui peuvent-être difficiles à suivre : l'un avec des chiffres et l'autre en bleu clair avec des points. Rocher Canon s'étend sur deux collines et sa géographie est très déroutante lors d'une première visite. Le circuit orange situé sur la première colline a de très bons passages, Le (12) est pour ceux qui apprécient l'humidité. Le (22) est expo et demande une bonne parade et un crash pad. Le circuit descend ensuite dans une vallée remplie de fougères où l'on trouve de nombreux passages rouge et blanc. La traversée (23) est très difficile et très épuisante. Le circuit va ensuite à travers les fougères pour rejoindre la crête. Le bloc Canon géant à 2b n'est pas du tout effrayant. Le (36) est un superbe passage qui se débute en traversée puis suit un surplomb (au-dessus du sentier bleu). Faites attention aux randonneurs en cas de chute. Pour finir le circuit redescend la colline et devient difficile à suivre mais il offre cependant de bons passages plus faciles. La dalle (43) n'est peut-être pas idéale pour une fin de circuit. Elle est un peu effrayante car la sortie est exposée et est de plus assez glissante.

Orange 32 - 4a+; Adrian Sims

This is good circuit for a reasonably competent climber coming to Font for the first time, but not ideal for a beginner. It consists of a real mixture of problems and without too many nasty delights in waiting. It's also a very easy circuit to locate and only a minute from the car. Rocher Canon is one of the main areas for climbing in the forest and hence there are eight circuits here. There are even two blue ones that intermix, highly confusing or what; one blue circuit has plain numbers, the others is light blue plus a dot. Rocher Canon is spread over two hillsides and the geography is very confusing on your first visit. The Orange circuit weaves its way around the first hill, including a lovely main passage area with tiny corridors leading off it to give some good problems; the wriggle-squirm at (12) is for those that enjoy damp experiences. The first half culminates with a very challenging highball at (22), and a problem that many will hail a good spotter & crash pad. The back of this block leads to a somewhat entertaining jump off a pedestal to another block, before dropping down into a fern filled valley. Here there are many red and white problems, often indicated by the constant thumping of muscle toned bodies onto crash pads. The traverse at (23) is a nasty on-sight that pumps you solid, especially if you take the hard option of not using any holds on top of the block. The circuit then battles through ferns and up the hill to the crest of the ridge, problems intermixed with rock that keeps you off the ground for most of the way. The giant Canon block at the top of the hill succumbs with a 2b and is not really frightening at all. (36) is a gem of a problem that traverses first, and then fights it's way up an overhanging groove (above the blue footpath), be careful not to wipe out a rambler if you fall here. Following the circuit down the hill and around to the finish is confusing, but does throw in some very good easier problems. The slab finale at (43) is maybe just what you don't want at the end of a tiring circuit. It has the crux is at the very top and certainly feels a bit scary. It also is quite slippy, and can prise the magician accolade from beneath your fingertips.

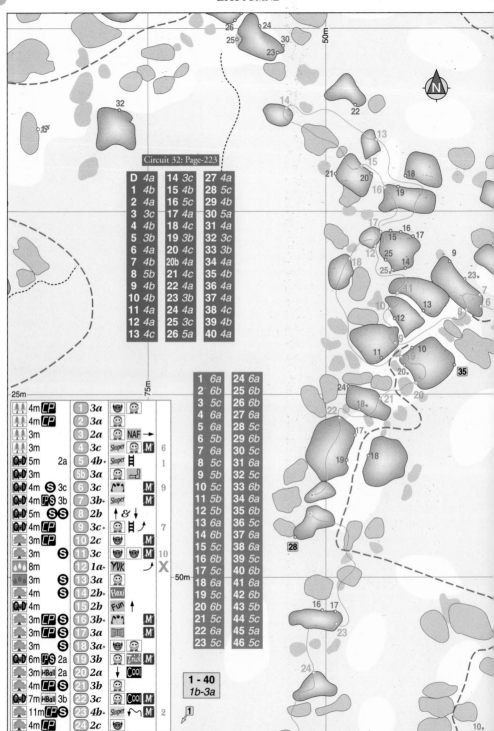

Circuit 32: Page-223

D	4a	14	3c	27	4a
1	4b	15	4b	28	5c
2	4a	16	5c	29	4b
3	3c	17	4a	30	5a
4	4b	18	4c	31	4a
5	3b	19	3b	32	3c
6	4a	20	4c	33	3b
7	4b	20b	4a	34	4a
8	5b	21	4c	35	4b
9	4b	22	4a	36	4a
10	4b	23	3b	37	4a
11	4a	24	4a	38	4c
12	4a	25	3c	39	4b
13	4c	26	5a	40	4a

1	6a	24	6a
2	6b	25	6b
3	5c	26	6b
4	6a	27	6a
5	6a	28	5c
6	5b	29	6b
7	6a	30	5c
8	5c	31	6a
9	5b	32	5c
10	5c	33	6b
11	5b	34	6a
12	5b	35	6b
13	6b	36	5c
14	6b	37	6a
15	5c	38	6a
16	6b	39	5c
17	5c	40	6b
18	6a	41	6a
19	5c	42	6b
20	6b	43	5b
21	5c	44	5c
22	6a	45	5a
23	5c	46	5c

1 - 40
1b-3a

1	3a		
2	3a		
3	2a	NAF →	
4	3c	Sloper	6
5	4b+	Sloper	1
5b	3a		
6	3c		9
7	3b+	Sloper	
8	2b	↑ & ↓	
9	3c+		7
10	2c		
11	3c		10
12	1a+	YUK	X
13	3a		
14	2b+	Flexi	
15	2b	Fun	
16	3b+		
17	3a		
18	3a+		
19	3b	Trick	
20	2a	Cool	
21	3b		
22	3c	Cool	
23	4b+	Sloper	2
24	2c		

25m

75m

50m

50m

Tracé original - 1950's; 1999 (Emmanuel Rémont)

25m

P

P ⊕ page-**218**

MOON
TM

0m

Orange 22 - 3c: Anna Péter

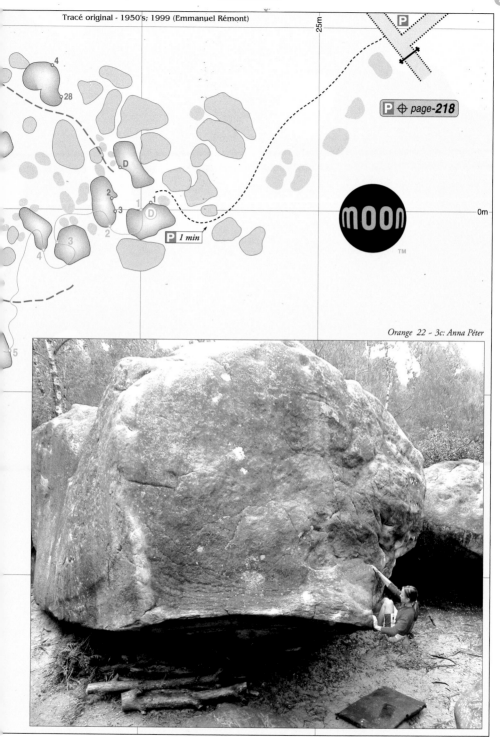

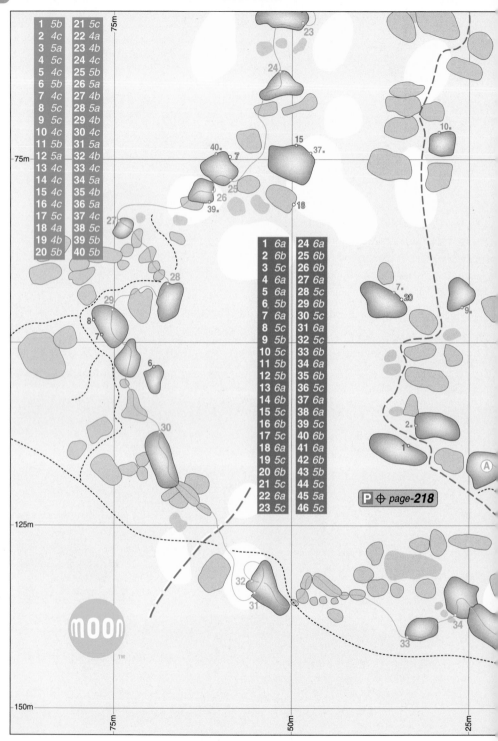

1	5b	21	5c
2	4c	22	4a
3	5a	23	4b
4	5c	24	4c
5	4c	25	5b
6	5b	26	5a
7	4c	27	4b
8	5c	28	5c
9	5c	29	4b
10	4c	30	4c
11	5b	31	5a
12	5a	32	4b
13	4c	33	4c
14	4c	34	5a
15	4c	35	4b
16	4c	36	5a
17	5c	37	4c
18	4a	38	5c
19	4b	39	5b
20	5b	40	5b

1	6a	24	6a
2	6b	25	6b
3	5c	26	6b
4	6a	27	6a
5	6a	28	5c
6	6b	29	6b
7	6a	30	5c
8	5c	31	6a
9	5b	32	5c
10	5c	33	6b
11	5b	34	6a
12	5b	35	6b
13	6a	36	5c
14	6b	37	6a
15	5c	38	6a
16	6b	39	5c
17	5c	40	6b
18	6a	41	6a
19	5c	42	6b
20	6b	43	5b
21	5c	44	5c
22	6a	45	5a
23	5c	46	5c

P ⊕ page-218

Orange 23 ~ 4b+; Adrian Sims

7	*6c*	
8	*7a*	
0	*7a*	
4	*7a*	

🌳 11m CP S	(23) **4b+**	Sloper	2
🌳 4m CP	(24) **2c**		
Q-D 5m S	(25) **2c+**		
🌳 5m CP S	(26) **3b**		
🌳 4m CP S	(27) **2c**		
Q-D 4m S	(28) **3c+**	Cool	
👬 5m S	(28b) **4a**	Sloper Fun	
👬 6m	(29) **3b**	Sloper	
👬 5m CP 2a	(30) **3c**		
👬 5m CP 2a	(31) **3c**		
Q-D 4m CP S	(32) **4a+**		3
🌳 7m	(33) **4a**		4
🌳 9m HBall 2b	(34) **2b**	Fun	
Q-D 4m CP S	(35) **3a**		
Q-D 7m CP	(36) **3b**		
4m S S	(36b) **4a+**	Flexi Flexi	5
🌳 4m CP S	(37) **3c**	Fun	
Q-D 3m S	(38) **3a**		
🌳 11m CP S	(39) **4a**		8
👬 2m	(40) **3b+**		
👬 3m	(41) **3b**	CRIMP	
🌳 3m HBall 3a	(42) **3a**		
👬 7m CP S	(43) **4a**	CRIMP	
	Magicien total		

C'est l'un des meilleurs circuits de Fontainebleau puisqu'il offre une diversité de passage depuis de petites dalles jusqu'à des passages expos. Le circuit est divisé en deux parties complètement séparées et s'approche plus facilement depuis la partie centrale. Il est difficile de trouver le départ du circuit, mais il vaut la peine de persévérer la recherche. Le circuit a beaucoup changé aux cours des décennies avec l'apport de variantes et de nombreuses améliorations. Le 4e passage est un bon échauffement en vue de l'arête plutôt haute du (6). La section Est se termine avec une petite marche de 70m vers la plage de sable du 91.1. Vous arriverez finalement au (27) situé sur la partie centrale Manhattan avec le premier passage expo. Il n'est pas très difficile, mais paraît très haut (7-

8m). Ces blocs géants ne voient pratiquement jamais le soleil et restent donc frais ce qui est idéal pour essayer les passages les plus difficiles. Ne manquez pas le (28b) qui est un mur géant expo, suivi d'une descente terrifiante depuis une hauteur de 6m grâce à une chaîne. Le circuit offre des voies techniques demandant beaucoup de puissance jusqu'à la fin. L'arête du (47) est intimidante mais une bonne manière de terminer ce long circuit. Vous serez sans arrêt surpris par l'escalade de ce massif et serez chanceux si vous effectuez chaque passage à vu.

Orange 28b - 3a; Avril Joubert-Laurencin

This is one of the great Fontainebleau circuits, giving a complete mixture of climbing from small slabs to radical highballs. The circuit divides into two completely separate parts, and is most easily approached via the main central – tower block area on your first visit. Finding the start is awkward but worth the perseverance (not being helped since there are 2 number 10 problems marked, one at the end of the eastern section and the other at the beginning of the high sandy sector). The circuit has changed over the decades with many improvements and variations added. There isn't a blue circuit here so you can appreciate why there is a high density of grade 4 problems. A new excellent gain is to add a traverse for the start, so at least you are slightly warmed up for the first problem which seems quite airy. The 4th problem (especially if you add the twirl back through the hole at the end), will again warm you up well in preparation for another airy adventure on the high arête of (6). The eastern section finishes with a short 70m walk back up to the sandy open area of the main high point of 91.1 metres. This area comprises of smaller boulders on the outside that throw in some fiendishly technical problems and test your fingertips very nicely. Eventually you arrive at (27) on the central Manhattan area, the first highball/deathball on the circuit, and with a your heart thumping no doubt. It's happily not that hard but seems immeasurably high (7-8m). These giant blocks in the centre barely allow sunlight into the corridors between them, keeping the walls cool for harder desperates. They give fabulous fun; make sure not to miss (28b) which is a superb wall highball, followed by the terrifying and gripping chain descent from this 6m overhanging block. The circuit continues to provide powerful and technical gems and certainly keep going to the very end. Taking the final (47) problem straight over the arête is quite daunting, but a lovely way to finish this long circuit - with a whizz or a thump. You will be constantly surprised by the climbing here and be very lucky if you onsight every problem. Happily the nasties are low down – with perhaps (25) being the only exception. You have been warned, stay cool man!

Orange 47 - 3c+; Friederike Jung

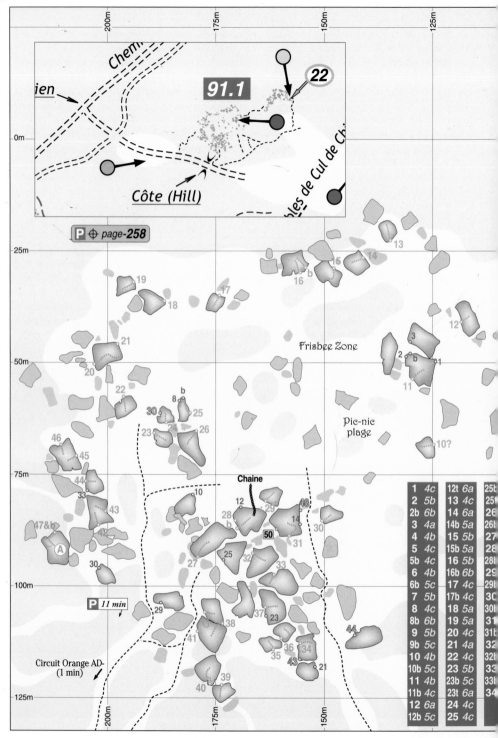

200m · 175m · 150m · 125m

Chem...

...ien

91.1

22

0m

Côte (Hill)

...bles de Cul de Ch...

P ⊕ page-258

25m

13

19
18
17
15 14
16 b

Frisbee Zone

50m

21
20
22
b
8
30 25
24 26
23
46
45
44
33
43
47&b
A
30

3
2 b 1
11
12?

Pic-nic plage

10?

75m

Chaine
10
12
28 29
b
50 14
48
30
31
27 25 32 33

100m

P 11 min

29

37
38
23
36 34
35
43 21
44

Circuit Orange AD-
(1 min)

40 39

125m

200m · 175m · 150m

1	4c	12t	6a	25t
2	5b	13	4c	25t
2b	6b	14	6a	26
3	4a	14b	5a	26t
4	4b	15	5b	27
5	4c	15b	5a	28
5b	4c	16	5b	28t
6	4b	16b	6b	29
6b	5c	17	4c	30
7	5b	17b	4c	30t
8	4c	18	5a	31
8b	6b	19	5a	31t
9	5b	20	4c	32
9b	5c	21	4a	32t
10	4b	22	4c	33
10b	5c	23	5b	33t
11	4b	23b	5c	34
11b	5b	23t	6a	
12	6a	24	4c	
12b	5c	25	4c	

TROIS PIGNONS - 91.1 - (AD+/Orange)

m HBall 2a	1 2a	3b →	
m	2 2c		.M.
m Ⓢ	3 3b	CRIMP	↑
0m Ⓢ	4 4a	Pump BUZZ .M.	
m	5 4a	Sloper	9
m HBall 3a	6 3a		Ⅲ
m	7 3c		
m	8 3c		
m	8b 4c+		
m	9 3a		7
m Ⓢ	10 3c+	Sloper	
m	10b 3a	⌒²1	
m	11 3b	Flexi .M.	
m	12 4a+	Sloper ⌒²1 .M.	
m	13 4a		10
m CP	14 4b	CRIMP .M.	5
m	15 2c	Fun	
m	16 5a	Sloper (4b)	2
m Ⓢ	16b 5a		1
m	17 3b		
m	17b 4a	⌒²1 .M.	
m	18 3c	Pump Sloper →	
m CP	19 5b-	CRIMP	3
m Ⓢ Ⓢ	20 3b		
m	21 3b		
m	22 2c	Flexi	
m	23 3b	⌒²1	
m Ⓢ	24 3b		
m CP Ⓢ	25 4a	Sloper .M.	5
m CP Ⓢ	26 3c	Flexi .M.	
m DBall 2b	27 2b	COol .M.	
8m Ⓢ	28 3b	Fun →	
m HBall 3a	28b 3a	⌒²1 .M.	
m	29 2c		
m	30 3c	Sloper Ⅲ	
m Ⓢ	31 4a	.M.	
m Ⓢ	32 3b	COol Ⅲ	
m Ⓢ	33 2b		
m Ⓢ	34 3b		
m	35 3a	Sloper	
m Ⓢ	36 3a	→	
m Ⓢ	37 3b		
m	38 3c		
m	39 3a	Ⅲ	
0m HBall 2c	40 2c	COol	
2m HBall 2b	41 3a		
m Ⓢ	42 2c		
m HBall 3b	43 3b	Flexi ⌒²1 .M.	
m Ⓢ	44 3c+	⌒²1	
m	45 4c	CRIMP .M.	4
m Ⓢ	46 3a		
m Ⓢ Ⓢ	47 3c+	.M.	
m Ⓢ	47b 4a	Pump .M.	8

Magicien total

1 - 50
1c-3c

Cul de Chien
(3 mins) →

P 15 min

Tracé - Monique et Wladimir Fédoroff,
Alain Laloup, Pierre Nédelec et André Schwartz
- Oleg Sokolsky

Ⓓ GPS-N31
E 464-541
N 5358-408

Orange 16b - 5a; David Durand

Orange 1 - 4a; Jingo

C'est un immense circuit avec 73 voies et de nombreuses variantes qui vous garderont occupées pendant une éternité. Le circuit orange se mêle aux circuits bleu et noir qui sont extrêmement difficiles et donnent des passages très athlétiques. Le cadre est magnifique, haut placé dans la forêt avec de belles vues sur le massif des Trois Pignons. Prenez la peine d'aller jusqu'à la fin du circuit puisque la vue depuis le (73) est imprenable. Le sentier très populaire des "25 bosses" est situé sur ce massif et il vous arrivera certainement de rencontrer des marcheurs plus fatigués que vous ne le serez. Le départ du circuit est difficile à trouver, mais vous serez récompensés par un très bon premier passage (1). Pour suivre ce circuit il vaut mieux garder un œil sur les flèches en haut des rochers. Il est aussi conseillé de séparer ce circuit en trois sections pour trois jours différents. Si vous le débutez de bonne heure ce circuit est agréable lors de journées chaudes puisque les deux tiers des voies sont exposées sud-ouest et restent à l'ombre jusqu'à l'heure du déjeuner. Prévoyez un pique-nique et une sieste puisque la majorité des voies difficiles sont situées à l'est et sont plus fraîches en fin de journée. Du fait de sa haute position, ce circuit est l'un de ceux qui sèchent le plus rapidement. Gros sablon est bien connu pour ses passages exposés qui sont pour la plupart sur le circuit noir et qui peuvent être grimpés en toute sécurité avec une bonne parade et des crash pads. Il y a également quelques voies engagées sur l'orange qui ne sont pas trop difficiles et qui peuvent encore une fois se faire avec une bonne parade. Le circuit est très long et il arrive souvent que les grimpeurs abandonnent le dernier tiers du circuit. Attention aux derniers passages en fin de circuit qui paraîtront probablement plus difficile du fait de votre niveau de fatigue. N'oubliez pas d'apporter suffisamment d'eau pour apprécier pleinement ce marathon.

Orange 3 - 4a; Jingo

A low flying Jingo !

Secteur 56-57

This is a mammoth circuit by any standards, with 73 set problems alone and countless variations to keep you busy for ages. It is also comically intermingled with the psycho blue and psychotic black circuits - should you require any extra exercise, bone rearrangement or mental fragmentation. The setting is magnificent and follows one of the highest ridges in the forest with views that are extensive and look south across the whole of the Trois Pignons massif. It is worth pulling out the stops to get to the end, since the view from the last problem (73) towards Rocher Fin is a gem and incredibly satisfying. The popular '25 Bosses' footpath runs along the top this ridge here, it's a full body work out, so expect the ramblers to be more exhausted than you are. Finding the start is a bit tricky but worth persevering, since problem (1) is very good indeed. To follow this circuit, you must keep a close eye on the arrows on top of the rock, which means carrying a crash pad is a bit of a non starter. Splitting the circuit into 3 sections for 3 separate days is also a good idea - then bring a pad for the last sector only. It's a good circuit to do on a hot day if you start early, the first 2/3rds face south west and stay in the shade until lunchtime; also, a lot of problems stay permanently in the shade too. Take a leisurely picnic and siesta, since the majority of hard problems in the last part face east and cool nicely for the evening. As it's high up, you are likely to get any cool breeze that is going, and is certainly one of the quicker areas of the forest to dry. Gros Sablons is famous for its highball problems, but most of these are on the black circuit and are often tackled with an army of spotters and crash pads. There are quite a few high balls on this Orange, but none are ridiculously difficult and feel ok'ish with an attentive person spotting. The circuit is long and feels even longer; not surprisingly, the last third of the circuit often proves too much for many. A lack of traffic means that the trees in this part invariably need pruning to find some of the problems. Be careful with some of these problems in the last part, you will be tired and can easily suffer from cramp – especially on the last problem as you lock off your arm. You need to carry plenty of water for this enjoyable Marathon.

Highball secteur 28

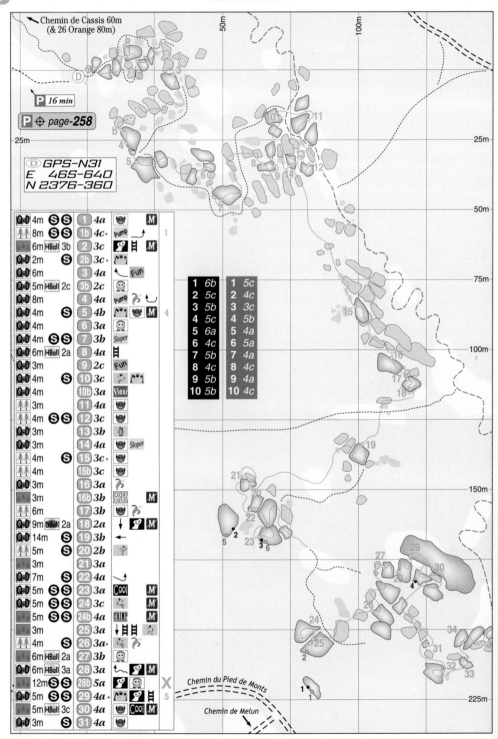

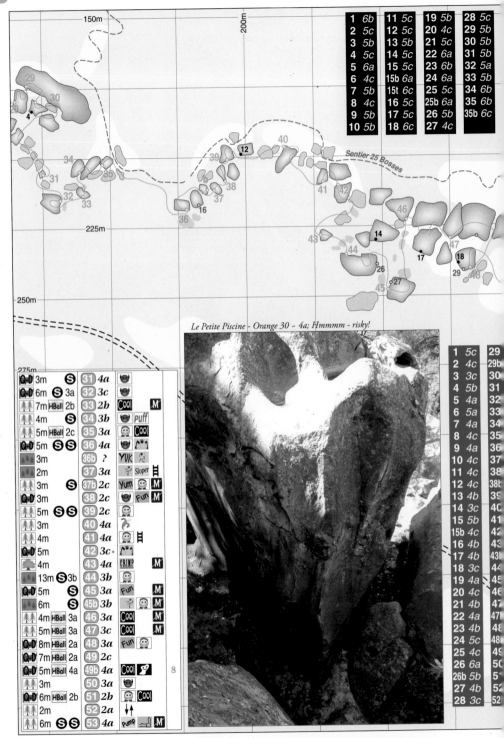

1	6b	11	5c	19	5b	28	5c
2	5c	12	5c	20	4c	29	5b
3	5b	13	5b	21	5c	30	5b
4	5c	14	5c	22	6a	31	5b
5	6a	15	5c	23	6b	32	5a
6	4c	15b	6a	24	6a	33	5b
7	5b	15t	6c	25	5c	34	6b
8	4c	16	5c	25b	6a	35	6b
9	5b	17	5c	26	5b	35b	6c
10	5b	18	6c	27	4c		

Sentier 25 Bosses

Le Petite Piscine - Orange 30 - 4a; Hmmmm - risky!

Q-D 3m S	31 4a	1 5c	29
Q-D 6m S 3a	32 3c	2 4c	29b
🌲 7m HBall 2b	33 2b Cool M	3 3c	30
🌲 4m S	34 3b Puff	4 5b	31
🌲 5m HBall 2c	35 3a Cool	5 4a	32
Q-D 5m SS	36 4a	6 5a	33
3m	36b ? YUK	7 4a	34
2m	37 3a Sloper	8 4c	35
🌲 3m S	37b 2c Yum M	9 4a	36
Q-D 3m	38 2c Fun M	10 4c	37
🌲 5m SS	39 2c	11 4c	38
🌲 3m	40 4a	12 4c	38b
🌲 4m	41 4a	13 4b	39
Q-D 5m	42 3c+	14 3c	40
🌳 4m	43 4a CRIMP	15 5b	41
13m S 3b	44 3b M	15b 4c	42
Q-D 5m	45 3a Fun M	16 4b	43
6m S	45b 3b M	17 4b	43b
🌲 4m HBall 3a	46 3a Cool M	18 3c	44
🌲 5m HBall 3a	47 3c Cool M	19 4a	45
Q-D 8m HBall 2a	48 3a Fun	20 4c	46
Q-D 7m HBall 2a	49 2c	21 4b	47
Q-D 5m HBall 4a	49b 4a Cool	22 4a	47b
🌲 3m	50 3a	23 4b	48
Q-D 6m HBall 2b	51 2b Cool	24 5c	49
🌲 2m	52 2a	25 4c	50
🌲 6m SS	53 4a Pump M	26 6a	51
		26b 5c	52
		27 4b	53
		28 3c	

8

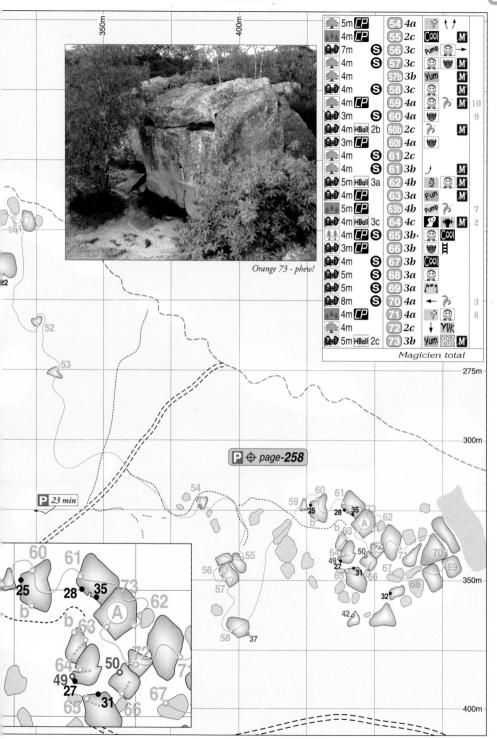

Orange 73 - phew!

5m CP	54	4a			
4m CP	55	2c	Cool		M
7m S	56	3c	Pump		→
4m S	57	3c			M
4m	57b	3b	Yum		M
4m S	58	3c			M
4m CP	59	4a			M
3m S	60	4a			
4m HBall 2b	60b	2c			M
3m CP	60l	4a			
4m S	61	2c			
4m S	61	3b			M
5m HBall 3a	62	4b			M
4m CP	63	3a	Fun		M
5m CP	63b	4b	Pump		
4m HBall 3c	64	4c			M
4m CP S	65	3b+		Cool	
3m CP	66	3b			
5m S	67	3b		Cool	
5m S	68	3a			
5m S	69	3a			
8m S	70	4a	←		
4m CP	71	4a			
4m	72	2c	↓	YUK	
5m HBall 2c	73	3b	Yum		M

Magicien total

350m / 400m

275m

300m

P ⊕ *page-258*

P 23 min

275m
300m
350m
400m

Ce circuit est situé prés le circuit Bizons enfant, mais il se cache derrière des arbres et est introuvable pour ceux qui ne savent pas où se trouvent les blocs de départ. Il y a deux circuits, le rouge et l'orange qui offrent de bons passages avec de très bonnes aires de réception et qui pour la plupart restent ombragés toute la journée. C'est un circuit idéal, en particulier durant les journées de canicule, pour les grimpeurs moins expérimentés et qui apprécient des sites sympa comme ceux du Cul de Chien et Rocher des Potets. Il y a 46 passages sur ce circuit qui sont bien plus faciles que ceux du circuit orange des Gorges d'Apremont. Les voies des petits blocs se succèdent et testent l'habileté des grimpeurs avec par exemple des rétablissements à une main et de larges cannelures. Il y a de nombreuses traversées ce qui peut-être un peu fastidieux cependant il y en a des excellentes que vous pouvez faire à vu. Il est parfois difficile de débuter certains passages puisque les prises sont assez hautes et il devient quelquefois utile de doubler le crash pad. Cependant vous aurez toujours besoin d'habileté et d'expérience pour faire ces passages. Les blocs sont arrondis et certains ressemblent un peu à de gigantesques bisons ! Il y a quelques passages assez horribles, le (32b) étant le pire de tous. Nous l'avons ôté ainsi que certains autres de notre défi du magicien. Le niveau de difficulté se situe aux alentours de 4a-4c offrant des voies qui mettront au défi les grimpeurs de ce niveau. Vous quitterez ce circuit exténué du fait des nombreuses voies à faire. C'est l'endroit idéal pour s'entraider à résoudre des passages et pour un groupe de grimpeurs de même niveau.

Orange 22b – 4b+; Dan Barbour   *Orange 20 – 4b; Gemma Lovering*

Orange 33 - 4c; Michael Gerrard

This circuit is only 100m away from the Bizons kids circuit, but it lurks behind trees and will remain hidden from those without the knowledge of where to locate the starting boulders. There are two circuits here, a red and an orange. Neither are world class or stunning, but do offer some really good bouldering with exceptionally good landings, plus it has the added advantage of shade on most of the problems all day. For those climbers not so experienced and enjoy the fun locations of Cul de Chien and Rocher des Potets, this is an ideal choice for a hot sunny day in a heatwave. With 46 problems on the circuit, there is a lot to go round, plus the red problems are very well intermingled to test any tip top rock monkeys in the group. It also serves as an excellent back up location when you go to try the mind testing orange circuits at the Gorges d'Apremont. Many climbers end up getting freaked out after the first few problems and go for this plan B. Here you can easily wield your crash pad around to make the problems nice and cosy. The small boulder problems arrive in fast succession, testing most skills from one handed mantelshelfs to flared grooves, plus flexible high step ups. There are a lot of traverses which can be a bit tedious, however, they are good ones with 'holds on,' that allow you to on-sight them with a good chance of success. Getting off the ground here on many problems is a lot of the difficulty and doubling up the crash pads often helps to reach the starting holds. You still need skill and canny climbing knowledge to progress up the problems though. The boulders are mostly rounded, somewhat resembling gigantic wild buffalo (Bizons) perhaps! There are a few really nasty problems up these rounded humps, with (32b) getting the fiendish award as the nastiest. We've taken this and a few others out of our Magicien challenge, since the best grade for climbing this circuit is around 4a-4c, and this area presents an ideal challenge for climbers of this standard. You don't come away from here remembering many of the problems; there are a few perhaps, with (20) being the classic if you get it sorted out first time, and the groove of (33) – because it can spit you out endless times. You leave here pretty exhausted because there is a lot to do in a day. It's a great place to help one and another to solve problems together, and ideal for a group of friends of similar standard.

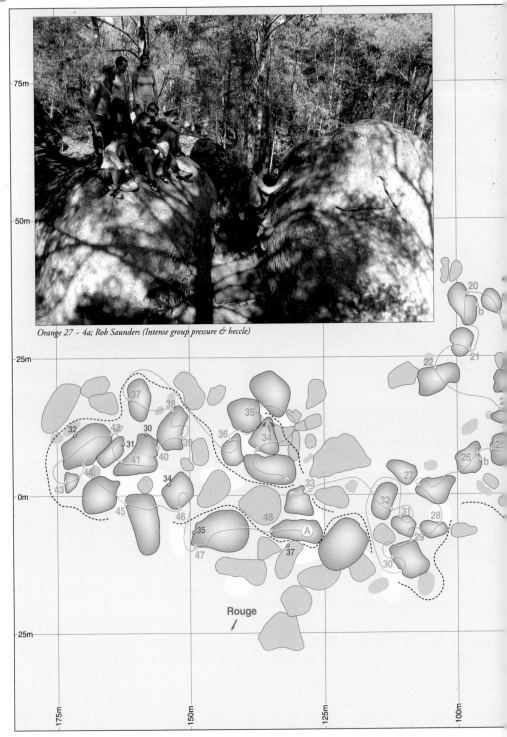

Orange 27 - 4a; Rob Saunders (Intense group pressure & heccle)

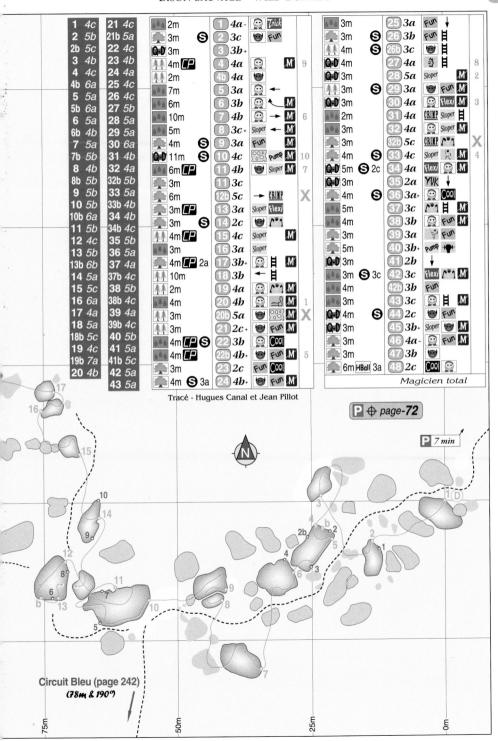

Tracé - Hugues Canal et Jean Pillot

Magicien total

P ⊕ page-72

P 7 min

Circuit Bleu (page 242)
(78m & 190°)

"LE PAPILLON - THE BUTTERFLY"

Bleu 12 - 4b: Sophie Clement

Au milieu de la forêt des Trois Pignons, il y a la plage du Cul de Chien, un désert avec des blocs marbrés de par leur immense popularité. Le dimanche la plage est envahie de paniers de pique-nique, de visiteurs prenant un bain de soleil et d'enfants jouant au volley-ball et au frisbee. L'approche depuis le nord est la plus facile pour trouver les blocs qui marquent le début de ce circuit. C'est un circuit assez long avec 50 voies, mais très varié avec des traversées, des passages courts mais athlétiques et quelques mouvements puissants. Pour pouvoir faire toutes les voies il faut grimper à environ 5b. Les passages les plus difficiles ne sont pas de très bonne qualité, il vaut mieux donc se contenter de faire ceux qui ont des cotations plus faciles ce qui maintient le challenge du magicien à 5a. Les blocs sont en majorité petits avec des aires de réception sableuses donc bonnes. Au secteur de la plage il y a également un circuit jaune et un rouge qui ne sont pas sévères à part pour les quelques passages du "toit". C'est le lieu idéal pour une journée relaxe et totalement magique au lever ou au coucher du soleil.

Les Sables de Cul de Chien

Bleu 37 – 5a+; Signe Seidelin

Bleu 36 - 5b+; Sebastien Kalaydjian

At the centre of the Trois Pignons forest there is the Cul de Chien beach, a desert with boulders that gleam from intense popularity. It's a sumptuous area with golden sand and where every day there are blue skies. Lets face it, everyone loves going to the beach, and laying out nicely coloured towels – the colours red, black and amber oddly spring to mind. Kids play volleyball & frisbee, making sure that the sand is kicked across your picnic should the mayonnaise lid be off, and screaming especially loudly if you have a hangover; a Sunday at Cul de Chien is usually full with this jamboree of jolly events. The blue circuit at Cul de Chien crescendos to its finish at this mêlée, but starts its life in a completely different location and with a very different character, some 500 meters north and deep in the pine forest. Approaching from the north is by far the easiest way to actually find the green boulders which mark the start of this circuit 'Le Papillon.' We named it this because it starts off life slowly wiggling around the first 8 green problems - before spending the rest of its time happily dancing around the desert from one boulder to another. It's a long circuit with 50 problems, and feels so because there is quite a lot of additional climbing in the earlier part of the circuit, and walking through sand slowly wears you down by the end of the day. There are a mixture of traverses, short powerful problems, and a few desperate power moves thrown in. You need to climb 5b to do all the problems, but the hard problems are not that interesting - they have either worn out, or will very soon. The ideal climbing here is in the lower grades on stronger rock, hence making it far more practical to keep the magician challenge at 5a. The boulders are mostly small, with excellent soft sandy landings and friendly in character. At the Le Plage area in the south, you can also find a yellow and red circuit, neither of which are that serious apart from the few problems on the high 'Toit.' For a relaxed day out it's ideal, and at sunrise or sunset – it's magical.

Bleu 50 ~ 5b; David Vonberg

TROIS PIGNONS - CUL DE CHIEN - (D-/Bleu)

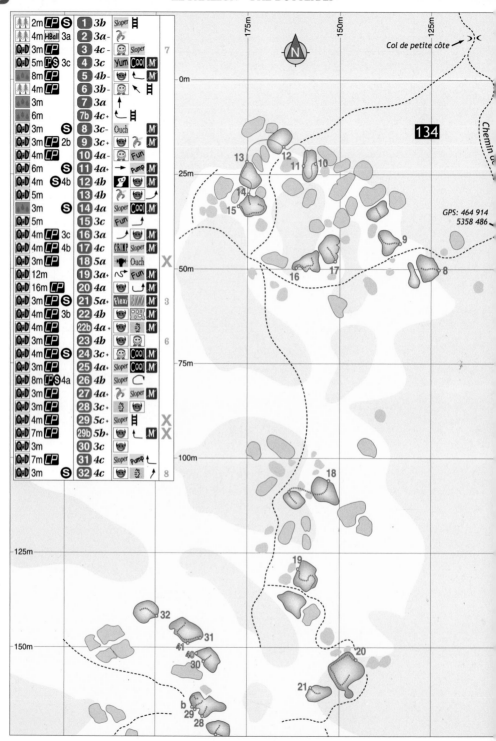

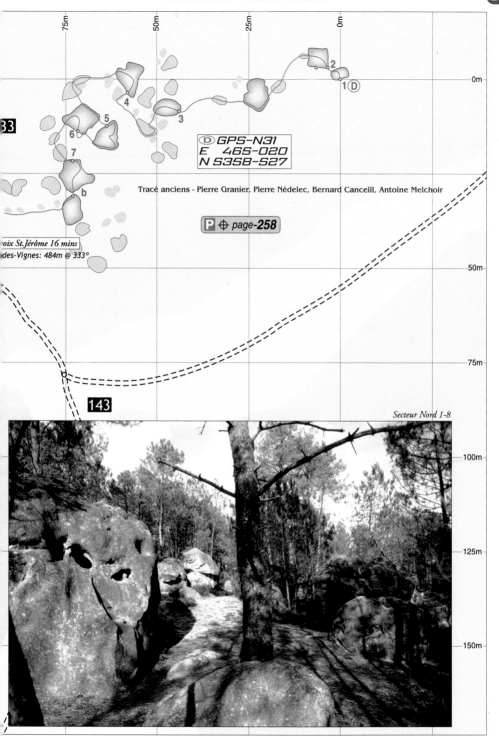

75m 50m 25m 0m

0m

2

1 D

33

4

3

5

6

7

D *GPS-N31*
E 46S-020
N 535B-S27

b

Tracé anciens - Pierre Granier, Pierre Nédelec, Bernard Canceill, Antoine Melchoir

P ⊕ *page-258*

oix St.Jérôme 16 mins
des-Vignes: 484m @ 333°

50m

75m

143

Secteur Nord 1-8

100m

125m

150m

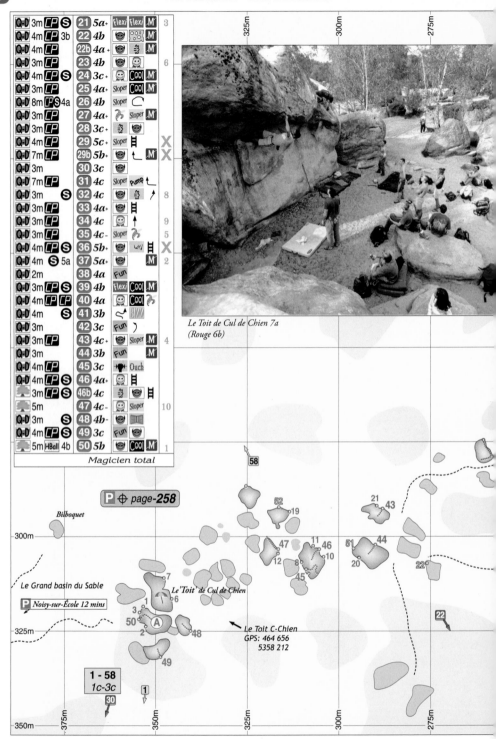

Le Toit de Cul de Chien 7a
(Rouge 6b)

P ⊕ page-258

Bilboquet

300m

Le Grand basin du Sable

P Noisy-sur-École 12 mins

325m

350m

Le 'Toit' de Cul de Chien

Le Toit C-Chien
GPS: 464 656
5358 212

1 - 58
1c-3c

Magicien total

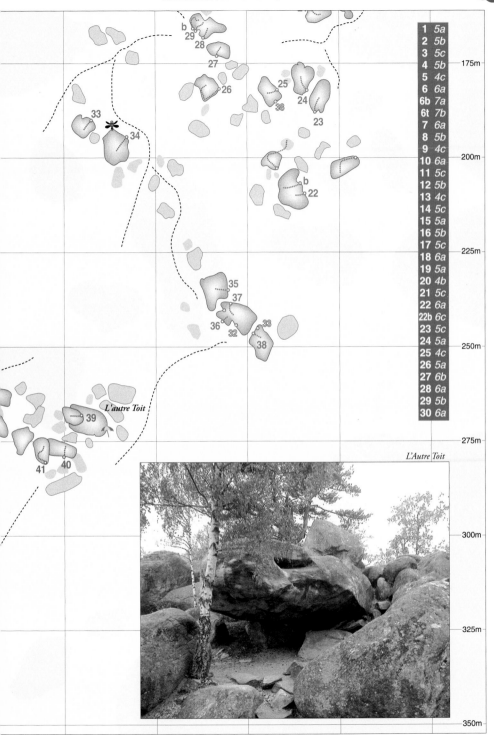

TROIS PIGNONS - CUL DE CHIEN - (D-/Bleu)   179

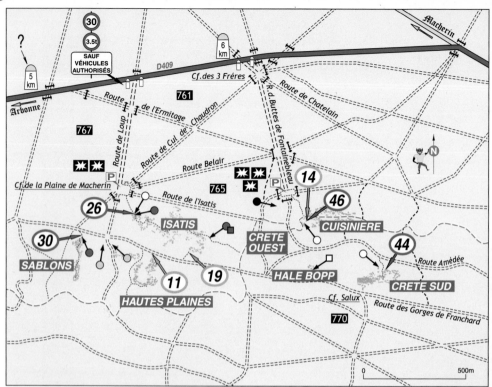

Circuit	Cot.	Ang.	Prob-Var	Bois	Expo	Info
SABLONS (p 209)						
● D	3b-6b		40 & (8)	🌊	CP	CRIMP
● TD	4b-6c		25	🌳	CP	CRIMP
♦ ABO	6c-8a		45	🌳	SCP	
SABLONS/HAUTES PLAINES						
○ PD	2a-3a		20	🌳	Yum	Fun
HAUTES PLAINES (p 90)						
○ PD+	2a-3c		25 & (4)	🌳	CP	😊
● AD+	1c-4c		37 & (7)	🌳	SCP	Fun
■ TD	5b-6b		7	🌳	CP	😊
♦ ABO	7a-7c		13	🌳	SS	😊
ISATIS OUEST (p 140 & 186)						
▫ PD+	2a-3b		40	🌊	CP	
▫ AD-	3b-4b		16	🌊	CP	😊
○ AD+	2a-5b		45 & (7)	🌊	CP	CRIMP
● D	2c-5a		48 & (1)	🌊	CP	CRIMP
■ D	4a-5a		20	🌊	CP	😊
● TD	4c-6a		47	🌳	CP	😊
■ TD	5c-6a		11	🌳	CP	😊
○ ED-	5c-6c		50&(16)	🌳	SCP	😊
♦ ABO	6b-8b		72	🌳	SCP	😊
ISATIS EST						
■ TD	5a-6c		30	🌲	CP	😊
♦ ABO	7c-8b		8	🌲	SCP	😊
CUISINIÈRE - CRÊTE NORD (p 108 & 310)						
○ AD+	2b-4b		19	🌲	HBall	COOl
● TD-	3a-6b		30 & (2)	🌲	CP	CRIMP
■ TD	5a-6b		31	🌲	CP	😊
○ ED-	5c-6c		48&(11)	🌲	SCP	😊
□ ED+	6a-7a		34	🌲	SCP	😊
♦ ABO	7b-8b		38	🌲	SCP	😊
CUISINIÈRE - CRÊTE OUEST						
● ED+	6a-7b		24&(14)	🌲	SCP	
CUISINIÈRE - CRÊTE SUD (p 298)						
● TD-	3b-6b		30 & (3)	🌲	HBall	COOl
CUISINIÈRE - CRÊTE SUD & HALE BOPP						
□ ED+	6a-8b		94	🌲	HBall	COOl

"Puck" était le nom d'un groupe de grimpeurs qui tracèrent et défrichèrent de nombreux circuits à Fontainebleau, comme ce circuit bleu de Franchard Isatis. De nombreux arbres sont cependant toujours présents et ils offrent un ombrage agréable en été. Il y a un grand nombre de blocs qui sont verts d'apparence mais comme c'est un endroit fréquenté les prises ne sont pas humides. Le sol est par contre souvent frais et un crash pad est utile pour garder les pieds secs. Le site se divise en 4 parties. Dans la première, les passages ne sont pas très difficiles, mais les faire à vu n'est pas aisé. Le rétablissement (21) vaut la peine d'être étudié avant d'être grimpé. La deuxième section a de grands blocs avec des cotations 6b-7c. La troisième partie du circuit offre des passages très divertissants sur des blocs beaucoup plus petits. La quatrième et dernière section a des blocs géants avec des passages expos, mais dont les sorties ne sont pas difficiles.

Bleu 21 - 4b+; Will Cross

Bleu 48 - 3b; Reto Schild

The word 'Puck' was the name of the group of climbers who initially traced a lot of circuits here in Fontainebleau. They put in an enormous amount of work to clear the moss and transform malaria ridden jungle into fingertip crunching and forearm pummelling climbing areas. This circuit is set in deep forest and would have looked very different before its exploration and development. Today, the paths around these superb boulders are well worn and the passing of millions of climbers each year leaves little chance for even a blade of grass to grow. Fortunately wisdom prevails and all the trees have been left, leaving a good canopy of shade over the outcrop and making it a perfect place to visit on a hot summer's day. Many of the boulders are green, but the holds are so often frequented that they never gather moss, stay damp, or stay gripped for very long. It won't be on your list of places to visit after it's rained, but it does dry out and is still worth a look in winter if you can stand the hot aches in your fingertips afterwards. The ground beneath does stay damp, making a wide crash pad invaluable. The outcrop splits into four sections. You are greeted upon arrival with a superb set of 4m boulders, high enough but not really dangerous. Here the blue, red and white circuits start together so you will be in the company of some highly toned bodies, cruising effortlessly. The problems may not be that hard, but keeping the on-sight sheet clean is difficult since the blue problems are less easy to read for the lowest grade. The problems flow nicely until perhaps (18), where you get a slab so typical with Font; with magnifying glass at hand you inspect the wall in front of you, after spotting no holds at all, you then pull on imaginary crimps and levitate upwards effortlessly. The mantel at (21) is likely to claim a few more victims who don't look at a problem before leaping straight onto it. The circuit then reaches a second set of giant boulders that offers many 6b-7c problems, it tip toes through this very carefully, stealing the good easier problems. The third part of the circuit takes you through rapid growing ferns to much smaller boulders that give amusing and pleasant problems. You finally end up at the 4th sector, which comprises of several giant boulders. All are highball, but none of the climbing is hard at the top outs.

Bleu 26 ~ 5a+; Stephanie Draussin

Bleu 30 ~ 4b+; Mike Kenny

Bleu 18 – 5a; Mike Cooper

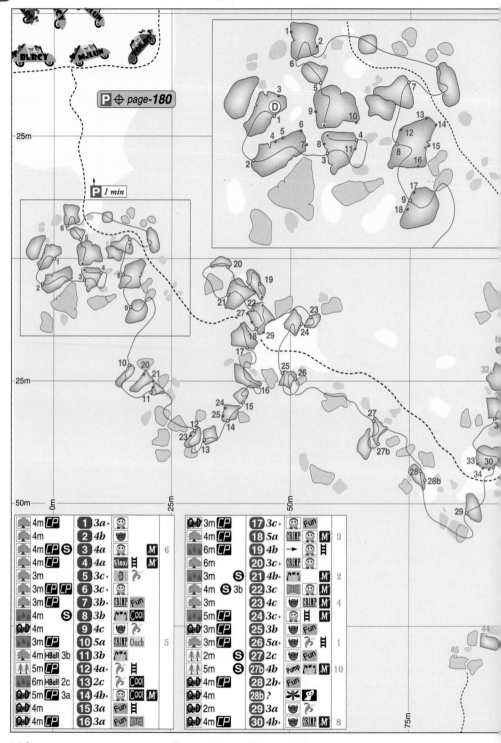

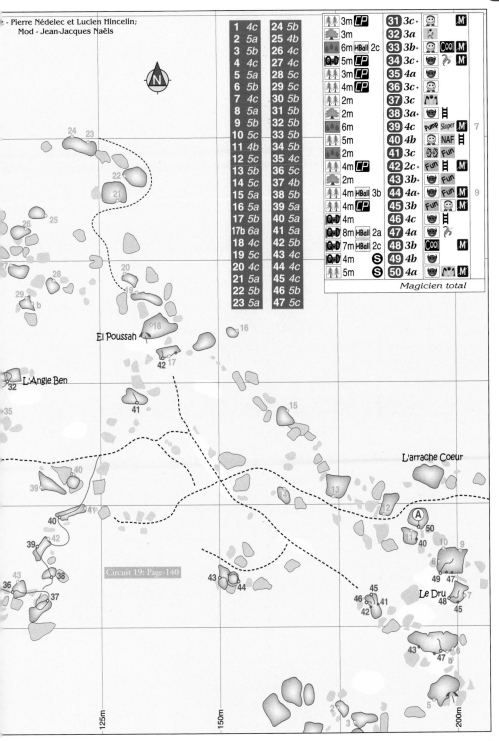

- Pierre Nédelec et Lucien Hincelin;
Mod - Jean-Jacques Naëls

1	4c	24	5b	
2	5a	25	4b	
3	5b	26	4c	
4	4c	27	4c	
5	5a	28	5c	
6	5b	29	5c	
7	4c	30	5b	
8	5a	31	5b	
9	5b	32	5b	
10	5c	33	5b	
11	4b	34	5b	
12	5c	35	4c	
13	5b	36	5c	
14	5c	37	4b	
15	5a	38	5b	
16	5a	39	5a	
17	5b	40	5a	
17b	6a	41	5a	
18	4c	42	5b	
19	5c	43	4c	
20	4c	44	4c	
21	5a	45	4c	
22	5b	46	5b	
23	5a	47	5c	

3m	31	3c+
3m	32	3a
6m HBall 2c	33	3b+
Q-D 5m	34	3c+
3m	35	4a
4m	36	3c+
2m	37	3c
2m	38	3a+
6m	39	4c
5m	40	4b
2m	41	3c
4m	42	2c+
2m	43	3b+
4m HBall 3b	44	4a+
4m	45	3b
Q-D 4m	46	4c
Q-D 8m HBall 2a	47	4a
Q-D 7m HBall 2c	48	3b
Q-D 4m S	49	4b
5m S	50	4a

Magicien total

El Poussah
42 17
L'Angle Ben
32
35
16
15
L'arrache Coeur
13
14
12
40
39
41
Circuit 19: Page 140
A
50
11 40
10
43
44
8
49 47
45
Le Dru
46 41
42
48 57
45
39
42
38
37
36
43
47

125m 150m 200m

Orange 1 - 4a; Catherine Smith

Ce circuit n'est pas destiné aux nerveux et doit être évité par les grimpeurs avec des compétences limitées. C'est un circuit plutôt classique qui sera apprécié par les âmes aventureuses. Il y a seulement 28 passages listés, mais à ceux la s'ajoutent des variantes très divertissantes. Le départ est technique, joli et sympa mais dès le passage expo (2) vous prendrez la décision de continuer le circuit ou d'abandonner. Assurez-vous de trouver le tunnel (16) puisqu'il est amusant. Le bac de sable au (20) s'est tassé c'est pourquoi il est nécessaire d'utiliser une grosse pierre pour atteindre les premières prises. Le circuit devrait peut-être se terminer au (26) puisque d'une part c'est le meilleur passage et que d'autre part il est situé en haut de la colline. Pour le conquérir il faut être capable de faire une traversée, d'avoir de la puissance et enfin de maîtriser les rétablissements.

Orange 2 - 4b; Jingo

Orange 15 - 4c; Jingo

Orange 26 - 4c+; Oddarne Steffensen

This is not a circuit for anyone of nervous disposition, and is to be avoided by those with limited ability. It is very much a circuit classique, enjoyed by those with adventurous spirit, combined with good technical perfection. If you finish it in one piece, then you obviously qualify as a good on-sight climber. Usually, even the most abstentious of climbers will be reaching for a stiff drink to calm their nerves after the completion of this world class circuit. There are only 28 listed problems to occupy you, but in addition there is a huge amount of intermediary climbing that is fully entertaining! You hardly touch the ground once you have started, but there are a few starts unfortunately that have worn away into sandpits. The start is technical, nice, and even fun, but as you turn the corner to look at problem (1), you will know what you are in for. Problem (2) is one where you decide if you want to continue or not, so be warned. It's a classic highball that offers you that point of no return, and with difficulty. (3) is a most bizzare but ingenious problem of bridging out over a chasm, then scuttling along via an undercut onto mushroom holds - be prepared to be perplexed; thereafter the circuit weaves its way up the hill, going up chimneys and down passages, with the painted arrows being essential to follow. You'll know if you need to go on a diet after you've done (13). Following the circuit downhill is a bit tricky but make sure you find the amusing tunnel at (16). The big loop at the bottom is worth following for some nice climbing before you reach the lovely fun arête of (18). By (20) you realise that you are on a full aerobic workout and will need enduring circuit stamina to start from the ground. The sand pit at (20) has sunken, so a handy big stone allows the first holds to be reached; the top proving a test of nerves for anyone. (This block will start to lean as the ground erodes further). Maybe the circuit should end at (26), because it is the best problem on the circuit and is at the top of the hill; it requires a whole host of skills, from being able to read a good traverse, then power, and finishing with a delicate and flexible mantel. There are some cute additional last tricks & jumps to amuse those who have lasted the course. You end up on top of the hill with a lovely position, with a feeling of travelled through, rather than over, the chaos of the Gorges d'Apremont.

Orange 3 - 3c; Catherine Smith

GORGES D'APREMONT - CHAOS - (AD+/Orange) 191

Tracé - Pierre Mercier

1	5c
2	4a
3	4a
4	4a
5	3c
6	4c
7	5b
8	5b
9	5c
10	4c
11	5b
12	4a
13	4c
14	5a
15	5b
16	4a
17	5b
18	4c
19	5a
20	6a
21	5a
22	5b
23	5a
24	6a
25	6a
26	5b
27	5a
28	4c
29	6a
30	5b
31	5a
32	4a

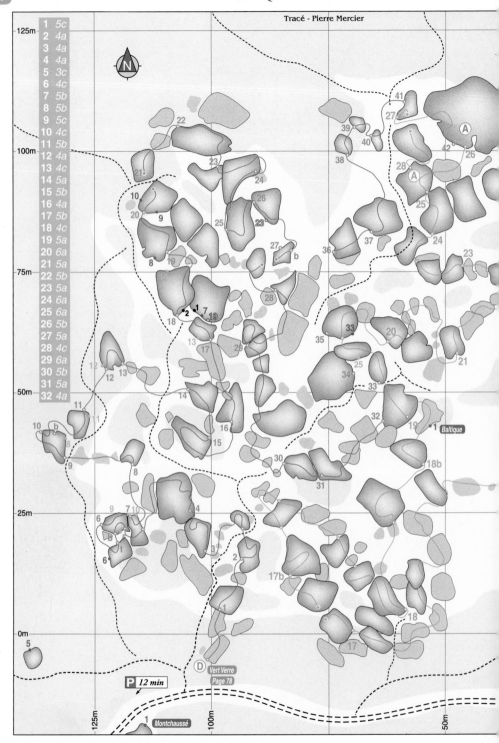

Vert Verre
Page 78

P 12 min

Montchaussé

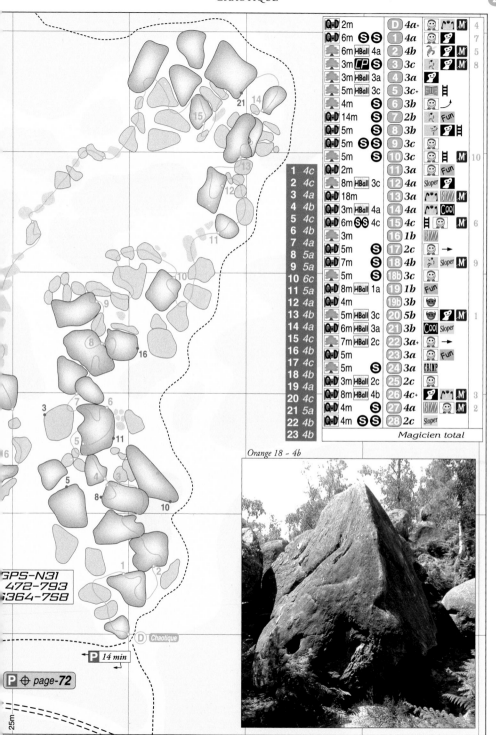

Orange 18 - 4b

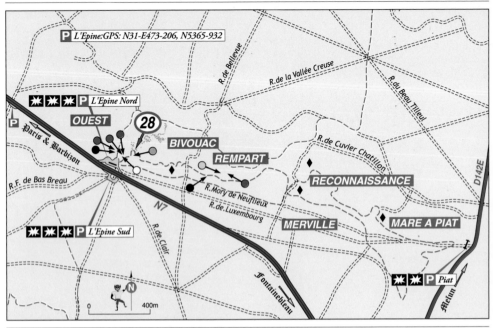

L'Epine:GPS: N31-E473-206, N5365-932

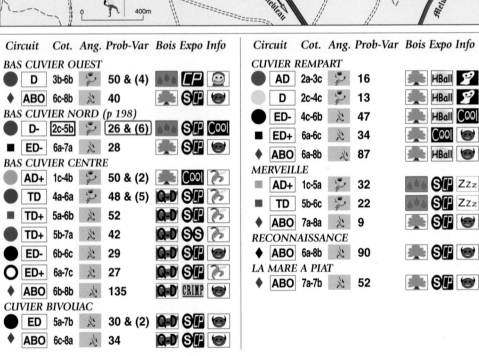

Circuit	Cot.	Ang.	Prob-Var	Bois	Expo	Info
BAS CUVIER OUEST						
● D	3b-6b		50 & (4)		CP	
♦ ABO	6c-8b		40		SP	
BAS CUVIER NORD (p 198)						
● D-	2c-5b		26 & (6)		SP	Cool
■ ED-	6a-7a		28		SP	
BAS CUVIER CENTRE						
● AD+	1c-4b		50 & (2)		Cool	
● TD	4a-6a		48 & (5)	Q-D	SP	
■ TD+	5a-6b		52	Q-D	SP	
● TD+	5b-7a		42	Q-D	SS	
● ED-	6b-6c		29	Q-D	SP	
○ ED+	6a-7c		27	Q-D	SP	
♦ ABO	6b-8b		135	Q-D	CRIMP	
CUVIER BIVOUAC						
● ED	5a-7b		30 & (2)	Q-D	SP	
♦ ABO	6c-8a		34	Q-D	SP	
CUVIER REMPART						
● AD	2a-3c		16		HBall	
● D	2c-4c		13		HBall	
● ED-	4c-6b		47		HBall	Cool
■ ED+	6a-6c		34		Cool	
♦ ABO	6a-8b		87		HBall	
MERVEILLE						
■ AD+	1c-5a		32		SP	Zzz
■ TD	5b-6c		22		SP	Zzz
♦ ABO	7a-8a		9		SP	
RECONNAISSANCE						
♦ ABO	6a-8b		90		SP	
LA MARE A PIAT						
♦ ABO	7a-7b		52		SP	

2nd Fontainebleau bouldering guide in production
for every level of boulderer - Cuvier Special

www.jingowobbly.com
Visit our website to see new titles in production

C'est un secteur tres fréquenté du fait de ses nombreux passages renommés, de ses aires de réception exceptionnelles et de son apparition dans de nombreuses vidéos d'escalade. C'est par contre un massif un peu bruyant de par sa proximité à la N7, mais l'escalade y est superbe malgré quelques voies faciles qui sont assez patinées. Pour ceux qui recherchent un circuit un peu différent, calme et tranquille nous vous conseillons ce circuit bleu. C'est un circuit très technique où les 4c sont parfois plus difficiles que certains 5b. Il y a un bon nombre de passages exposés tel le (14b) qui heureusement n'est pas trop difficile. Réussir le défi du magicien sur ce circuit est possible. Pour les grimpeurs un peu plus puissant il y a quelques variantes à 5c-6b qui sont assez techniques et peu fréquentées. Le circuit est au milieu des bois et les voies bénéficient d'un bon ombrage. Un bon choix pour les chaudes journées d'été.

Bleu 24 ~ 5a; Jim Bacon

For a lot of climbers, the name Bas Cuvier is synonymous with super hard test piece climbs that bring most first time visitors back to earth immediately, with a resounding thud onto the crash pad. It's an exceptionally busy sector, due to the high density of problems with good landings, and featuring in just about every bouldering video ever made. However, it's a terribly noisy location and is only metres away from one of the busiest roads in France (N7). It is also the first convenient stop off point by criminals, searching the car parks in the forest for cars to break into! The climbing on the other hand is superb, if somewhat polished on many of the easier problems that have been notoriously undergraded through history. (Our other Fontainebleau guidebook covers the main sector of Cuvier problems.) For anybody willing to search out something different, try out this old style circuit that wanders up the hill through the Amazonian sized, giant ferns – and happily escapes the traffic rumble the best it can. It's a climbing tour, and one that's completely different. You have to be prepared to travel between problems (and the occasional naff problem), but you are rewarded with quietness and solitude that is unheard of at central Bas Cuvier. Most of the holds have been sparred traffic, hence your feet can actually stay on the rock without skidding off at every instant. It's a technical circuit where often the 4c's are more likely to spit you off than the harder 5b's. You don't have to be very strong and there are a wide variety of problems that have great charm. There is a good sprinkling of highballs in the middle of the circuit, with (14b) amusingly rating as a deathball - fortunately it's not very hard. (16) may bring on the collywobbles a bit sharpish for those short on reach. Getting the magicien tick here is quite possible, but getting the complete clean sheet would be exceptional. For the very strong, this area provides quite a few off circuit 5c-6b problems that are technical and thoughtful, and with the added benefit of nearly always being nice and quiet. The circuit is set in lovely woodland, with many of the desperates enjoying excellent shade during the day. A perfect choice for that hot summer day perhaps.

Bleu 22 – 5b; Jim 'the sizzler'

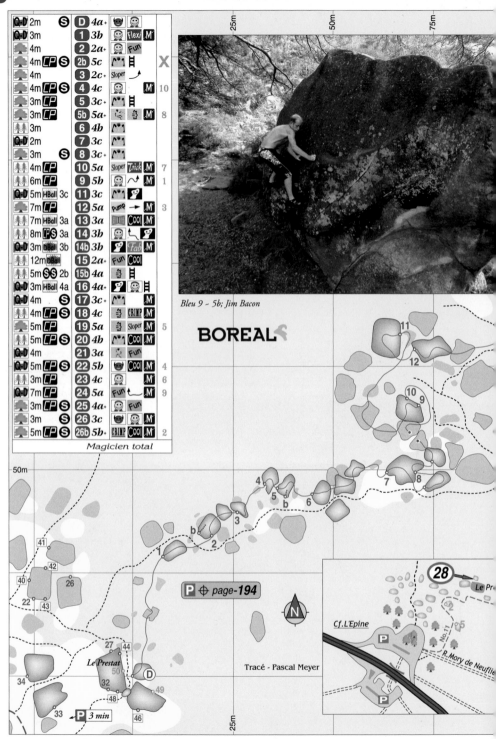

Bleu 9 ~ 5b; Jim Bacon

BOREAL

page-194

Tracé - Pascal Meyer

3 min

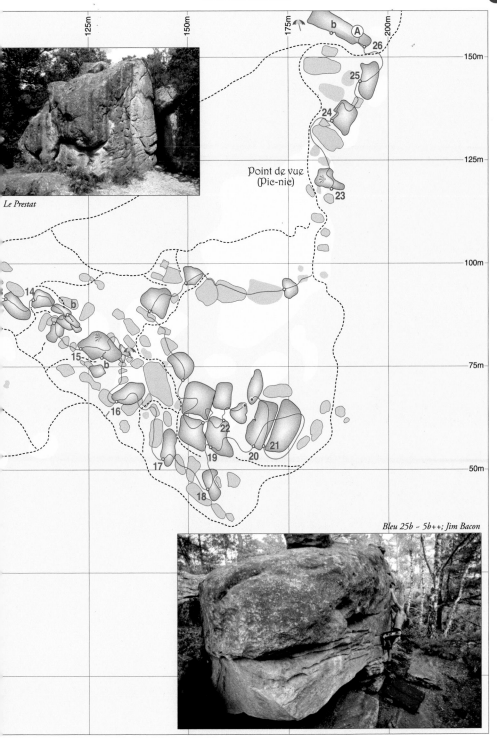

Le Prestat

125m   150m   175m   200m

150m

Point de vue
(Pic-nic)

125m

100m

75m

50m

Bleu 25b ~ 5b++; Jim Bacon

"WLAD THE MAN"

Ce massif est très proche du parking et offre une bonne sélection de passages de moyen niveau ce qui explique qu'il soit l'un des sites les plus populaires de Fontainebleau. Les trois premiers passages sont tout simplement excellents, mais leurs hauteurs s'amplifient avec le (2) qui fera trembler les grimpeurs un peu hésitants. Les voies (3-12) sont techniques mais de faible hauteur, pas plus de 3m, et avec des sorties qui ne sont pas trop difficiles. Nous avons indiqué sur notre colonne du magicien les passages à omettre pour le défi à vu. En milieu de circuit il y a une sélection de voies très sympa et c'est là où le sentier des 25 bosses vient se mêler aux blocs. Le (26) est un passage parfait en revanche le (30) est plutôt dangereux car le bloc est perché au-dessus d'un gouffre. Pour finir il y a sur le plateau de superbes passages en rouge à essayer une fois le circuit bleu terminé. Le surplomb final est effrayant et demande de la puissance, des doigts forts et une bonne technique, la conclusion parfaite à un superbe circuit.

Bleu 26

TROIS PIGNONS SUD - LE POTALA - (D-/Bleu)

Bleu 38 – 5a; Tom Poyser

Rocher du Potala is quite a short walk from the car park and with a good range of mid grade problems, which makes it one of the more popular areas of Fontainebleau. Blue problems of 4a-5a seem to be the natural flavour of the rocks, and hence this circuit is the most complete and follows the full extent of the boulder layout. The blue (D), can be quickly reached by following a small footpath before you reach the main outcrop and orange start. The first three problems on the blue are simply excellent, but get higher and higher, with number (2) guaranteed to get the legs shaking of any hesitant or indecisive climber. I can at least tell you that the rest of the circuit has much smaller problems, so don't get phased out straight away and walk straight back to the car park. Problems (3-12) are a complete delight of low technical problems, not really getting higher than 3m and with very reasonable top outs. There are a few comic additions to the blue circuit in this early part, such as imaginary crimps combined with polished footholds that need humungous power, usually way beyond the ability of your average blue standard climber. We illustrate in our magician column, which problems to leave out for the on-sight challenge. The central area has a lovely collection of problems, and is where the 25 Bosses footpath intertwines through the boulders. This presents an endless supply of ramblers chirping, 'bonjour,,, incroyable,' at every other second. You crimp on in desperation, showing no signs of effort and reply 'bonjour, c'est facile,' then thud onto the crash pad after they've disappeared around the next boulder. Problem (26) is simply a gem, an ideal boulder problem. At (30) there is a giant block, perched over a horrible chasm. The problem itself is a reach one and on slightly dodgy holds, but the variation below is very dangerous since loose rock; we left this out of our challenge since the risk seems pointless. The final plateau area is certainly not to be missed and has some super red problems to go and thrash at when you have finished the circuit. The final overhang is daunting; power and finger strength combined with technique, the perfect finale to a super circuit.

Bleu 10 - 4b; Régis Guillot

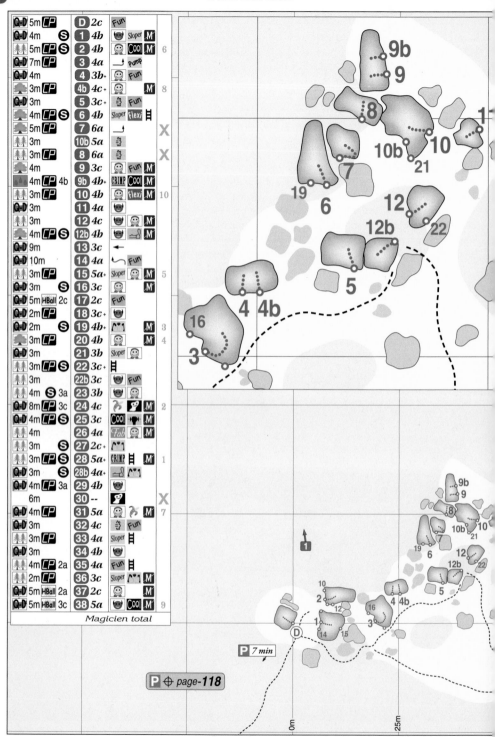

Q-D 5m CP	D 2c	Fun	
Q-D 4m S	1 4b	Sloper M'	
5m CP S	2 4b	COOl M'	6
Q-D 7m CP	3 4a	Pump	
Q-D 4m	4 3b+		
3m CP	4b 4c+	M'	8
Q-D 3m	5 3c+	Fun	
4m CP S	6 4b	Sloper Flexi	
5m CP	7 6a		X
3m	10b 5a		
3m CP	8 6a		X
4m	9 3c	Fun M'	
4m CP 4b	9b 4b+	CRIMP COOl M'	
3m CP	10 4b	Flexi M'	10
Q-D 3m	11 4a		
3m	12 4c	M'	
4m CP S	12b 4b	M'	
Q-D 9m	13 3c	←	
Q-D 10m	14 4a	Fun	
3m CP	15 5a+	Sloper	5
Q-D 3m	16 3c	M'	
Q-D 5m HBall 2c	17 2c	Fun	
Q-D 2m	18 3c+		
Q-D 2m S	19 4b+	M'	3
3m CP	20 4b	M'	4
Q-D 3m	21 3b	Sloper	
3m CP S	22 3c+		
3m	22b 3c	Fun	
4m S 3a	23 3b		
Q-D 8m CP 3c	24 4c	M'	2
Q-D 4m CP S	25 3c	COOl M'	
4m	26 4a	Fab M'	
3m S	27 2c+		
3m CP S	28 5a+	CRIMP M'	1
Q-D 3m S	28b 4a+		
Q-D 4m CP 3a	29 4b		
6m	30 --		X
Q-D 4m CP	31 5a	M'	7
Q-D 3m	32 4c	Fun	
3m CP	33 4a	Sloper	
Q-D 3m	34 4b		
4m CP 2a	35 4a	Fun	
2m CP	36 3c	Sloper M'	
Q-D 5m HBall 2a	37 2c	M'	
Q-D 5m HBall 3c	38 5a	COOl M'	9

Magicien total

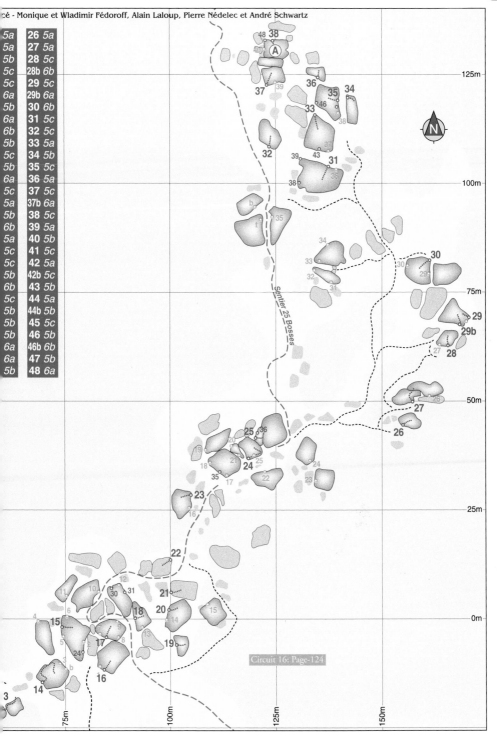

cé - Monique et Wladimir Fédoroff, Alain Laloup, Pierre Nédelec et André Schwartz

5a	26	5a
5a	27	5a
5b	28	5c
5c	28b	6b
5c	29	5c
6a	29b	6a
5b	30	6b
6a	31	5c
6b	32	5c
5b	33	5a
5c	34	5b
5b	35	5c
6a	36	5a
5c	37	5c
5a	37b	6a
5b	38	5c
6b	39	5a
5a	40	5b
5c	41	5c
5c	42	5a
5b	42b	5c
6b	43	5b
5c	44	5a
5b	44b	5b
5b	45	5c
5b	46	5b
6a	46b	6b
6a	47	5b
5b	48	6a

Circuit 16: Page-124

C'est un circuit très tranquille à seulement quelques mètres d'Isatis. Les blocs sont situés sur la colline avec la majorité des passages exposés au nord ce qui les laisse vert et humide. Il y a une crête qui protège les rochers du vent ce qui rend le circuit rouge et les variantes souvent très humides. Le circuit bleu ne souffre pas autant de l'humidité, mais les passages sont très techniques. Malgré le terrain pentu, les aires de réception sont excellentes et avec un crash pad et une bonne parade c'est un circuit tres agréable. La majorité des passages ont une hauteur de 3 mètres avec des cotations moyennes de 4c. Le (22) devrait être sur le circuit rouge et nous l'avons remplacé par une variante du (19) rouge plus sympa qui suit une arête. Nous avons également rajouté un toit assez divertissant (39) de l'ancien circuit rouge. Le circuit se termine en haut de la colline et offre des voies de qualité du début jusqu'à la fin.

Bleu 7 ~ 4a; Nick Dill

Secteur 12 Bleu & 10 rouge

This is a quiet circuit that lurks away in the woods, yet is only a few hundred yards from the ever popular Isatis area. The first few boulders are nicely positioned out in the open since the great storm of 1999, but the young fir trees seem to be rocketing up and will no doubt enclose the start of the circuit and conceal it back to dim shade. These boulders are stepped up the side of the hill, with most problems facing north and consequently remain somewhat green and damp in anything other than a dry spell. The substantial ridge protects the rocks from the prevailing winds and results in a constantly high level of humidity, often making the red circuit and off circuit problems greasy and skin shredding. The blue circuit is far more amenable and doesn't suffer so much from inherent dampness, nearly all the problems are purely technical, making them easy going for your fingertip skin. Not to say that you are in for an easy day here, far from it since the technicality of the bouldering here is tremendous. It's an ideal place for your first blue circuit if you are strong on technique and lack the arm power needed for places such as Cul de Chien or Roche aux Sabots. Even though the circuit is set on quite a steep hill, the landings are generally very good. With a crash pad and spotter, the blue becomes a very friendly circuit. Your tour starts very sensibly with two casual problems, but then throws in a gem of a problem at (3), a speciality without holds and might use up all of your 10 falls. The circuit then settles down to a wonderful succession of 3 metre problems that all hover around the 4c grade. There have been many changes in colour and tracing of the circuits here in the past, and doubtless to say that further mutations will happen. Therefore we have simply set out the circuit problems as you are likely to approach them going up the hill, avec your pad. We have omitted any foot traverses on the circuit because they simply get polished to hell on popular circuits. Blue (22) should be on the red circuit, 'crimp-ouch,' and we have replaced it with a nice variation of (19) red, taking a lovely line up the arête. We also have sneaked in the superb fun roof (39) from the old red circuit of a bygone age. The circuit finishes high up the hill and keeping quality problems right through to the finish. It's a shady circuit, 'an affair with quite a few problems,' be dynamic and have the odd 'fling.'

Bleu 25b - 5b; Nick Dill

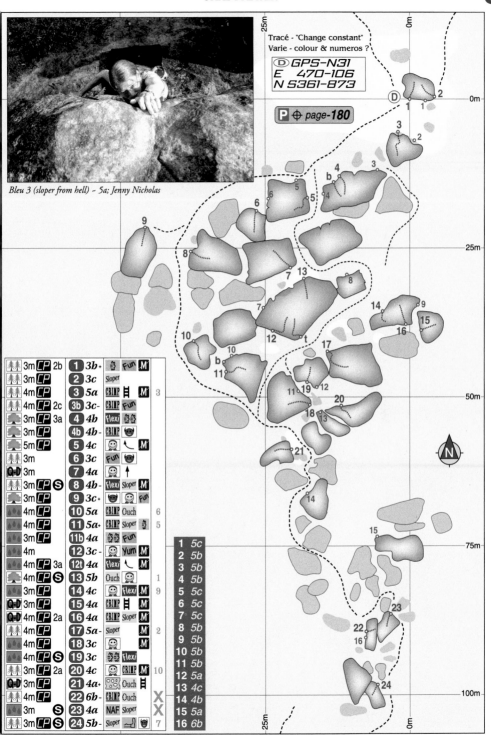

Tracé - "Change constant"
Varie - colour & numeros ?

D *GPS-N31*
E   470-106
N S361-873

P ⊕ *page-180*

Bleu 3 (sloper from hell) ~ 5a; Jenny Nicholas

3m CP 2b	**1** 3b+	Fun	M			
3m CP	**2** 3c	Sloper				
4m CP	**3** 5a	CRIMP	M	3		
4m CP 2c	**3b** 3c-	CRIMP Fun				
3m CP 3a	**4** 4b	Flexi				
3m CP	**4b** 4b-	CRIMP				
5m CP	**5** 4c	M				
3m	**6** 3c	Fun				
Q-D 3m	**7** 4a	↑				
3m CP S	**8** 4b-	Flexi Sloper M				
3m CP	**9** 3c+	Fun				
4m CP	**10** 5a	CRIMP Ouch	6			
4m CP	**11** 5a+	CRIMP Sloper	5			
3m CP	**11b** 4a	Fun				
4m	**12** 3c-	Yum M				
4m CP 3a	**12t** 4a	Flexi M				
4m CP S	**13** 5b	Ouch	1			
3m CP	**14** 4c	Flexi M	9			
Q-D 3m CP	**15** 4a	CRIMP M				
Q-D 4m CP 2a	**16** 4a	CRIMP Sloper M				
4m CP	**17** 5a-	Sloper M	2			
4m CP	**18** 3c	M				
4m CP S	**19** 3c	Flexi				
3m CP 2a	**20** 4c	CRIMP M	10			
Q-D 3m CP	**21** 4a+	Ouch				
4m CP	**22** 6b-	CRIMP Ouch	X			
3m S	**23** 4a	NAF Sloper	X			
3m CP S	**24** 5b-	Sloper	7			

1	5c
2	5b
3	5b
4	5b
5	5c
6	5c
7	5c
8	5b
9	5b
10	5b
11	5b
12	5a
13	4c
14	4b
15	5a
16	6b

FRANCHARD - SABLONS - (D-/Bleu)

Bleu 40 ~ 4a; Jenny Nicholas

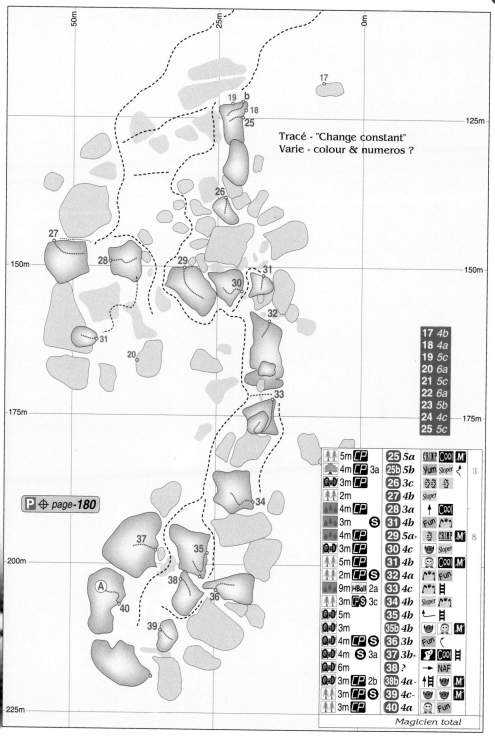

Tracé - "Change constant"
Varie - couleur & numeros ?

P ⊕ page-*180*

17	4b	
18	4a	
19	5c	
20	6a	
21	5c	
22	6a	
23	5b	
24	4c	
25	5c	

Magicien total

Le Diplodocus

Ce circuit est court avec des aires de réception excellentes, mais les voies sont difficiles à faire à vu. Nous avons omis deux passages sur notre liste du défi du magicien ; le (11) car son niveau de difficulté dépend de la taille du grimpeur et la dalle (14) dont la difficulté varie selon les conditions atmosphériques. Néanmoins c'est un circuit sympa et un bon grimpeur devrait pouvoir remporter le défi du magicien. Les blocs sont éparpillés sur le sable nu et la plupart des passages sont seulement de 3 mètres de haut. Au (12) sur le bloc du Diplodocus, nous vous conseillons de finir tout droit ce qui est moins dangereux que d'aller vers la droite et abstenez-vous d'utiliser la bouche fragile du dinosaure. Il vaut la peine de faire le (23b) avant le (23) car ce dernier vous permet de terminer en beauté en haut du diplodocus. En résumé c'est un circuit très sympathique et tranquille, qui sèche rapidement et où vous pouvez facilement vous déplacer avec un crash pad.

Bleu 9 – 5b+; Lukasz Markiewicz

Bleu 21 (Le réta du gibbon) ~ 3c+; Jingo

This circuit is famous for being an 'easy touch' for a blue because it's short in length, and the landings are so good that you can thrash away forever until you get up the problems. It's also a very popular hangout and is easy to pick up the beta on problems. If you try it as a strict on-sight challenge (only possible on midweek mornings), it can catch you out, since you need some very awkward and elusive tricks to unlock a few of the wicked problems. We have left two problems off our challenge for the magic tick; (11) is purely a reach problem that only goes at 6a+ or harder for short people, and Teflon Slab (14) gets anything from 5b-6b - depending on the conditions of the day and the stickiness of rubber on your boots. Notwithstanding this, it's a nice and challenging circuit and fiendishly canny in parts. A good strong climber is likely to get the magician tick here– but only just. Many of the problems have two obvious ways of doing them, but fortunately only one that is easy. Be warned to have a few goes in hand for the very last problem (23), since in hot and sweaty conditions it can easily present a continual failing point, leaving you dumped in the sand pit at the base, whimpering with your old dog accolade. The blocks casually rest in a sandy arena, with most problems being only 3 metres high. The central front face of the Diplodocus has a mouth that you could pull on and climb up. It is only joined by thin parts of sandstone at either side and will collapse one day if enough people pull on it; so it might be better to avoid climbing this line and leave this wonderful piece of rock intact. At (12) on the giant Diplodocus block, finish intelligently straight up, a lot less dangerous than drifting right and avoids utilising the fragile mouth of the giant Diplodocus. Adding (23b) is fun, and is much better to do before the final problem of (23); then you can finish direct to the top of the giant Diplodocus as a grand finale. You could design a red circuit here but it would be small and naf, the area just doesn't suit really hard bouldering The cheeky circuits of yellow and orange however make it an ideal venue for a mixed group with beginners. You will find it a lovely and relaxed spot, quick drying, and easy to move around with a big crash pad.

Bleu 23 – 5b+; Baptiste Provini

Q-D 4m	S	D 4c		M
Q-D 4m	S	1 4c		10
Q-D 4m	S	2 4a+		
Q-D 3m	S	3 4a		M 9
Q-D 5m	2a	4 3b	Pump Sloper	
Q-D 4m	S	5 4b	Sloper	6
Q-D 3m	4a	6 4a		M 8
Q-D 3m		7 3c+		
Q-D 3m		8 3b		
Q-D 3m	S	9 5b+	CRIMP	M 2
8m		10 4a	→ Pump	
Q-D 3m		11 6a+		X
7m	HBall 2a	12 3b	Fun Cool	

Q-D 3m	13 5a	Sloper	
Q-D 5m CP S	14 6a		M
Q-D 3m CP S	15 4c		M 5
Q-D 4m 3a	16 4a		
3m CP S	17 4c		4
Q-D 4m PS 2b	18 4b		
3m CP S	19 3c		
2m CP S	20 4b		M 7
8m HBall 3b	21 3c+	Cool	M
Q-D 4m CP S	22 5a	Sloper	3
Q-D 7m S 2a	23 5b+		M 1

Magicien total

Rocher du Général
150 metres

Circuit 7: Page-64

1	3b	13	4c
1b	2c	14	4a
2	4a	14b	3c
2b	3a	15	3a
3	3c	15b	3a
4	2c	16	3c
5	5b	16b	3b
6	3c	17	3b
7	3c	18	3a
7b	2b	19	2c
8	4a	20	2c
9	3a	21	3a
10	3c	22	3b
11	2c	23	4b
12	3b		

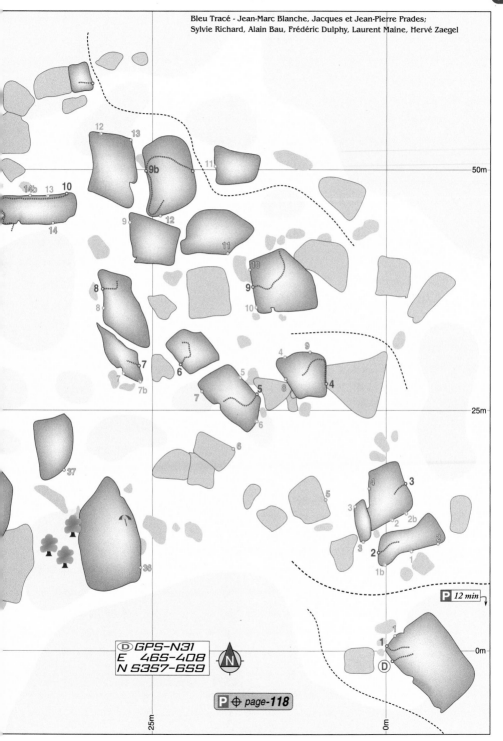

Bleu Tracé - Jean-Marc Blanche, Jacques et Jean-Pierre Prades; Sylvie Richard, Alain Bau, Frédéric Dulphy, Laurent Maine, Hervé Zaegel

GPS-N31
E 465-408
N 5357-659

P ⊕ page-118

P 12 min

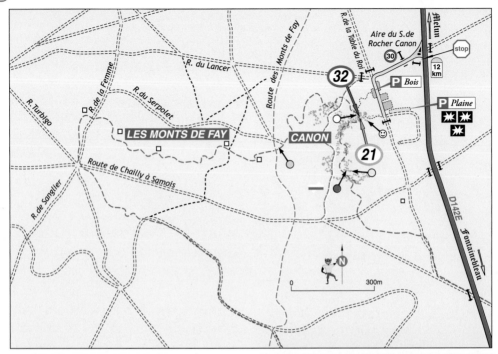

ROCHER CANON

Circuit	Cot.	Ang.	Prob-Var	Bois	Expo	Info
😊 ENF	1-2	🏃	40 & (9)	Q-D	Yum	Fun
⬤ PD	1b-3b	🏃	40	💧💧💧	Yum	Fun
⬤ AD	1a-4b	🏃	42 & (3)	🌳	CP	😊
⬤ D	3b-5c	🏃	40 & (2)	💧💧	PS	CRIMP
⬤ D+	2b-5c	🏃	40	🌳	PS	😊
⬤ TD+	5b-6b	🏃	46 & (2)	🌳	PS	😊
■ TD+	5b-6c	🏃	23	🌳	PS	😊
O ED+	6c-7b	🏃	24 & (2)	🌳	PS	😊
♦ ABO	7a-8c	🏃	45	🌳	PS	😊

LES MONTS DE FAŸ
| ■ TD+ | 5c-6c | 🏃 | 7 | 💧💧 | PS | 😊 |
| □ ED+ | 6c-7c | 🏃 | 8 | 🌳 | PS | 😊 |

ROCHER CANON (p 150 & 223)

Bleu 16 – 5c; Dave Brown

PHOTO: ALEX MESSENGER

MOON
100% CLIMBING

KATHERINE SCHIRRMACHER
BRAD PITT 7C+
STANAGE PLANTATION, PEAK DISTRICT

WWW.MOONCLIMBING.COM

moon

219

Nous avons appelé ce circuit moustique car ils sont nombreux sur ce massif durant l'été. C'est certainement l'un des circuits les plus désorientant et nous vous conseillons d'éviter sa deuxième partie si la végétation est humide car vous serez complètement trempés. Le (8) vous garantira un séjour à l'hôpital si vous chutez sans parade dans le chaos de blocs. Les (16) et (28) sont difficiles c'est pourquoi nous les avons omis sur notre liste ainsi que le (8). Aucun passage n'est vraiment exposé cependant nous vous conseillons une parade et un bon crash pad. De nombreux blocs ont leur sommet courbé ce qui fera plaisir a tous ceux qui aiment faire des rétablissements sur un bras. C'est un circuit un peu frustrant avec des lignes difficiles à comprendre. Cependant il est possible d'inspecter les voies depuis d'autres blocs et d'essayer les mouvements. Il est également réalisable à vu par la majorité des grimpeurs. Comme nous l'avons indiqué auparavant la fin du circuit reste vert et il vaut mieux grimper sur ce massif lors d'une période sèche.

Bleu 18 - 4c; Pascal Fillon

Bleu 38 - 4c; Fiona Murray

The circuit has been very aptly named, primarily because if you stand around still for too long, you are likely to get munched by one of the many passing mosquitos that seem to inhabit this area in summer. The circuit also traces a bewildering passage through the forest like a demented insect, going round on itself, crossing back through itself - and then does its best to loose you in the thick ferns of the latter part. Don't even think of attempting the back half of the circuit if there is any moisture on the undergrowth, you'll get completely soaked. It's certainly one of the most disorientating circuits you are likely to find – or not, depending on your level of perseverance. It also has a few nasty bites – No. (8) is guaranteed to put you in hospital if you fall unspotted into the chaos of boulders beneath. (16) just try pulling on quartz slopers on a beastly hot summers day. (28) Nice, but way too stiff for a happy 4b/c on-sighter. These three problems are way in excess to the rest of the circuit, so we have left them out of our on-sight challenge here; don't worry - you still get 39 problems to go at. For a circuit without any highballs, it still presents a good heady challenge and a spotter is well recommended. Most of the landings have been pounded into submission over the years and leaving a great many tree roots exposed, hence a good crash pad is essential. The boulders are mostly well separated and terrain is fairly level, so carrying your biggest pad doesn't present too much of a problem. A lot of the boulders curve at the top, so enthusiasts of the inverted hand single arm mantel will do well on many of the top outs – grabbing the on-sight prize from those who loose it all trying to top out. It is a slightly infuriating and annoying circuit with about 6 problems that are one move wonders, and a few top outs that naturally cop out. All said, there are always adjacent boulders to inspect the problems from and work out the moves, plus casual areas to flop out and rest between problems. This circuit really does give a realistic on-sight opportunity for many climbers. The very end part stays quite green, so choose a day at the end of a dry spell and have a toothbrush at the ready.

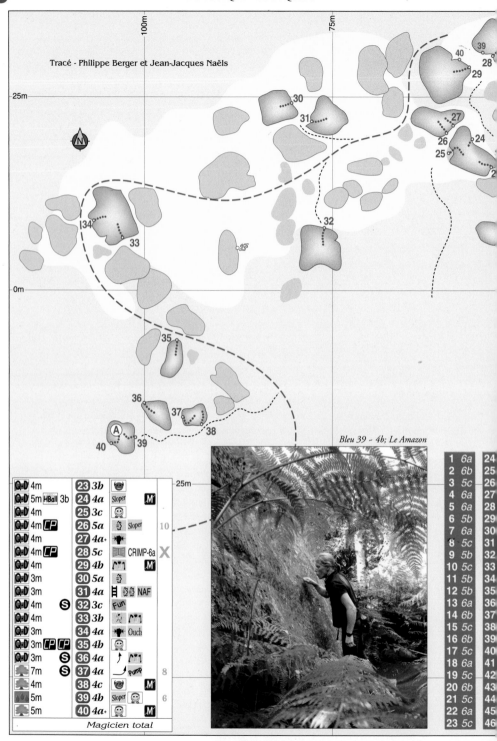

Tracé - Philippe Berger et Jean-Jacques Naëls

Bleu 39 - 4b; Le Amazon

Q-D 4m	**23** *3b*	
Q-D 5m HBall 3b	**24** *4a*	Sloper
Q-D 4m	**25** *3c*	
Q-D 4m *CP*	**26** *5a*	Sloper 10
Q-D 4m	**27** *4a+*	
Q-D 4m *CP*	**28** *5c*	CRIMP-6a
Q-D 4m	**29** *4b*	
Q-D 3m	**30** *5a*	
Q-D 3m	**31** *4a*	NAF
Q-D 4m **S**	**32** *3c*	Fun
Q-D 4m	**33** *3b*	
Q-D 3m	**34** *4a*	Ouch
Q-D 3m *CP* *CP*	**35** *4b*	
Q-D 3m **S**	**36** *4a*	
7m **S**	**37** *4a*	Pump 8
4m	**38** *4c*	
5m	**39** *4b*	Sloper 6
5m	**40** *4a+*	
	Magicien total	

1	6a
2	6b
3	5c
4	6a
5	6a
6	5b
7	6a
8	5c
9	5b
10	5c
11	5b
12	5b
13	6a
14	6b
15	5c
16	6b
17	5c
18	6a
19	5c
20	6b
21	5c
22	6a
23	5c

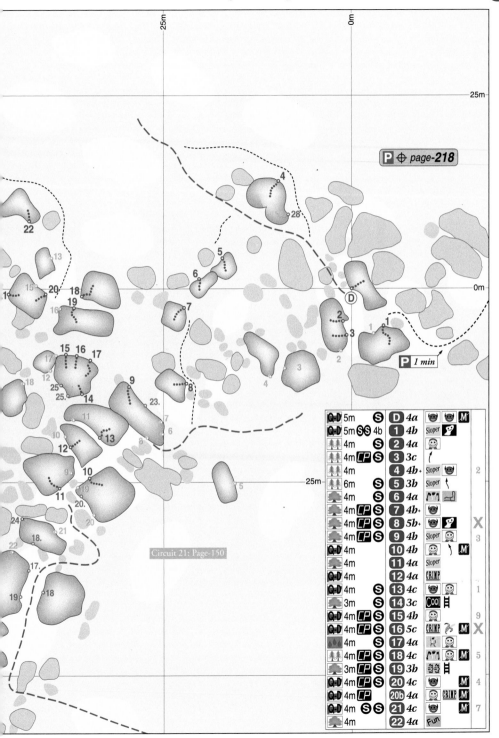

P ⊕ *page-218*

Circuit 21: Page-150

Q-D 5m	S	D 4a	😊 😊 M	
Q-D 5m SS 4b		1 4b	Sloper 👻	
↟↟ 4m	S	2 4a	😊	
↟↟ 4m		3 3c	↑	
↟↟ 4m		4 4b+	😊	2
↟↟ 6m	S	5 3b	Sloper ↖	
☘ 4m		6 4a	🦎 ⬚	
☘ 4m CP	S	7 4b-	😊	
☘ 4m CP	S	8 5b-	😊 👻	X
☘ 4m CP	S	9 4b	Sloper 😊	3
Q-D 4m		10 4b	😊 ↘ M	
☘ 4m		11 4a	Sloper	
Q-D 4m		12 4a	CRIMP	1
Q-D 4m	S	13 4c	😊 😊	
☘ 3m	S	14 3c	COOL ॥	
Q-D 4m CP	S	15 4b	😊	9
Q-D 4m CP	S	16 5c	CRIMP 🦎 M	X
☘☘ 4m	S	17 4a	🙈 🦎	
↟↟ 4m CP	S	18 4c	🦎 😊 M	5
☘ 3m CP	S	19 3b	❋❋ ॥	
Q-D 4m CP	S	20 4c	😊	4
Q-D 4m CP		20b 4a	😊 CRIMP M	7
☘ 4m	SS	21 4c	😊 M	
☘ 4m		22 4a	Fun	

C'est le massif le plus populaire de Fontainebleau. Il peut y avoir jusqu'à 300 grimpeurs le dimanche qui doivent parfois faire la queue pour faire les voies. Il y a cependant divers circuits et de nombreuses variantes qui permettent de satisfaire une telle popularité. Les aires de réception sont en général excellentes ce qui est une bonne chose car les voies sont patinées. Le grès de ce site contient beaucoup de quartz ce qui le rend très glissant et je défie quiconque à trouver de l'adhérence sur les prises du (36), qui sont glissantes comme de la glace. Les blocs ont souvent de gros trous tel du gruyère; certains offrent même des prises géantes alors que d'autres ont des aplats. Le mot glace évoquera la sensation que vous éprouverez dans vos doigts surtout en automne lorsque les jours sont froids. Après le (11), les arbres ombragent la plupart des passages du circuit

ce qui est plutôt agréable lors des chaudes journées d'été cependant il est préférable de débuter le circuit de bonne heure puisque les aplats du (16) sont suffisamment difficiles lorsqu'il fait frais. Les 15 premières voies sont faciles et banales comme en salle d'escalade. À partir du (16) le circuit devient plus intéressant. Le (18) est une traversée superbe qui peut-être faite à tout niveau de difficulté en débutant à 5a. Le (32) n'est pas difficile mais classique. Les prises sont évidentes, mais effectuer les mouvements au-dessus d'une aire de réception peu accueillante demande une bonne technique. Le Pod (40) est un bijou qui peut-être grimpé de 5 manières et à 5 niveaux de difficulté différents. Assurez-vous également d'avoir quelques essais de magicien sur le (45). Pour apprécier au mieux ce circuit nous vous conseillons de bien nettoyer les semelles de vos chaussures pour garantir une bonne adhérence.

Bleu 43 - 5a; Jo Montchaussé

Bleu 18 - 5b+; Jacky Godoffe

Trois Pignons - La Roche aux Sabots - (D/Bleu)

The name we have given to this circuit offers a few clues. To start with, this outcrop is the busiest in the whole of Fontainebleau, and on a busy Sunday afternoon there can be up to 300 people bouldering here, so it's no problem to find queues here. Fortunately, there is a whole mixture of circuits, plus many off circuit problems to accommodate such popularity and feverish enthusiasm. The landings are generally flat and good, which is just as well since rock has become very polished in places. The sandstone here is high in quartz content, making it was slippery even before the sand crystals had been ground out by successive generations of feet. I defy anyone to find any possible friction on the central foothold of (36), 'slippery as Ice' is the term that comes to mind. These cubic boulders often have luscious big holes, which resemble Emmenthal cheese; some offering giant jugs, yet others triumphantly disappointing, with large slopers that seem clandestinely polished to the uninitiated. The term 'Ice' will conjure up the feeling in your fingertips here on a cold autumn day. A lot of the problems on this blue circuit seem to face away from the sun, with trees shading most of the circuit after problem (11). This does however make it quite an attractive proposition on a warm day in summer, but make sure you get the circuit underway early since the slopers on (16) are ghastly enough when it is cool. The first 15 problems are a bit simple and mundane like a climbing wall, you don't really have to engage your brain until (16), where suddenly the circuit gets interesting and becomes more cerebral than giant pocket cranking. (18) is a superb traverse fest and can be climbed at any grade from 5a upwards. Problem (32) is not hard, but is a classic the first time you do it. The holds are obvious, but working out the body movements above an awkward landing takes 'careful judgement with technique.' The Pod at (40) is another gem, it can easily be climbed 5 different ways at 5 different grades. The easiest way is 4c, but it's for you to find that method – no clues given. Make sure you have a few magician falls in hand for (45), again it has many ways to be climbed, but some are not that easy. Perfectly clean soles are the key to enjoying this circuit, otherwise you will be slipping off all over the place - and have to go to the back of the queue.

Bleu 40 ~ 4c; Nadine Chelon

Bleu 27 - 5a; Jo Montchaussé

Special bread day in Milly-la-Forêt

Milly-la-Forêt: 2 shops that sell excellent artisan bread - 7 days
Vaudoué: Small tiny shop near church, only mornings. (1)
Arbonne-la-Forêt: Small epicerie that sells a selection of bread (3p)
Barbizon: Excellent artisan bread shop (3), general shop open 7 days
Chailly-en-Bière: Good shop
Malesherbes: 2 very shops offering good selection of artisan bread, plus cakes and soft goo - 7 days
Fontainebleau: Various shops in town, difficult to find easy parking.
Musardière camping: baguette van in summer only - 8.30-9am

Barbizon fayre

Milly-la-Forêt: Market day on thursdays-pm. Excellent selection of small shops in village centre, plus casino-shop that stays open late. S Intermarche (1-7) on W/edge of town with fish shop (1) - reasonable size; big champion store a few km NW of town. Both sell petrol. A good bookshop opposite the market hall that sells other climbing guidebooks.
Arbonne: Small shop with selection of foods, open 7 days, but closes 12.30-15.30 (3p). Two very good local vegetable farm shops.
Barbizon: Some very good shops in a very stylish long street, a coffee bar next to a good international newsagent. Mainly art galleries.
Chailly: Not a big village, but shopping is far quicker than going up to the carrefour.
Achères: Tiny village shop - hopefully will survive.   [Key; 1-Mon / 7-sun red closed]

Milly-la-Forêt

Villiers: Giant carrefour and Decathlon store.
La Chapelle: Out of town to East - big store.
Fontainebleau: Champion - medium sized near station at Avon - busy & parking dodgy.
Malesherbes: Intermarche down the backstreets.

Bleu 46 - 4b; Jo Montchaussé

	#	Grade	Icons
Q-D 4m S 3b	1	4a-	Fun · M
Q-D 4m CP	2	4a	
Q-D 4m CP	3	4b	Flexi · Fun
Q-D 3m	4	4c	
Q-D 3m	5	4b+	Fun
Q-D 4m	6	4b+	M
Q-D 3m	7	4c	· 10
Q-D 3m	8	3c	
Q-D 3m	9	4c	M · 7
Q-D 4m CP	10	4b+	Sloper · Cool · M
Q-D 3m	11	3b	M
Q-D 5m CP S	12	5a	
Q-D 3m S	13	4a-	
Q-D 4m S	14	4a	Cool · M
Q-D 3m	15	4a+	Sloper · M
Q-D 4m	16	5a-	Sloper · Cool · 1
Q-D 3m CP	17	4b	CRIMP · ( )
Q-D 9m S	18	5b-	Pump
3m CP	19	4b+	Sloper · M
Q-D 5m CP 3a	20	3c+	M
5m CP 2c	21	3c	Cool · CRIMP · M
Q-D 4m CP	22	4b+	(
4m CP S	23	5b	CRIMP · M · 2
3m S	24	4b+	M · 8
Q-D 4m CP	25	4a	Sloper · M
5m S	26	4c+	Pump · M · 6
Q-D 5m CP	27	5a	Cool · M
Q-D 5m CP	28	3b-	Cool · M
4m S	29	5a	Fun · 9
4m CP	30	4a+	CRIMP
Q-D 3m CP	31	3b	
Q-D 4m P S 4c	32	4c+	CRIMP · M · 4
Q-D 5m HBall 3c	33	4a	Cool · M
Q-D 4m CP	34	4a	M
Q-D 3m	35	3c	Fun
Q-D 3m	36	5c+	CRIMP · Ouch · X
Q-D 3m	37	4b	
Q-D 3m CP	38	4b-	M
Q-D 4m CP 3b	39	3b-	3
Q-D 4m CP	40	4c	BN · M
Q-D 3m CP	41	3c	CRIMP · M
Q-D 3m	42	4a-	Flexi · Fun
Q-D 5m CP	43	5a	CRIMP
4m CP 2a	44	4b+	Sloper
4m CP	45	5b	M · 5
5m CP 3a	46	4b	Fun · M

Magicien total

Bleu 45 – 5b; Jo Montch...

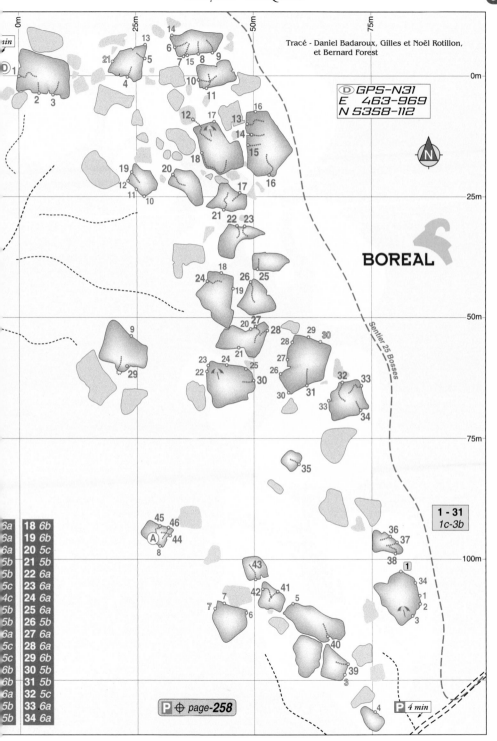

Tracé - Daniel Badaroux, Gilles et Noël Rotillon, et Bernard Forest

Ⓓ GPS-N31
E 463-969
N 53S8-112

BOREAL

Sentier 25 Bosses

1 - 31
1c-3b

P ⊕ page-258

P 4 min

6a	18	6b
6a	19	6b
6a	20	5c
5b	21	5b
5b	22	6a
5c	23	6a
4c	24	6a
5b	25	6a
5b	26	5b
6a	27	6a
5c	28	6a
5c	29	6b
6b	30	5b
6b	31	5b
6a	32	5c
5b	33	6a
5b	34	6a

Bleu 1 - 3b+; Jim Bacon

Si vous souhaitez grimper les circuits des Gorges d'Apremont, il vous faut un bon mental car les blocs sont en général tres hauts. Cependant la plupart des voies du circuit bleu sont sur des rochers plus petits ce qui plaira à ceux qui souhaitent éviter une visite à l'hôpital. De plus les blocs du début de circuit sont bien ombragés. Il y a également un circuit blanc pour les enfants et de nombreuses variantes faciles dans les cotations 2 et 3. Tout cela rend le massif très populaire. Le circuit bleu est un bon défi et il n'est pas trop horrible puisqu'il est possible d'éviter les blocs les plus hauts. En général les aires de réception sont bonnes et il est facile de transporter un crash pad entre les blocs. Le fait que ce circuit soit populaire est une bonne chose puisqu'il y a souvent un grimpeur disponible pour vous aider sur un passage ou pour vous offrir une parade qui vous permet de mieux apprécier les rétablissements en haut des blocs. Le nom de tempête a été donné à ce circuit puisqu'il débute tranquillement mais indique qu'il y a des voies féroces à l'horizon. Le (20) a la forme d'un gros nuage. En milieu de circuit, la nature des voies change pour faire place à une succession de passages difficiles. Heureusement au (36) les choses se calment et les blocs deviennent plus sympathiques. Le circuit se termine tranquillement avec cependant quelques passages qui vous surprendront surtout après avoir surmonté une tempête de difficultés. Attention aux (21) et (32) qui sont extrêmement difficiles et qui vous renverront certainement sur le crash pad (nous ne les avons pas inclus sur la liste du défi du magicien). C'est un superbe circuit qui testera votre technique et qui est très difficile à faire à vu pour le défi du magicien.

Bleu 14 - 4c+; Michel

Bleu 21 - 5c; James Bacon

To climb any of the circuits at the Gorges d'Apremont, you need a good head, because the blocks are usually on the large side of big! The major part of this blue circuit however is on smaller blocks, which makes it perhaps the most appealing circuit to the general climber visiting Gorges d'Apremont, and certainly will appeal to those who like keeping out of hospital. The boulders at the beginning of the circuit form a cluster of small blocks that enjoy dappled shade. There is also a white children's circuit plus a mixture of off circuit easy problems in the grades of 2-3. These together make a pleasant starting area and is consequently - deservedly popular. The blue circuit though as a complete outing, is a big challenge, and is a classic circuit offering a full on experience. It's not a nasty circuit, since the highballs announce themselves very well and can be left for those days when you are feeling exceptionally strong and confident. For the majority of the problems, the landings are good and it is very easy to carry a large crash pad between the boulders. It's popularity can be useful since there is often someone around to show you how to do a problem, plus having a spotter enables you to 'enjoy' the mantelshelf top-outs. With reasonable descriptive thought, we've given this circuit the name of 'The Tempest.' It starts very quietly, just rumbling along but with the inkling that there might be some ferocious problems appearing on the horizon, sooner or later. No (20), is shaped like a billowing cloud and certainly will have you suddenly huffing and puffing. The whole nature of the circuit changes midway to a storm of hard problems coming in constant succession with no let up. Then at (36) the battering relents fortunately; the highballs you are then confronted with are a lot more friendly. The circuit finally settles down to a quiet finish, but not without the outbreak of a few problems to catch you out, especially having been exhausted by the storm that you have just weathered. Watch out for the couple of nasty lightning strikes thrown in at (21) and (32). These are exceptionally difficult and highly likely to send you back to earth with a series of continual loud thundering bangs onto the crash pad. (We haven't included these in the magician challenge). It's a great circuit and a superb test of all round technique, it's also a very difficult one to get the magician on-sight tick.

Bleu 37 - 3c; James Bacon

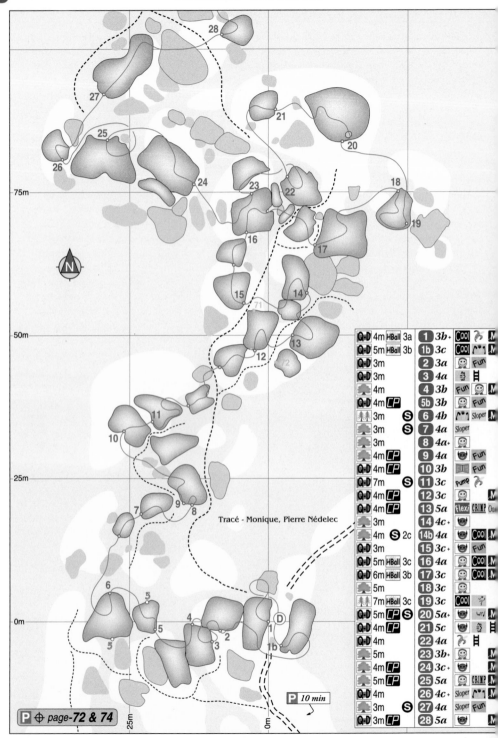

Tracé - Monique, Pierre Nédelec

Q-D 4m HBall	1	3a
Q-D 5m HBall	1b	3b
Q-D 3m	2	3a
Q-D 3m	3	4a
4m	4	3b
Q-D 4m CP	5b	3b
3m S	6	4b
3m S	7	4a
3m	8	4a+
4m CP	9	4a
Q-D 4m CP	10	3b
Q-D 7m S	11	3c
Q-D 4m CP	12	3c
Q-D 4m CP	13	5a
3m	14	4c+
4m S 2c	14b	4a
Q-D 3m	15	3c+
Q-D 5m HBall	16	4a
Q-D 6m HBall	17	3c
3m	18	3c
7m HBall	19	3c
Q-D 5m CP S	20	5a+
Q-D 4m CP	21	5c
Q-D 4m	22	4a
3m	23	3b+
4m CP	24	3c+
5m CP	25	5a
Q-D 4m	26	4c+
3m S	27	4a
Q-D 3m CP	28	5a

P ⊕ page-**72 & 74**

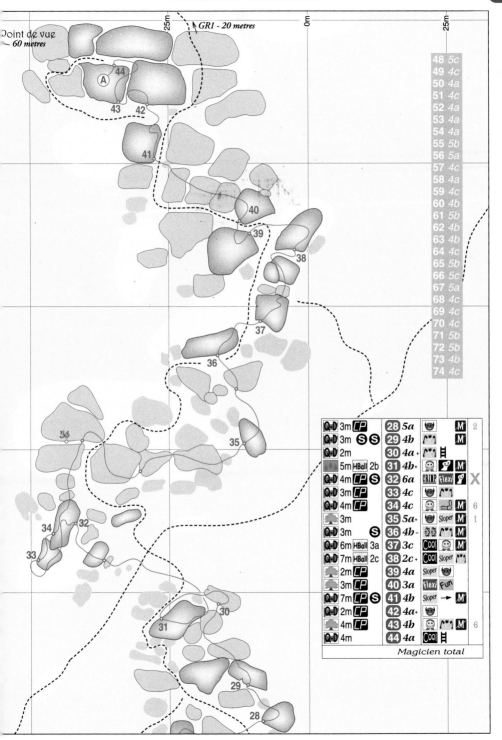

Départ

Il est facile de deviner la raison pour laquelle ce circuit s'appelle les traversées. De par sa nature c'est un circuit qui sera adoré par certains et hais par d'autres. Nous l'aimons car il est différent et qu'il est situé dans la forêt loin des nombreux randonneurs et des touristes qui visitent Barbizon. Je vous recommande d'aller sur ce site seulement par temps sec puisque de nombreux blocs sont couverts de lichen rendant les passages difficiles même lorsqu'ils sont secs. Cependant de nombreux rochers sont situés en hauteur et sèchent assez rapidement si le vent souffle. Le circuit se déroule sur les deux versants de la colline et par temps pluvieux le début du circuit reste souvent humide alors que les autres blocs sont secs. Nous vous conseillons d 'avoir un crash pad bien qu'il n'y ait pas autant de blocs en-dessous des voies comme dans les Gorges opposées. Ils manquent de bonnes prises sur ce circuit, mais les passages sont cependant excellents telle la dalle du (32) qui n'offre aucune prise. Le (13b) est très exposé mais c'est un passage superbe qui vaut la peine d'être essayé par tous ceux qui le peuvent. Le circuit culmine avec les (16) et (18) où la première arête est un échauffement alors que la deuxième est impressionnante et d'une qualité stupéfiante. Les grimpeurs de moyen niveau se souviendront longtemps du (18). Soyez prudents avec ce dernier car il vous conduira à l'hôpital si les choses tournent mal. Le (36) est parfait pour terminer le circuit. Il y a quelques passages supplémentaires sur le dernier bloc géant qui sont à essayer s'il vous reste un peu d'énergie. Le circuit a un côté un peu magique et il est très traditionnel de Fontainebleau. Le choix idéal pour ceux qui recherchent quelque chose de différent.

Bleu 18 - 5a+; Jimbo

Gorges d'Apremont - Bizons Sud - (D/Bleu)

Bleu 13b - 3c; Jingo

There are no prizes for guessing why we called this circuit Les Traverses! It's a circuit that will definitely have those who love it, and those who despise it. We like it - because it's different. It is set deep in the woods with a magical rocky situation, quiet and nicely away from the millions of ramblers that trundle down the GR1 and sentier of 25 (million) Bosses, or the hundreds of thousands of tourists that gush out of the executive coaches into Barbizon. I would only recommend a visit to this spot during a dry spell, since many of the problems are coated in a protective green lichen that is disconcerting and difficult enough to grapple with when it's dry! If there's any moisture on the ferns – you'll get a soaking too. This said however, a lot of the boulders are high

up and do dry out quite quickly when a wind is blowing. The circuit is set on two sides of the hill, leaving the start often damp, but with the problems later on in the circuit having dried out. It's slightly rocky territory and bringing a crash pad is a wise move, however it's still relatively friendly – unlike the chaotic Gorges across the road. There's no shortage of excellent problems, just a big shortage of excellent holds - the slab at (32), resplendent of having any holds on it! We have omitted the traverse at (1) from the magician challenge since it is not that brilliant and hardly an on-sight, practical challenge for the grade. Even though (13b) is a highball, it's an excellent problem that is well worth doing for anybody of a reasonably competent standard. The circuit has 2 climax's (good eh!). You arrive at the twin blocks of (16) and (18), where the first arête is a warm up for the staggeringly good and impressive second arête, (double up the crash pad for this tick). Certainly, most mid grade climbers will remember (18) for quite a time afterwards! Think wisely at (30b), it takes an excellent line, but does go into the hospital zone if things go wrong. The finale (36) to the circuit is perfect, hard but not too hard, and a lovely way to finish off your visit here. There are other problems around the giant finishing block to enjoy if you are still going strong and have energy to burn. This circuit does have quite a magical feel to it and is very much a traditional circuit that wanders around the forest, an ideal choice if you are looking for something different.

Bleu 36- 5b; Jingo (Not many 5b's offer you a chance for a kip)

Tracé - Pierre Manuel; et refondu par Jean Pillot

Bleu (21) - Orange - (10)
78 metres @ 190°

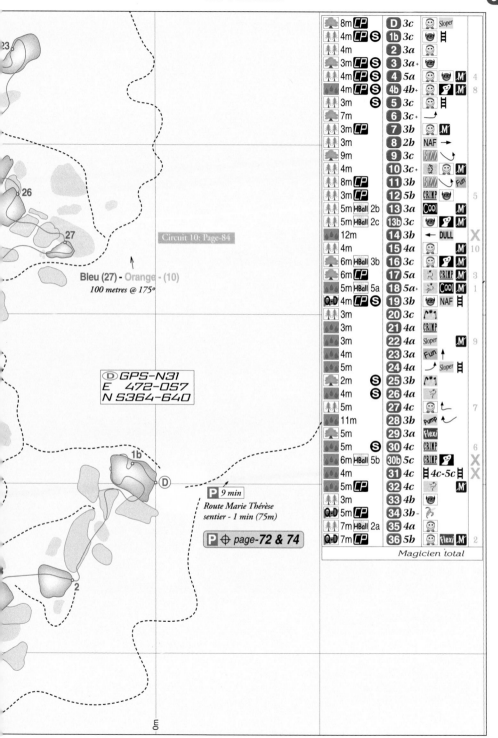

Circuit 10: Page-84

Bleu (27) - Orange - (10)
100 metres @ 175°

D GPS-N31
E 472-057
N 5364-640

P 9 min
Route Marie Thérèse
sentier - 1 min (75m)

P ⊕ page-72 & 74

Magicien total

C'est le site idéal si vous aimez les petits blocs dans un endroit calme ainsi que les circuits bleu et orange. Depuis le parking de Chanfroy le sentier forestier qui mène au massif est l'un des plus longs de Fontainebleau, parfait pour accéder en VTT (1km64). Soyez prêts pour un vent de face au retour et prenez le plus petit crash pad que vous avez. Après 17 minutes de marche un peu difficile, essayez de repérer un petit panneau dans les arbres pour le sentier de Bornage [785] qui vous emmène sur la gauche vers le haut de la colline. Les deux circuits débutent ensemble et, sur le topo, vous trouverez le circuit orange car tous les passages ont un niveau inférieur à 4 et qu'ils sont sympas à faire. La qualité du rocher est excellente, avec de très bonnes prises sur l'orange mais des aplats difficiles sur le bleu. Les blocs font face au sud et reçoivent beaucoup de soleil, et bien qu'ils soient sous

Bleu 2 - 5a; Nicholas Faussot

des hêtres ceux-ci sont bien séparés ce qui permet un séchage rapide. Les aires de réception sont pour la plupart sur terrain plat et donc très bonnes. Le sanglier, qui vit sur ce massif, retourne la terre en bas des blocs à la recherche de nourriture rendant le sol aussi moelleux qu'un crash pad. Cela explique également que les sentiers autour des blocs sont si usés mais les fougères très hautes sont elles complètement intactes. Avec 48 passages sur le circuit bleu et plus de 40 sur le circuit orange c'est le site idéal pour un groupe de grimpeurs de niveau différent. Pour notre défi du magicien, nous avons transformé le (29) en une cheminée sympa plutôt que d'abîmer vos doigts sur des grattons horribles ! La fin du circuit orange fera trembler de peur les grimpeurs débutants.

Bleu secteur 13-15

If you like low boulders in a quiet setting, and where a blue and orange circuit are intermingled, then this is the spot for you. If you want an extreme orienteering challenge, then by all means park at the Isatis car park and navigate your way south through the woods for a considerable time! For the practical, but slightly dull approach, park just beyond the big riding club at Arbonne-le-Forêt. The forest track leading from the parking at Chanfroy is one of the longest and straightest in Fontainebleau; perfect for access on mountain bike (1.64 km). It runs E-W so be prepared for a headwind on the return and take the smallest crash pad you have (and a sideways carrying mechanism). The track leaves the woods and opens up onto the Plaine de Chanfroy, so be wary of galloping jockeys thinking they are winning in the Prix de l'arc de Triomphe. After the somewhat arduous but rewardingly sunny 17 min stroll through an unforested part of the Forêt des Trois Pignons, you need to spot a small sign in the trees for the Bornage [785] footpath, that strikes leftwards up the hill to the north. You won't see any major geological or recognisable distinction, but this does mark the beginning of the Rocher de Milly ridge, and becomes the western edge of the Forêt de Fontainebleau. Both circuits start here together and we include the orange circuit on the topo since just about all the problems are below grade 4, you can try it out for fun. The rock is mostly good, offering nice chunky holds for the orange circuit, but difficult slopers on the blue problems. All of the climbing is set on a south-facing ridge and gets a lot of sunshine, since the forest consists of beech trees that are well separated and allow the rocks to dry quickly. The landings are mostly level and good to land on. The wild boar (Sanglier) that inhabit the area, and in search of a chumpy breakfast, dig up the base of the climbs to make the ground as soft as a crash pad. It also explains why the trails around the rocks are so well worn, but the ferns at head height are completely intact. With 48 problems on the blue circuit, and 40 plus variations on the Orange, it presents an ideal day out for a group of mixed climbers. For our magician challenge, we have dropped 26b (soft rock), and converted (29) to a fun chimney, why mercilessly crush your fingertips on painful crimps! The finishing uphill leap at the end of the orange circuit will definitely get the débutante climbers shaking with fear.

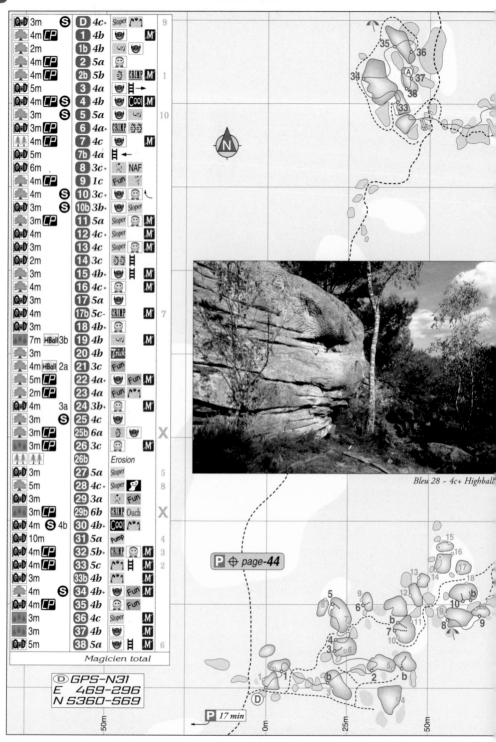

Q+D 3m	S	D	4c+	Sloper ^*1	9
4m CP		1	4b	M'	
2m		1b	4b		
4m CP		2	5a		
4m CP		2b	5b	CRIMP M'	1
Q+D 5m		3	4a	→	
Q+D 4m CP S		4	4b	COOl M'	
3m	S	5	5a		10
Q+D 3m CP		6	4a+	CRIMP	
4m CP		7	4c	M'	
Q+D 5m		7b	4a	←	
Q+D 6m		8	3c+	NAF	
4m CP		9	1c	Fun	
4m	S	10	3c+		
Q+D 3m		10b	3b+		
3m CP		11	5a	Sloper M'	
Q+D 4m		12	4c+	Sloper	
Q+D 3m		13	4c	Sloper M'	
Q+D 2m		14	3c		
3m		15	4b+	M'	
4m		16	4c+	M'	
Q+D 3m		17	5a		
Q+D 4m		17b	5c+	CRIMP M'	7
Q+D 3m		18	4b+		
7m HBall 3b		19	4b	M'	
3m		20	4b	Trick	
4m HBall 2a		21	3c	Fun	
5m CP		22	4a+	Fun M'	
2m CP		23	4a	Fun ^*1	
Q+D 4m 3a		24	3b+		
3m	S	25	4c		
3m CP		25b	6a		X
Q+D 4m		26	3c	M'	
		26b		Erosion	
Q+D 5m		27	5a	Sloper	5
5m		28	4c+	Sloper	8
Q+D 3m		29	3a	Fun	
3m CP		29b	6b	CRIMP Ouch	X
Q+D 4m S 4b		30	4b+	COOl ^*1	
Q+D 10m		31	5a	Pump	4
Q+D 4m CP		32	5b+	CRIMP M'	3
Q+D 4m CP		33	5c	^*1	2
Q+D 3m		33b	4b	^*1 M'	
4m	S	34	4b+	Fun M'	
Q+D 4m CP		35	4b	Fun	
3m		36	4c	Sloper M'	
3m		37	4b	M'	
Q+D 5m		38	5a	M'	6
				Magicien total	

Bleu 28 – 4c+ Highball

D GPS-N31
E   469-296
N S360-569

P ⊕ *page-44*

P 17 min

Tracé - Monique et Wladimir Fédoroff, Alain Laloup, Pierre Nédelec et André Schwartz

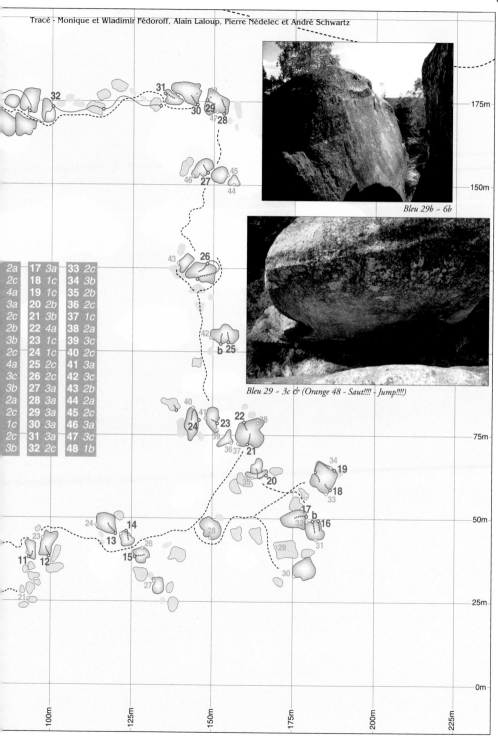

Bleu 29b - 6b

Bleu 29 - 3c & (Orange 48 - Saut!!!! - Jump!!!!)

2a	17 3a	33 2c
2c	18 1c	34 3b
4a	19 1c	35 2b
3a	20 2b	36 2c
2c	21 3b	37 1c
2b	22 4a	38 2a
3b	23 1c	39 3c
2c	24 1c	40 2c
4a	25 2c	41 3a
3c	26 2c	42 3c
3b	27 3a	43 2b
2a	28 3a	44 2a
2c	29 3a	45 2c
1c	30 3a	46 3a
2c	31 3a	47 3c
3b	32 2c	48 1b

Orange 8 ~ 5a; Matt Nicholson

Il faut faire beaucoup d'efforts pour atteindre le sommet de ce circuit que nous avons appelé Mont Blanc mais vous serez récompensé car c'est là où sont situés les meilleurs passages. Avec 70 voies et des variantes, c'est sans conteste le plus long circuit de ce guide et nous recommandons donc de le diviser en 2 pour deux jours d'escalade. La première partie, les "aiguilles de Chamonix," vous emmène sur le versant de la colline. La deuxième partie est située dans la forêt de pins. Nous avons inclus de nombreuses variantes assez difficiles puisque c'est un site idéal pour un groupe de grimpeurs aux habiletés diverses. Il y a suffisamment de voies de cotation 5 pour divertir les grimpeurs de bon niveau et les passages les plus faciles sont parfaits pour les grimpeurs de niveau moyen. Du fait que ce circuit soit séparé en 2 jours d'escalade, nous espérons que la deuxième partie garde sa popularité pour que les prises restent propres et sans lichen. Le circuit commence tout près du chemin des Béorlets. Le sentier à ce niveau est un magnifique chemin pavé qui descend la colline telle la Mer de Glace. Pour débuter, les passages sont sympas et offrent un excellent échauffement. Le (7) n'est pas très agréable et vous rappelle que les passages de niveau 5 peuvent être très dur. Après le (9) vous rejoignez le sentier des 25 bosses pour être confronté aux blocs géants des Aiguilles de Chamonix. Ils paraissent effrayants, mais ils ne sont pas trop difficiles si le temps est sec. Le circuit s'en va ensuite dans les bois pour rejoindre le (17), une méchante traversée suivie par un toit. Attention à la descente du (30) qui fera pleurer de peur les plus nerveux qui jureront sûrement de ne pas être capable de l'effectuer.

It will come as no surprise to anyone flicking through the tourist brochure to the Forêt de Fontainebleau, that a region cut through by several giant gorges will have its special own Grand Montange region. In keeping with tradition of understatement, we have named this circuit Mont Blanc of course. The summit is traditionally whale back shaped, it's quite a long slog up, and the best climbing actually lies on the little summits to the top. With 70 problems and a few variations, it is by far the longest circuit in the book and we recommend splitting it into a two-day event. The first part 'The Chamonix Aiguilles,' is a typical wandering circuit that makes an excellent tour up the hillside. The second part circumnavigates around an open picnic area, deep in the pine forest and is best suited for simply climbing individual problems. We have included a lot of hard variations with our interpretation of the circuit, because it is an ideal spot for a group of climbers of mixed ability. There are enough problems of grade 5 to keep it entertaining for good boulderers, plus the easier climbing is great for the middle grade climber. By splitting this giant circuit into these two separate days out, it will hopefully make the latter part more popular, and keep the vital holds free of lichen. The circuit starts only seconds off the Chemin des Béorlets, and opposite the finish of the Potala circuits. Here the track is a beautiful cobbled road in the forest, snaking its way down the hill like the Mer de Glace. The introduction problems are very pleasant and work as an excellent warm up before problem (6) a steep jaunt that tantalisingly doesn't allow you to bridge on the opposite wall. (7) is the first nasty and an excellent reminder that the 5th grade can be a tough step up. (8) is desperate for the short climber, but a superb problem nevertheless. You then squirm up (9) before rejoining the 25 bosses footpath, only to be confronted with the lovely collection of gigantic pointed boulders – the Chamonix Aiguilles, naturally. These look frightening - and are, but don't prove too difficult if conditions are dry. The circuit then wanders off into the woods for (17), strange you may think until you see the challenge; a mean traverse followed by a crux roof section that whams in a desperate set of finishing moves, it also separates the grade 4 and 5 climbers quite ruthlessly. The whole middle section of the circuit is a mixture of beguiling slabs and roofs that prove to be friendlier than they look. Peeping over the top of the descent for (30) will have those of nervous disposition crying with fear, and uttering 'I'm not going down f***ing that.' Part 1 of the circuit finishes with an excellent crescendo at (38), a good juggy outing for beginners, but also a very fine (b) version, which is a tricky technical tortional twisting and tantalizing tormentor.

Orange 25 ~ 4a; Fiona Murray

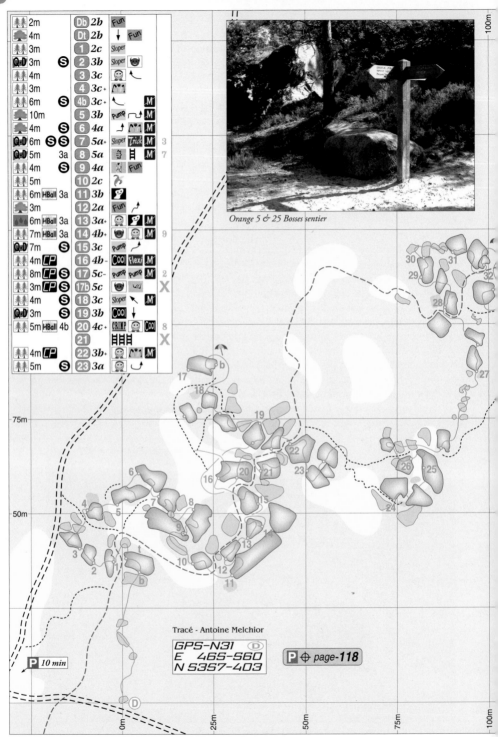

Orange 5 & 25 Bosses sentier

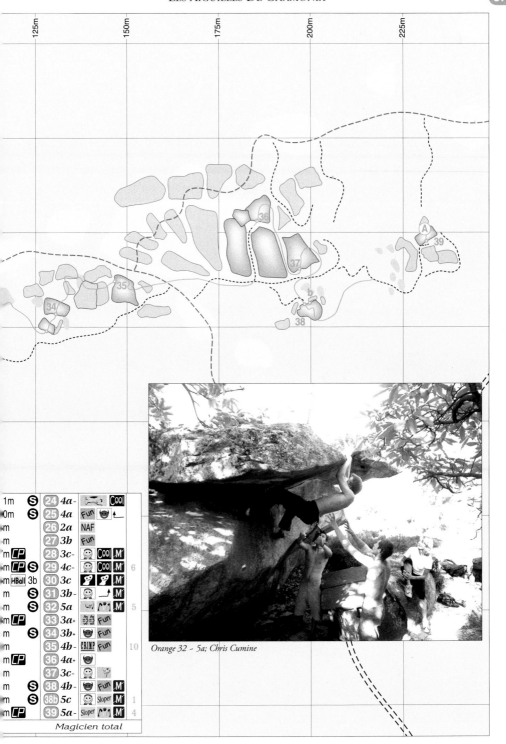

Orange 32 - 5a; Chris Cumine

1m	S	24	4a-		COOl
0m	S	25	4a	Fun	
m		26	2a	NAF	
m		27	3b	Fun	
m CP		28	3c-	COOl	M
m CP S		29	4c-	COOl	M
m HBall 3b		30	3c		M
m	S	31	3b-		M
m	S	32	5a		M
m CP		33	3a+	Fun	
m	S	34	3b+	Fun	
m		35	4b	CRIMP Fun	10
m CP		36	4a+		
m		37	3c-		
m	S	38	4b-	Fun	M
m	S	38b	5c	Sloper	M 1
m CP		39	5a-	Sloper	M 4

Magicien total

La deuxième partie du circuit peut-être rejointe en suivant le sentier des 25 bosses qui est balisé par des traits rouges, donc facile à suivre. Vous passerez un chaos de blocs à la fin du premier circuit puis un toit très connu (32). 60 mètres plus loin en haut de la colline, vous atteindrez les derniers blocs, et trouverez les (42) et (45) à gauche du sentier. Il y a un bon espace pour pique-niquer derrière le dernier bloc. De là tous les passages sont seulement à quelques pas et sont faciles d'accès avec un crash pad. Il y a de nombreuses arêtes et des murs qui une fois nettoyés offrent des voies de niveau 5. Ce site est très tranquille avec de belles vues sur 95.2. Il est bien ombragé grâce aux pins et est un meilleur choix que Diplodocus lorsque le temps est beau. Certains passages sont sympathiques, d'autres sont difficiles (56), certains sont horribles (55) et quelques-uns sont répugnants de difficulté (67). Si l'emplacement d'un site d'escalade et sa beauté naturelle sont aussi importants pour vous que de grimper alors ce circuit est idéal. Si vous mentionnez à un grimpeur de Cuvier que vous allez à Grand Montagne pour faire le Mont Blanc, il est certain qu'il ne comprendra pas pourquoi. Sans doute par manque d'appréciation de la sérénité de ce massif.

Orange 56 ~ 4a+; Matt Nicholson

The second part of the circuit can be easily reached by following the 25 bosses sentier, the footpath being well marked by red dashes and easy to follow. You know where you are by the chaos that it navigates at the end of the first part of the circuit, having passed the well known roof at (32) some 30 metres previously. Then up the hill and 60 metres further on, it reaches the final set of finishing blocs. Here you will easily see (42) and (45) on your left at the side of the path. An ideal place to picnic is behind the finishing block. From here all the problems are only a short walk and you can navigate the area very easily with a crash pad. There are also countless other arêtes and walls that will offer excellent grade 5 problems if you clean off the lichen. This whole area is very tranquil, with fine views over to the twin hills of 95.2 and beyond. It gets excellent shade from a reasonably open pine forest, and is a far wiser choice in good weather than greasy old Diplodocus. Some of the problems here are friendly, others are difficult (56), some are mean (55), and some are disgustingly hard (67). We cleaned up a huge amount of this area, but left (52) for those who enjoy, high-risk problems and perhaps have a rope to clean by abseil. If location and natural beauty are as important to you as is climbing, then this is an excellent choice. Just mention to a Cuvier slapper that you are off to Grand Montagne to climb Mont Blanc. They won't understand and will think you are off your trolley; but then again, they most probably wouldn't appreciate the quietness, fun and happy social conviviality that you get here.

Orange 50 – 4a; Chris Cumine

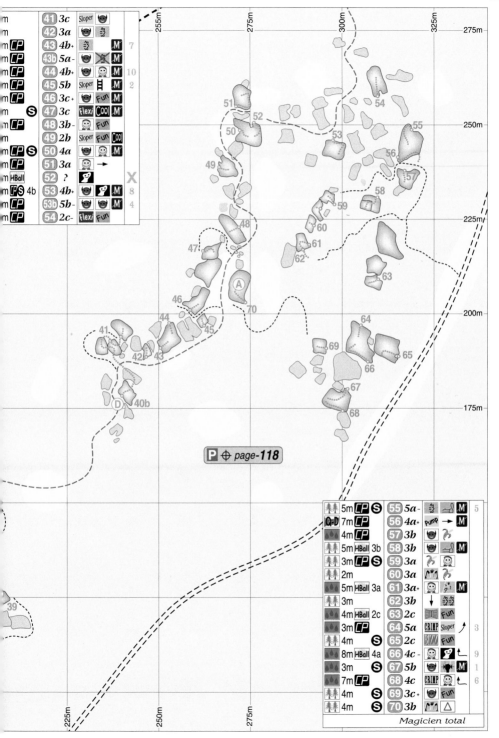

Circuit	Cot.	Ang.	Prob-Var	Bois	Expo	Info
LE PIGNON POTEAU						
PD	1b-3b		81&(23)	Q-D	CP	
GROS SABLONS OUEST (p 84)						
AD	2a-5a		40 & (2)	🌲	Yum	
ED+	6c-7b		6	🌲	S CP	
GROS SABLONS (p 164)						
AD+	2c-4c		73&(15)	🌲	HBall	
TD-	4a-5c		52 & (9)	Q-D	HBall	
ED-	4c-7a		35 & (4)	Q-D	HBall	
ABO	7a-8a		11	Q-D	HBall	Cool
95.2 OUEST (p 130)						
AD+	2a-4c		40 & (4)	Q-D	Cool	
95.2 EST (p 265)						
PD+	1c-3b		54&(12)	Q-D	Cool	
D	2c-5c		38 & (7)	Q-D	CP	
TD-	3c-5c		47&(12)	Q-D	CP	
ED-	4c-7a		37&(12)	Q-D	P S	
ABO	7a-8a		41	Q-D	P S	
ROCHER DES POTETS						
PD	1c-3c		42 & (1)	Q-D	Yum	
AD	1c-4b		36 & (2)	Q-D	Yum	
ROCHER DES SOURIS						
ABO	6a-7c		14	🌳	P S	
JEAN DES VIGNES (p 320)						
D+	3c-6b		35 & (8)	Q-D	S S	
ED+	6c-7b		9	Q-D	P S	Pump

Circuit	Cot.	Ang.	Prob-Var	Bois	Expo	Info
CUL DE CHIEN - NORD (p 177)						
D-	3a-5c		50 & (6)	🌲	Yum	Fun
CUL DE CHIEN (p 178)						
PD+	1c-3b		58 & (8)	Q-D	Yum	
TD+	4b-6b		30	Q-D	S CP	
ED	6b-7b		15	Q-D	CP	
ABO	7a-8a		12	Q-D	CP	Trick
91.1 (p 159)						
PD+	1c-3b		50&(20)	Q-D	CP	
AD+	2b-5a		47 & (7)	Q-D	HBall	Cool
TD-	3c-6b		34&(17)	Q-D	HBall	Cool
ED-	6a-7a		18	Q-D	DBall	
91.1 - OUEST						
AD-	2a-4b		37 & (7)	Q-D	Yum	Fun
ROCHER AUX SABOTS (p 231)						
ENF	1-2		40 & (8)	🌲	Yum	Fun
PD+	1c-3b		31 & (6)	Q-D	CP	
D+	3c-5c		46	Q-D	CP	
TD+	3c-6b		34	Q-D	CP	
ED	6a-6c		25	Q-D	P S	
ABO	7a-8a		45	Q-D	P S	CRIMP
ROCHER AUX OISEAUX						
ABO	6a-8a		27	🌳	P S	

BOREAL

JET SET 7a+, La Roche aux Sabots; Jacky Godoffe

Mile End Climbing Wall

London's premier climbing venue

- new outdoor bouldering and roped walls
- over 1500m² of quality climbing
- two mins from Mile End tube
- wide range of courses
- great atmosphere
- large car park

www.mileendwall.org.uk
020 **8980 0289**

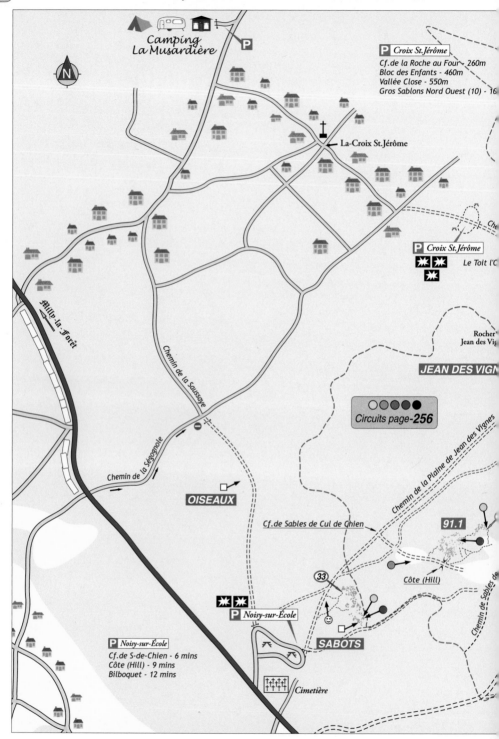

Camping
La Musardière

P

N

P Croix St.Jérôme
Cf.de la Roche au Four ~ 260m
Bloc des Enfants - 460m
Vallée Close - 550m
Gros Sablons Nord Ouest (10) - 16

La-Croix St.Jérôme

Fhilly-la-Forêt

Chemin de la Saussoye

P Croix St.Jérôme

Le Toit l'C

Rocher
Jean des Vig

JEAN DES VIGN

○○●●●
Circuits page-256

Chemin de la Plaine de Jean des Vignes

Chemin de la Ségognole

OISEAUX

Cf.de Sables de Cul de Chien

91.1

Côte (Hill)

33

Chemin de Sables de

SABOTS

P Noisy-sur-École

P Noisy-sur-École
Cf.de S-de-Chien - 6 mins
Côte (Hill) - 9 mins
Bilboquet - 12 mins

Cimetière

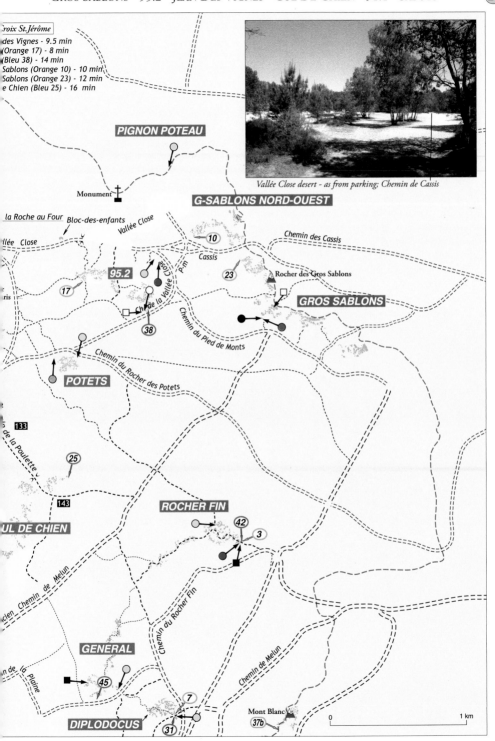

Croix St.Jérôme
des Vignes - 9.5 min
(Orange 17) - 8 min
(Bleu 38) - 14 min
Sablons (Orange 10) - 10 min
Sablons (Orange 23) - 12 min
e Chien (Bleu 25) - 16 min

PIGNON POTEAU

Monument †

la Roche au Four   Bloc-des-enfants   Vallée Close
llée Close

G-SABLONS NORD-OUEST

Vallée Close desert - as from parking; Chemin de Cassis

10

Cassis

Chemin des Cassis

95.2

17

ris

Ch. de la Vallée Clos

38

23   Rocher des Gros Sablons

GROS SABLONS

Chemin du Pied de Monts

Chemin du Rocher des Potets

POTETS

133

25

143

UL DE CHIEN

ROCHER FIN

42
3

Chemin du Rocher Fin

cien Chemin de Melun

Chemin de Melun

GENERAL

45

Mont Blanc

7

DIPLODOCUS

31

37b

0   1 km

Les discothèques ont souvent dans leurs noms des numéros tel le Club 100 par exemple, alors pourquoi ne pas appeler ce circuit Le Disco. C'est un site populaire avec de nombreux grimpeurs qui tentent les passages et oublient souvent d'utiliser leurs pieds de manière effective. La plupart n'arrivent jamais à faire les passages qu'ils essaient et finissent invariablement par être très fatigués et couverts de sueur. Le bruit constant des chutes sur les crash pad ressemble au bruit que produit un DJ sur sa platine de disque. Vous entendrez très certainement le bruit des grimpeurs sur les différents circuits (jaune, rouge et blanc) mais vous ne les verrez pas toujours car les blocs font parfois 5 mètres de haut. Ce n'est pas un circuit très grand donc nous vous conseillons d'ajouter les passages supplémentaires puisqu'ils sont excellents. Le haut de la colline offre la meilleure location des trois Pignons pour grimper et est également parfait pour exercer vos talents de photographe. Il y a de larges blocs avec de très bons passages et des aires de réception acceptables (avec une parade et un crash pad). Nous avons mis le (9) blanc sur notre liste du défi du magicien ce qui vous permettra de faire une voie blanche facile. Ce site est également le lieu parfait pour un pique-nique. Les passages s'améliorent en qualité et style jusqu'au (28) avant de changer pour offrir des voies qui demandent plus de puissance. Nous avons rehaussé le niveau de difficulté du (34) Ectoplasme, puisqu'il faut beaucoup de force en particulier dans les doigts. Attention au (38) qui est difficile et qui renverra de nombreux Vieux Chiens au parking la queue entre les jambes. Ce circuit est idéal pour les jours d'hiver ensoleillés et c'est l'un des circuits de la forêt qui sèche le plus rapidement. Il est cependant à éviter en été.

Bleu 22 ~ 4a-; Oli Korden

Bleu 16 – 5b; Trym Selland

"Le Disco"

Trois Pignons Nord - 95.2 - (D/Bleu)

Bleu 38 - 5a; Trym Selland

Nightclubs are often named after a number, like the 100 club etc, so why not call this circuit Le Disco. It's a popular hangout where you see lots of people struggling on desperates and slapping all over the place, and forgetting that really fancy footwork is the cool way to succeed. You might as well call it slap dancing, since most folk never seem to get up the problem they are trying, and invariably end up getting disgustingly hot and sweaty, and the young lads are always trying to pull. The constant all day echo of banging on crash pads, sounds like a demented DJ shuffling the turntable with the latest hip hop garage remix. Sound reverberates here, especially amongst the jumbled chaos of large blocks in the first half of the circuit, down at the bottom of the hill. You can hear people on different circuits, (yellow, red & white), but don't see them behind the boulders which are often up to 5 metres high. The first 12 problems on the side of the hill are superb and take very good direct climbing lines up the blocs. It's not a giant circuit, so include the extra (b) numbers since they are often very good problems themselves. Just before you get to the top of the hill, (13) is very likely to claim a few falls and for once is a problem that is actually easier for shorter climbers. The top of the hill is one of the most perfect bouldering locations in the Trois Pignons and ideal to get some photos of your mates climbing. There is a superb arrangement of large boulders with excellent problems of ideal length, high technicality and comfortable landings (with a spotter & crash pad). (15t) seemed a touch on the tough side so we omitted it from the magician challenge, but have inserted white (9), so you can at least have ticked an easy white problem (Boo, hoo, it should be on our circuit anyway). This area is also a perfect spot for a picnic and to re-supply yourself with energy for the second part. The problems simply keep on arriving in quality and style, crecsendoing with (28). It then subsides for a lower sector of more brutal power climbing before the superb sub-finale of (34) Ectoplasme, we upgraded it since you really do need power and fingertip strength. Make sure you have falls in reserve for (38), which is a real sting in the tail and likely to send many Vieux Chien's shuffling back to the car park with their tails between their legs. Ideal on a winter's sunny day and one of the fastest drying circuits in the forest; disgustingly too hot in summer.

Bleu 34 ECTOPLASME– 5a+; Fréderick Osseland

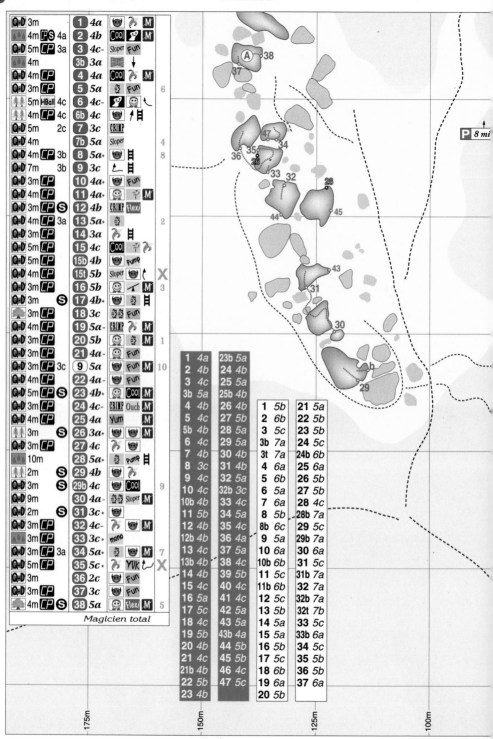

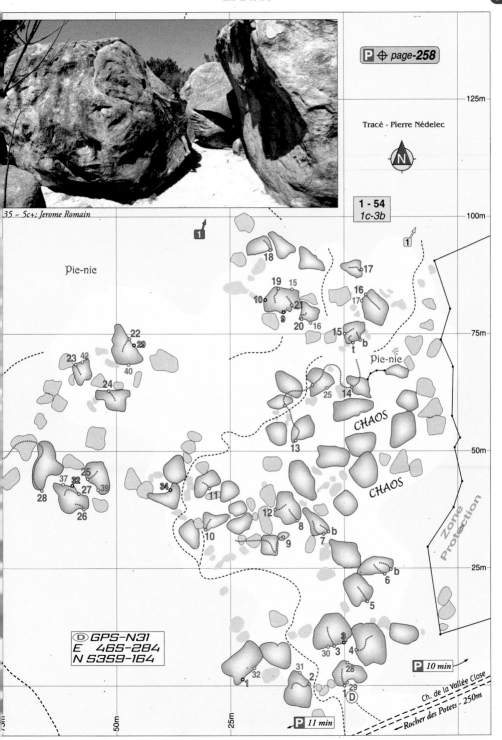

35 ~ 5c+; Jerome Romain

P ⊕ page-258

125m

Tracé - Pierre Nédelec

N

1 - 54
1c-3b

100m

Pic-nic

18

17

19   15

16

10   21   17

9   75m

20   16

15

b

t

Pic-nic

22

29

23 42

40

24   25   14

CHAOS

13   50m

CHAOS

34

25

37 32

27   39

28

26   11

12

10   8

9   7   b   25m

6   b

5

D GPS-N31
E   465-284
N 5359-164

3

30 3   4

32   28

31

2   29   P 10 min

1   1

Zone Protection

P 11 min

Ch. de la Vallée Close
Rocher des Potets - 250m

Rochers après le rain (rochers après la pluie) est une bonne manière de se souvenir de ce circuit. Ce site exposé sud et où le vent d'ouest souffle constamment, offre de superbes vues et, malgré les bruits de l'autoroute A6 proche, est très inspirant surtout lorsque le soleil brille. Les passages sur circuits jaune et bleu sont de très bonne qualité. Le circuit jaune demande beaucoup d'efforts et avec ses nombreux passages en cotation 3, il devrait presque figurer dans ce livre. Le circuit bleu monte et descend la colline à la manière de montagnes russes. Il est rempli de passages difficiles en cotation 4 avec certains encore plus difficiles, comme le (51) par exemple ''La Grande Ourse'' qui est assez effrayant. Le circuit est dans l'ensemble plutôt sympa avec des blocs de bonne hauteur. Les aires de réception sont bonnes mais parfois en pente et une parade est souvent la bienvenue. C'est un massif assez complexe par sa géographie et si vous fixez un rendez-vous avec d'autres grimpeurs, il peut être difficile de les retrouver. Nous vous conseillons de grimper avec des chaussons d'escalade confortables car vos pieds seront mis à l'épreuve sur de nombreuses voies. La plupart des blocs reçoivent le soleil toute la journée cependant les grands arbres un peu plus bas donnent de l'ombre

et certains passages en haut de la colline sont par ailleurs exposés nord. C'est donc le circuit idéal pour les journées chaudes de printemps ou d'automne. Les 4 passages les plus difficiles sont exceptionnellement bons et sont plus appropriés pour ceux qui souhaitent essayer les 20 variantes. Prenez en considération les problèmes d'érosion lorsque vous descendez la colline et essayez autant que possible de rester sur les blocs afin de ménager le sol.

Bleu 51 - 5a; Wobbly

Bleu 48 - 4c

Rochers aprés le rain (Rocks after the rain) – is a good way to remember this circuit. It's a small area and set on a fine south-facing ridge, and therefore is constantly swept by the prevailing westerly wind. The position and views are tremendous to offer a really uplifting spirit on a sunny and windy day, even though the noise from the A6 motorway is ever present. This area offers plenty of high quality problems that are divided between two circuits; a yellow and a blue. We have included both circuits on the topo since they intermingle so well. The yellow is a demanding circuit with a substantial number of grade 3 problems, almost worth inclusion in the book on its own merit. It fortunately dodges the harder problems – hence we called it 'The Dodgems.' The blue meanwhile keeps going up and down the hill a lot – hence 'Roller Coaster.' It is jam packed with a relentless barrage of grade 4 hard problems, interspersed with even harder ones, (51) being the 'Big Dipper' and quite scary. It's essential character though is nice and friendly, a circuit with sensible sized problems. The landings are pretty good but often slope downhill, hence a spotter is very handy to stop you trundling pronto down the steep hill and grovelling around in the bushes. The sheer complexity of the area makes it difficult to casually find other climbers, so be careful if you are planning to meet anyone - arrange a particular spot. Comfortable climbing shoes are ideal for tramping around this classic style circuit, and I can promise that foot technique here is more rewarding than tight edging shoes. Most of the general areas gets all day sun, but the bigger trees low down offer dappled shade, also many of the problems in the unique gorge on the top of the hill face north; so it isn't such a bad choice for a hot autumn or spring day. We chose (5a) as the magician cut off grade for this circuit because it is a sensible challenge for most, however, it is still a technically fiendish challenge to pull off. The 4 harder problems are exceptionally good, but wow - a lot harder and are more suited to those trying the 20 or so off-circuit harder problems. Note: Moving around hillsides in the forest on soft soil causes ground slip erosion very easily, so be thoughtful when descending the hill, always try to stay on boulders or rock as this helps to protect against erosion.

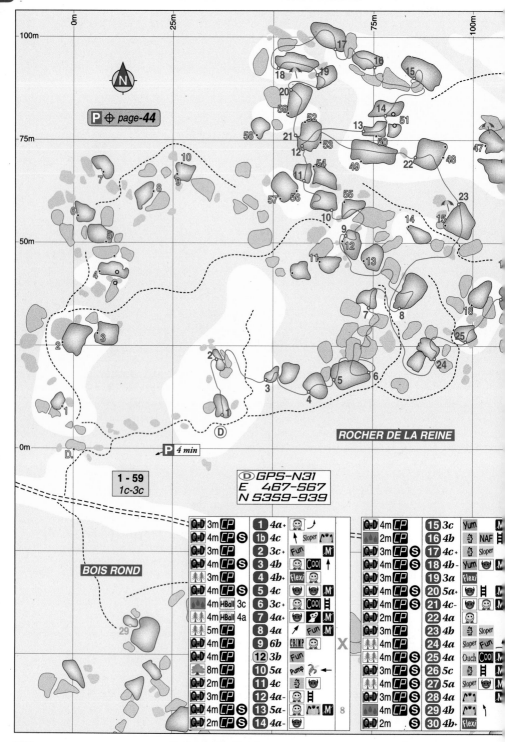

P ⊕ *page-44*

ROCHER DE LA REINE

P *4 min*

1 - 59
1c-3c

Ⓓ *GPS-N31*
E 467-567
N 5359-939

BOIS ROND

Q-D 3m CP	**1** 4a+	😊 ↝
Q-D 4m CP S	**1b** 4c	↖ Sloper ⌃^1
Q-D 3m CP	**2** 3c+	Fun .M:
Q-D 4m CP S	**3** 4b	😊 COOL ↑
🌲 3m CP	**4** 4b+	Flexi 😊
Q-D 4m CP S	**5** 4c	😊 .M:
🌲 4m HBall 3c	**6** 3c+	COOL ⊞
🌲 4m HBall 4a	**7** 4a+	🐾 .M:
🌲 5m CP	**8** 4a	↗ Fun .M:
Q-D 4m CP	**9** 6b	CRIMP 😊
♣ 8m CP	**12** 3b	Fun
Q-D 4m CP	**10** 5a	Pump ✂ ←
Q-D 2m CP	**11** 4c	😊 ⊞
Q-D 3m CP	**12** 4a-	😊 ⊞
Q-D 4m CP S	**13** 5a-	⌃^1 .M:
Q-D 2m CP S	**14** 4a-	😊 ⊞

Q-D 4m CP	**15** 3c	Yum .M:
2m CP	**16** 4b	🐾 NAF .M:
Q-D 3m CP S	**17** 4c+	🐾 Sloper
Q-D 4m CP	**18** 4b-	Yum 😊 .M:
Q-D 3m CP	**19** 3a	Flexi
Q-D 4m CP S	**20** 5a+	😊 ⊞ .M:
Q-D 4m CP S	**21** 4c-	😊 😊 .M:
Q-D 2m CP	**22** 4a	😊 😊
Q-D 3m CP	**23** 4b	🐾 Sloper
🌲 4m CP	**24** 4a	Sloper Fun ⊞
Q-D 3m CP S	**25** 4a	Ouch COOL .M:
🌲 4m CP S	**26** 5c	🐾 ⊞ .M:
🌲 4m CP S	**27** 5a	Sloper 😊 .M:
Q-D 3m CP S	**28** 4a	⌃^1 ⊞
🌲 4m CP S	**29** 4b	⌃^1 ↘
Q-D 2m S	**30** 4b+	Flexi

X

8

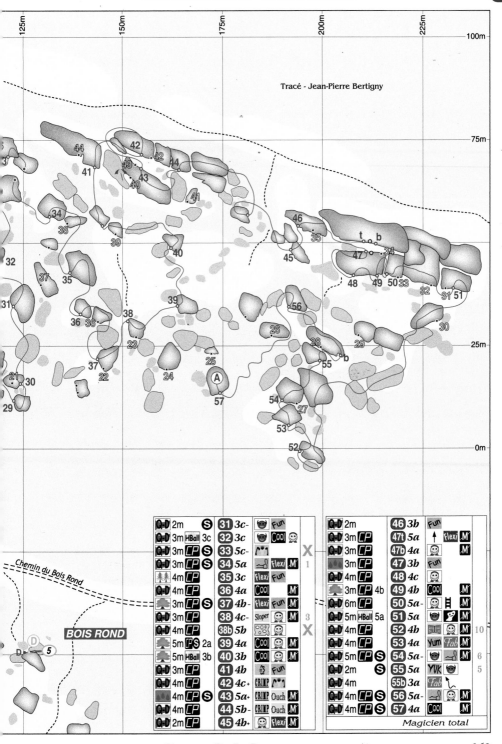

Tracé - Jean-Pierre Bertigny

Q-D	2m	S	**31**	*3c-*	Fun		Q-D	2m	**46**	*3b*	Fun
Q-D	3m	HBall 3c	**32**	*3c*	COOL		Q-D	3m	CP	**47t**	*5a*	Flexi .M¹
Q-D	3m	CP S	**33**	*5c-*	⌂¹		Q-D	3m	CP	**47b**	*4a*	.M¹
Q-D	3m	CP S	**34**	*5a*	Flexi .M¹			3m		**47**	*3b*	Fun
	4m	CP	**35**	*3c*	Flexi Fun		Q-D	4m	CP	**48**	*4c*	
Q-D	4m	CP	**36**	*4a*	COOL .M¹			3m	CP 4b	**49**	*4b*	COOL .M¹
	3m	CP S	**37**	*4b-*	Flexi Fun		Q-D	6m		**50**	*5a-*	.M¹
Q-D	3m	CP	**38**	*4c-*	Sloper .M¹		Q-D	5m	HBall 5a	**51**	*5a*	
Q-D	4m	CP	**38b**	*5b*			Q-D	4m	CP	**52**	*4b*	
	5m	P S	**39**	*4a*	COOL .M¹		Q-D	4m		**53**	*4a*	Yum Fab
	5m	HBall 3b	**40**	*3b*	COOL .M¹		Q-D	5m	CP S	**54**	*5a-*	
	3m	CP	**41**	*4b*	Fun		Q-D	2m	S	**55**	*5a*	YUK
Q-D	4m	CP	**42**	*4c+*	CRIMP ⌂¹			4m		**55b**	*3a*	Fab
	4m	CP S	**43**	*5a+*	CRIMP Ouch .M¹		Q-D	4m	CP S	**56**	*5a-*	.M¹
	4m	CP	**44**	*5b-*	CRIMP Ouch		Q-D	4m	CP S	**57**	*4a*	COOL .M¹
Q-D	2m	CP	**45**	*4b+*	Flexi					*Magicien total*

Chemin du Bois Rond

BOIS ROND

D — 5

Il est très facile de se perdre dans la forêt de Fontainebleau et la Canche aux Merciers est l'un des sites les plus déroutants. Les blocs qui se ressemblent tous sont éparpillés sur un sol plat et les nombreux arbres, mélange de pins, de hêtres, de chênes et de châtaigniers, ajoutent à cette confusion. C'est l'un des sites ou un GPS peut-être très utile surtout pour retrouver votre pique-nique. Ce circuit bleu est excellent et en dépit du (4) qui est un peu difficile la plupart des voies sont sympa et faciles avec de bonnes aires de réception. C'est également le site idéal pour l'utilisation d'un crash pad. Les arbres donnent beaucoup d'ombre surtout en début et fin de circuit et lors des chaudes journées d'été nous vous conseillons de garder les voies ombragées pour la fin. Les blocs se prêtent très bien au niveau de difficulté du circuit bleu demandant puissance et technique. Sur ce circuit, il vous arrivera de faire un passage en force pour réaliser peu après qu'un mouvement très technique aurait permis de le réaliser plus facilement, le (20) en étant un exemple parfait. Pour notre défi du magicien, nous avons fait 3 changements. Nous avons tout d'abord supprimé le (27) car il demande trop de puissance et qu'il est dangereux en cas de chute si vous n'avez pas de parade. Ensuite le (29) car les prises sont difficiles à atteindre et qu'il est assez humide et enfin le (31) qui devrait être sur un circuit ED. C'est un superbe circuit avec 44 passages et 6 variantes, un site idéal pour se perdre sans s'effrayer.

Bleu 4 - 5c; Severine Riandet: A casual approach, concentration and relief of success

Bleu 22 - 5b; Frederick Proville

Bleu 8 ~ 5a; Franck Benicy

Bleu 16 ~ 5a+; Francis Zerka

It's very easy to get lost in the forests of Fontainebleau; Canche aux Merciers being one of the most confusing areas that you are likely to find. Here the boulders are scattered over completely flat ground that never gives any indication to your movement or point of location. The mixture of pine, beech, oak and chestnut trees is homogenous everywhere, to further add complexity. Beguilingly, there are always memory defying groups of other boulders in every direction which all look the same. If this isn't enough to confuse you, remember that the blocs are steep on all sides making the descents difficult, so by the time you have walked around the top the boulder a few times and eventually got down, you have completely lost your sense of direction. It's one of the few places where a GPS device can be really helpful to locate your lost picnic hamper and champagne. This blue circuit is both excellent and well balanced. Apart from delivering a thumper of a problem at (4), it is mostly nice and easy to read with generally good landings throughout. It's a crash pad friendly location, with the trees giving a very good amount of shade to the start and at the end of the circuit. If it is a very hot day in summer, keep the shaded problems for the latter part of the day. The boulders here really suit blue style problems, with a lovely mixture of power and technicality. You can often do a problem here with humungous strength, only to after realise that a really technical move can unlock it at a far lower grade; with (20) being a fine example. We have included the best interesting variations to keep the circuit a good length, and given an alternative finish for short people (1.8m or less) on the last problem (44), so making the magic award a real possibility for a good all round climber. For our magical on-sight; we have made 3 changes. (27) deleted since it is purely a reach and power problem – and falling off it on your own could easily break your back if you are unspotted. (29) is again down to reach plus humidity free conditions. (31) direct up the slab at 6a-6b, should be on a ED (much harder) circuit anyway - so we recommend the fun 3c obvious version. In surmise, you can have a superb day here with the 44 problems plus 6 variations. It's simply a great place to get lost - without getting scared.

Bleu 14b - 5b; Ludovic Priami

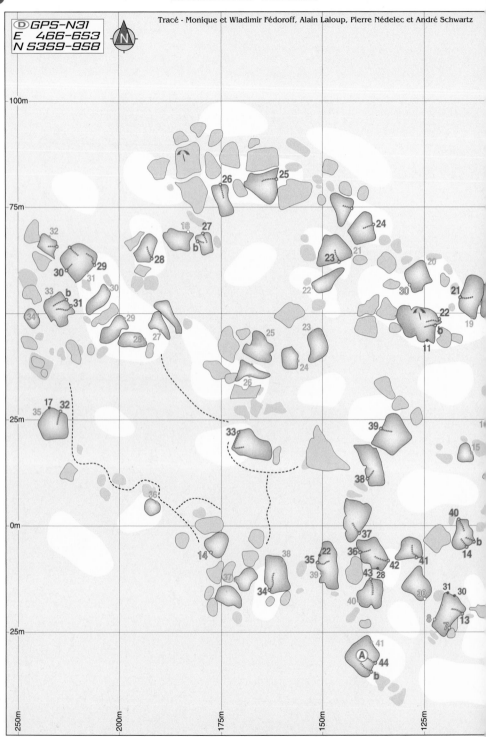

Tracé - Monique et Wladimir Fédoroff, Alain Laloup, Pierre Nédelec et André Schwartz

Ⓓ GPS-N31
E 466-653
N 5359-958

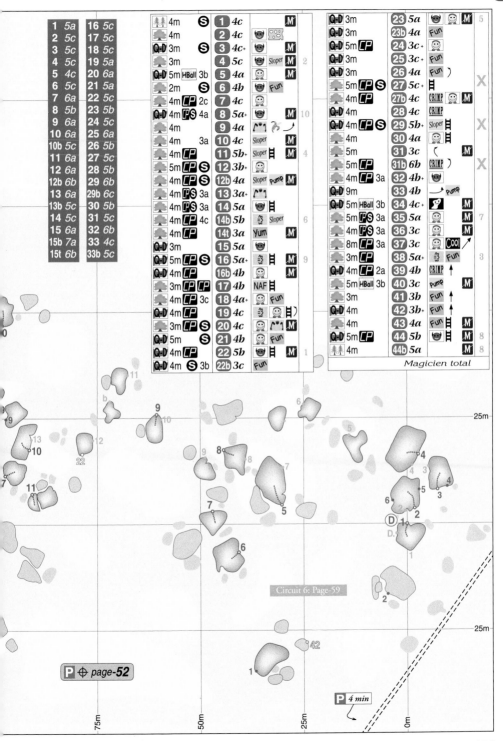

1	5a	16	5c						
2	5c	17	5c						
3	5c	18	5c						
4	5c	19	5a						
5	4c	20	6a						
6	5c	21	5a						
7	6a	22	5c						
8	5b	23	5b						
9	6a	24	5c						
10	6a	25	6a						
10b	5c	26	5b						
11	6a	27	5c						
12	6a	28	5b						
12b	6b	29	6b						
13	6a	29b	6c						
13b	5c	30	5b						
14	5c	31	5c						
15	6a	32	6b						
15b	7a	33	4c						
15t	6b	33b	5c						

Circuit 6: Page-59

P ⊕ page-52

25m

25m

75m   50m   25m   0m

Lors de votre première visite au site de Buthiers Canard, vous serez impressionnés par la dimension des blocs qui forment un magnifique chaos surplombant les restaurants et le parking. Certains blocs sont aussi grands qu'une maison. Le site est situé au-dessus de la route et offre un grès d'une épaisseur de 6 mètres. Il y a beaucoup de dièdres et de fissures ainsi que de très belles voies qui paraissent très effrayantes. Les passages du circuit bleu sont très hauts parfois dangereusement trop hauts. Cependant le niveau de difficulté n'est pas trop difficile. Vous aurez néanmoins besoin d'un bon mental et l'habileté de grimper des passages dans le 4. Le circuit débute par des passages assez faciles et pas trop techniques offrant un bon échauffement. Tout au long du circuit il y a de nombreux numéros et des flèches et parfois vous trouverez 2 numéros différents sur le même passage. Il y a même deux 35. (12t) est haut et dangereux parfait pour ceux qui aiment les dalles. Le (14) est probablement LE passage du circuit et demande un engagement total pour l'apprécier pleinement ! Du fait de leur hauteur, de nombreuses voies difficiles et hors circuit sont faites avec une corde (en moulinette). Faire la totalité du circuit bleu sans corde est un véritable défi, et si vous réussissez, vous serez récompensés par le sentiment d'avoir réalisé un véritable exploit – bonne chance.

When you first arrive at the Buthiers Canard massif, you will be impressed at the sheer size of the boulders, perched in a wonderful chaos that overlooks the restaurants and parking. No sooner than you have set foot outside the car, than you are literally scrambling around boulders the size of houses. Set high above the road, there is a 6 metre thick sandstone seam that runs for about 150 metres, and is left vertical where blocks have broken away. There are many corners, cracks and wonderful impending lines that look completely scary and death defying. If at this point you start to quiver and shake in your sneakers, don't change into you rock shoes since the blue circuit here takes on just about all open mouthed - jaw suspending, natural climbing lines. You are not only greeted with woeful high balls, but a reasonable indulgence of death balls too. There is one positive thing however, that the climbing just isn't very hard when it matters. I'm not saying that it's easy by any means, but your skills here need to be of firm mental control and competence in grade 4 level climbing, rather than having the outlandish power needed for many of the other blue circuits in the forest. You also get nicely broken in (hopefully rather than broken up), since the circuit starts

with easy grade highballs, and relatively low technical problems. There have been many attempts to form blue circuits at Canard over the years, resulting in a vast array of blue numbers and arrows all over the place. We have done our best to link most of these problems together in a coherent sequence. Some problems are marked with two different numbers together (5&6 on the same problem), and there are amusingly two number 35's. When you struggle mercilessly on the low (7) don't worry, you don't get highballs as viscous as this. (10) and (11) will generally sort out those climbers who are finding it just a bit too airy, we recommended a gracefull retirement to the bar for those in need of a stiff drink. (12t) offers a fine deathball for those who like slabs in the sky! (14) is most probably 'the problem' of the circuit and needs, "total commitment" for 'full enjoyment!' This is then followed with a countless barrarge of highballs until (23); when at last you can be joined by the rest of your team of spotters who decided to skip most of the first 23 problems. There are still another terrific 17 problems of smaller nature offering great bouldering. A lot of the hard off circuit problems are done here on a top rope – they're "BIG," By solo climbing the blue circuit, you take on a real challenge, but then are rewarded by real achievement - good luck.

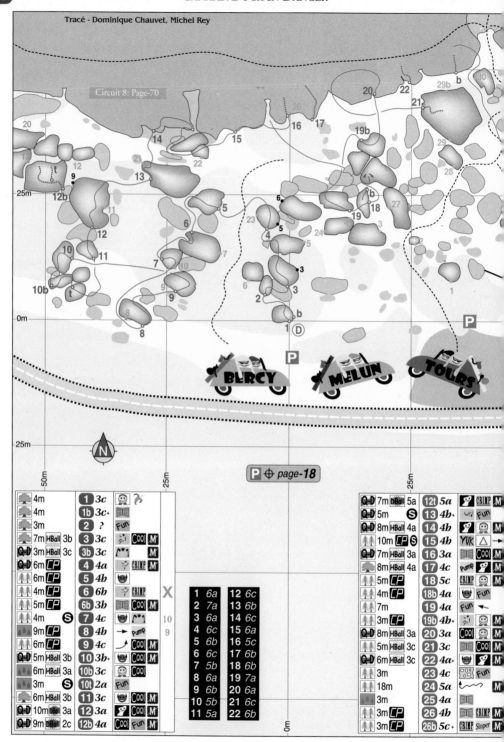

Tracé - Dominique Chauvet, Michel Rey

Circuit 8: Page-70

⊕ page-18

🌲 4m	**1** *3c*			
🌲 4m	**1b** *3c+*			
🌲 3m	**2** *?*			
🌲 7m HBall *3b*	**3** *3c*	Cool .M		
Q-D 3m HBall *3c*	**3b** *3c*	^1 .M		
Q-D 6m CP	**4** *4a*	CRIMP .M		
🌲🌲 6m CP	**5** *4b*			
🌲🌲 4m CP	**6** *6b*	CRIMP		
🌲🌲 5m CP	**6b** *3b*	Cool .M	X	
🌲🌲 4m Ⓢ	**7** *4c*	^1	10	
🔥 9m CP	**8** *4b*	→ Pump	9	
🌲🌲 6m CP	**9** *4c*	Cool .M		
Q-D 5m HBall *3b*	**10** *3b+*	Cool .M		
🔥 6m HBall *3a*	**10b** *3c*	Cool		
🌲 3m Ⓢ	**10t** *2a*	Fun		
🌲 6m HBall *3b*	**11** *3c*			
Q-D 10m ▦ *3a*	**12** *3a*	Cool .M		
Q-D 9m DBall *2c*	**12b** *4a*	Cool Fun .M		

1 *6a*	**12** *6c*
2 *7a*	**13** *6b*
3 *6a*	**14** *6c*
4 *6c*	**15** *6a*
5 *6b*	**16** *5c*
6 *6c*	**17** *6b*
7 *5b*	**18** *6b*
8 *6a*	**19** *7a*
9 *6b*	**20** *6a*
10 *5b*	**21** *6c*
11 *5a*	**22** *6b*

Q-D 7m DBall *5a*	**12t** *5a*	CRIMP	
Q-D 5m Ⓢ	**13** *4b+*	Fun	
Q-D 8m HBall *4a*	**14** *4b*	.M	
🌲 10m CP Ⓢ	**15** *4b*	YUK △	
Q-D 7m HBall *3a*	**16** *3a*	Cool .M	
🌲 8m HBall *4a*	**17** *4c*	Pump .M	
🌲 5m CP	**18** *5c*	CRIMP .M	
🌲 4m CP	**18b** *4a*	Fun	
🌲 7m	**19** *4a*	Fun ←	
🌲 3m CP	**19b** *4b+*	.M	
Q-D 8m HBall *3a*	**20** *3a*	Cool .M	
🌲 5m HBall *3c*	**21** *3c*	Cool .M	
Q-D 6m HBall *3c*	**22** *4a+*	.M	
🌲 3m	**23** *4c*	Fun	
🌲 18m	**24** *5a*	.M	
🌲 3m	**25** *4a*		
🌲 3m CP	**26** *4b*	CRIMP .M	
🌲 3m CP	**26b** *5c+*	CRIMP Sloper .M	

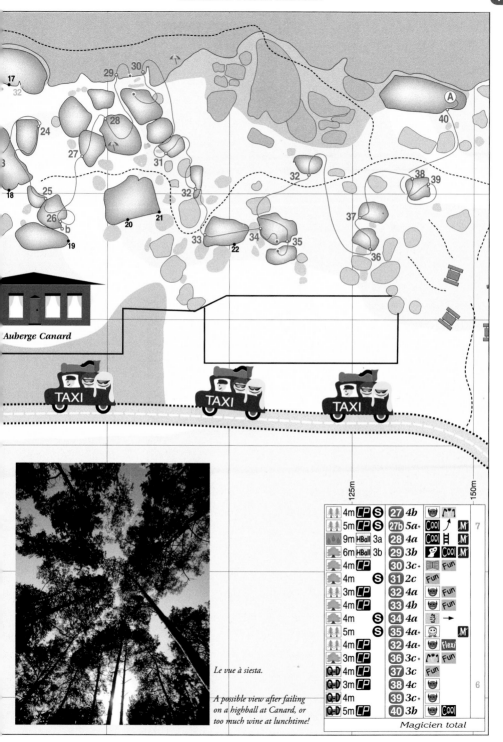

Auberge Canard

Le vue à siesta.

A possible view after failing on a highball at Canard, or too much wine at lunchtime!

🌲	4m	CP	S	**27**	*4b*	😊	🏃1	
🌲	5m	CP	S	**27b**	*5a+*	Cool	↗	M
🌲	9m	HBall	3a	**28**	*4a*	Cool	⊞	M
🌲	6m	HBall	3b	**29**	*3b*	🐸	Cool	M
🌲	4m	CP		**30**	*3c+*	😊	Fun	
🌲	4m		S	**31**	*2c*	Fun		
🌲	3m	CP		**32**	*4a*	😊	Fun	
🌲	4m	CP		**33**	*4b*	😊	Fun	
🌲	4m		S	**34**	*4a*	🐸	→	
🌲	5m		S	**35**	*4a+*	😊		M
🌲	4m	CP		**32**	*4a+*	😊	Flexi	
🌲	3m	CP		**36**	*3c+*	🏃1	Fun	
Q-D	4m	CP		**37**	*3c*	Fun		
Q-D	3m	CP		**38**	*4c*	😊		
Q-D	4m			**39**	*3c+*	😊		
Q-D	5m	CP		**40**	*3b*	😊	Cool	
					Magicien total			

C'est sans aucun doute l'un des meilleurs circuits de la forêt. Il est assez long et peut-être divisé en deux secteurs. Le secteur du matin a des blocs de bonne taille qui bénéficient d'un bon ensoleillement. Heureusement les passages les plus difficiles sont exposés nord. En été si vous passez une journée entière sur ce site, prévoyez un pique-nique que vous

Bleu 8 - 5a+; Sandy Ogilvie

pourrez apprécier en haut de la colline. Le secteur de l'après-midi suit un amas de blocs ombragés par les châtaigniers. C'est un circuit sympa et divertissant. Nous n'avons pas tenu compte des variantes trop difficiles et avons essayé de garder le circuit simple et continu. Pour un grimpeur d'assez bon niveau, il est intéressant d'essayer le défi du magicien avec un maximum de 10 chutes. Pour ce défi, il vous faudra bien comprendre les passages ainsi qu'une bonne endurance pour pouvoir grimper toute la journée. Les 57 passages sont d'un standard assez élevé et nécessitent d'être alerte tout au long du circuit surtout à la fin car ils deviennent plus difficiles surtout lorsque votre force s'amenuise. La plupart des passages difficiles ont des techniques tres variées et ils testeront vos faiblesses plutôt que vos points forts.

Bleu 27 - 4b; Sandy Ogilvie

Bleu 46 ~ 5a; Sandy Ogilvie

This is without doubt, one of the finest of the circuits in the forest. It is a full length outing that will keep you on your toes all day long, and splits very nicely into two half's. The morning sector follows a whole array of good sized boulders that get excellent sunshine, being set on the side of a hill (sandy desert). Fortunately, the hardest problems in the morning face north and can be dispatched in fine fashion without greasing off, 'too often.' If you have all day here in summer with long evenings, you can find time to enjoy a fine picnic on the golden sand at the top of the hill; before the afternoons entertainment which follows a track of scattered boulders, shaded in the lush chestnut 'Châtaignier,' forest. It naturally works well as an all day outing and certainly packs a full punch with 57 problems, with only a couple being naff. It's a fun entertaining circuit too with some traverses that are very possible, they're slightly blind and leave you completely pumped, (stepping off to look at the holds, is not allowed on the magician challenge). Problems (1) and (3) will certainly warm you up in fine style. We have left any desperate variations out, modified (12) to a sensible straight up, and tried to keep the circuit nice and continuous. A really top level climber might get the total clean on-sight, but it's best nail biting enjoyment, will be had by a relatively good climber trying to keep a magic score to a maximum of 10 falls. This challenge is very much about reading the rock and having enough finger and arm stamina to keep going all day. The 57 problems of a sustained high standard necessitate you to be sharp and alert during the entire circuit, especially at the end with so many hard problems coming at you when the light is fading along with your strength. Nerves can play havoc if you only have a few falls left when attempting the desperado problems at the very end of the circuit. You don't have to be a very powerful climber to do well on this one, since many of the hard problems are technical, crimpy slabs. The biggest downfall for most climbers is that the hard problems seem to cover a large range of techniques, so it tests more your weaknesses than your strengths. It's a circuit where you can have a clean sheet up to problem 35 and still blow the magician tick, be on your guard at all times!

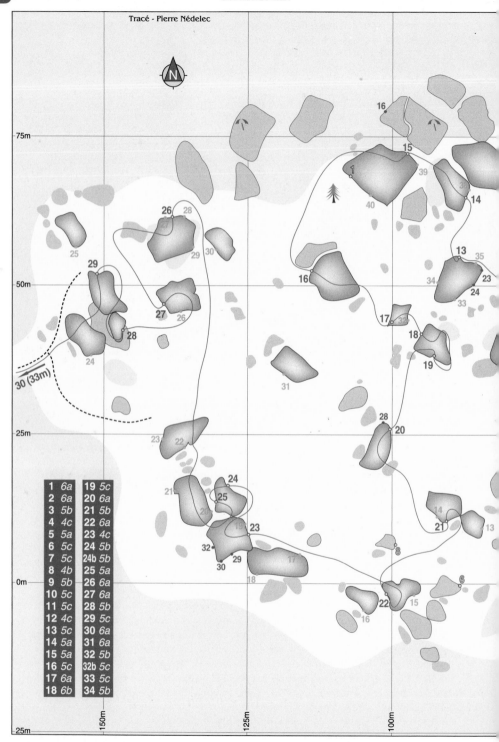

Tracé - Pierre Nédelec

1	*6a*	**19**	*5c*
2	*6a*	**20**	*6a*
3	*5b*	**21**	*5b*
4	*4c*	**22**	*6a*
5	*5a*	**23**	*4c*
6	*5c*	**24**	*5b*
7	*5c*	**24b**	*5b*
8	*4b*	**25**	*5a*
9	*5b*	**26**	*6a*
10	*5c*	**27**	*6a*
11	*5c*	**28**	*5b*
12	*4c*	**29**	*5c*
13	*5c*	**30**	*6a*
14	*5a*	**31**	*6a*
15	*5a*	**32**	*5b*
16	*5c*	**32b**	*5c*
17	*6a*	**33**	*5c*
18	*6b*	**34**	*5b*

30 (33m)

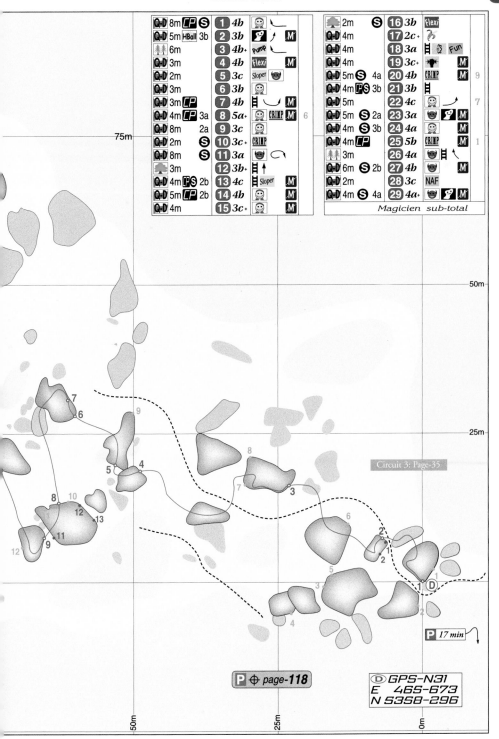

Q-D 8m *CP* S	**1** 4b		
Q-D 5m HBall 3b	**2** 3b		.M'
🌲 6m	**3** 4b+ Pump		
Q-D 3m	**4** 4b+ Flexi		.M'
Q-D 2m	**5** 3c Sloper		
Q-D 3m	**6** 3b		
Q-D 3m *CP*	**7** 4b		.M'
Q-D 4m *CP* 3a	**8** 5a+ CRIMP		.M'
Q-D 8m 2a	**9** 3c		6
Q-D 2m S	**10** 3c+ CRIMP		
Q-D 8m S	**11** 3a		
🌳 3m	**12** 3b+		
Q-D 4m *PS* 2b	**13** 4c Sloper		.M'
Q-D 5m *CP* 2b	**14** 4b		.M'
Q-D 4m	**15** 3c+		.M'

🌳 2m S	**16** 3b Flexi		
Q-D 4m	**17** 2c+		
Q-D 4m	**18** 3a	Fun	
Q-D 4m	**19** 3c+		.M'
Q-D 5m S 4a	**20** 4b CRIMP		.M' 9
Q-D 4m *PS* 3b	**21** 3b		
Q-D 5m	**22** 4c		7
Q-D 5m S 2a	**23** 3a		.M'
Q-D 4m S 3b	**24** 4a		.M'
Q-D 4m *CP*	**25** 5b CRIMP		.M' 1
🌲 3m	**26** 4a		
Q-D 6m S 2b	**27** 4b		
Q-D 2m	**28** 3c NAF		
Q-D 4m S 4a	**29** 4a+		.M'
	Magicien sub-total		

75m

50m

25m

Circuit 3: Page-35

P ⊕ page-**118**

Ⓓ GPS-N31
E 465-673
N 5358-296

P 17 min

50m 25m 0m

16m	30 4a	Pump / Sloper
Q-D 3m S	31 4b	M
5m CP	32 4a+	
4m CP	33 5a	CRIMP ↰ M
3m	34 4a	Sloper
9m	35 3a	NAF →
10m S	36 4a+	Pump
2m	37 4b+	Sloper
Q-D 4m S	38 4a	M
Q-D 3m S	39 3b	
8m S	39b 5a	Flexi M
3m CP	39t 5a+	Sloper M
Q-D 3m	40 2c	Fun
4m	41 4c+	Sloper ↗ M
3m CP	41b 5a	
5m S	42 4b+	Fun M
5m CP	42b 5b	M
6m HBall 4b	43 4c	Sloper M
Q-D 4m S	44 3c	M
3m	45 3c+	CRIMP
Q-D 4m PS 4c	46 5a	M
Q-D 11m CP	47 4a	Pump Fun
	48 3a	
4m	49 3c	
4m PS 3c	50 4b	
4m CP S	51 3b	Sloper
4m S 3c	52 3c	
6m HBall 2c	53 3b	Fun M

Magicien total

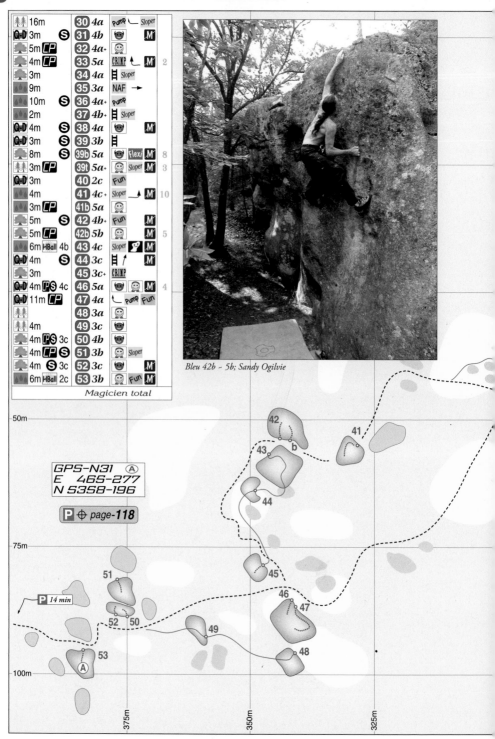

Bleu 42b – 5b; Sandy Ogilvie

GPS-N31 Ⓐ
E 46S-277
N S3S8-196

P ⊕ page-118

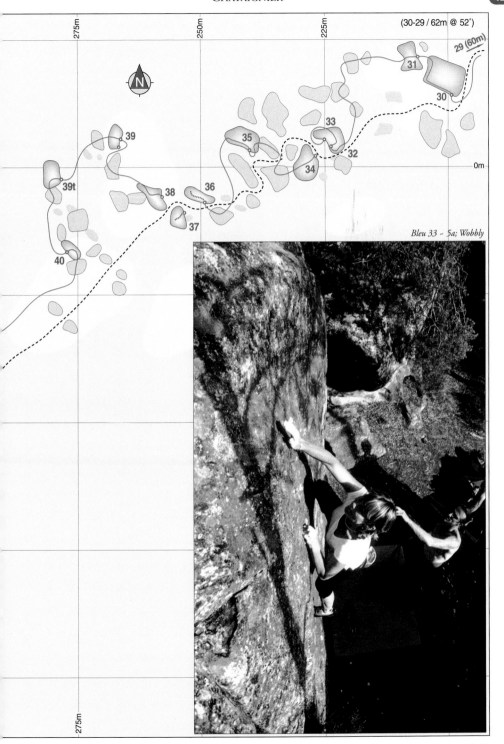

(30-29 / 62m @ 52˚)

29 (60m)

31

30

39

39t

38

36

35

33

32

34

37

40

0m

275m

250m

225m

275m

Bleu 33 ~ 5a; Wobbly

Ce n'est pas un circuit pour ceux qui sont peu sérieux ou qui ont peu d'aptitude mais il est cependant idéal pour les grimpeurs d'un bon niveau avec de bonnes compétences. Si vous avez l'habitude de grimper sur de petits blocs, ce circuit sera totalement effrayant et lorsque vous le finirez, il vous laissera tout tremblant près de la piscine de Buthiers. C'est un superbe circuit qui garde les passages les plus hauts pour la fin lorsque vos bras sont bien fatigués. Les passages difficiles paraissent très difficiles cependant les aires de réception sont pour la plupart bonnes ce qui permet d'abandonner un passage et de sauter en toute sécurité. Les sorties de la majorité des blocs demandent des nerfs solides et non pas une technique infaillible. Nous avons ajouté la dalle technique

Bleu 12 ~ 4c; Daniel Bethelot

du noir (2) car elle est sympa et très plaisante à 5a+ et bien trop facile pour un noir. Le (23) est le premier passage très haut. Nous vous conseillons un peu de repos après le (27) pour pouvoir finir le circuit. Pour la fin du circuit un crash pad et une bonne parade sont conseillés. Cependant pour une bonne dose d'adrénaline rien de telle que de grimper le circuit tout seul, en hiver, à vu, lorsque la nuit tombe et que les blocs sont humides. Alors sans aucun doute vous tremblerez près de la piscine (Shaking by the pool).

Bleu 7 ~ 5b; Florence Pistré

Bleu 8- 5a; Adeline Rix

This is not a circuit for the light hearted or incapable. It is ideal for good climbers that are partial adrenaline junkies and with a pretty good level of competence. For the boulderer only used to small problems, it is a circuit that really gets you gripped and frightened, leaving you at the end of the circuit near the swimming pool – shaking with fear. It's a truly great Fontainebleau circuit, because it saves all the best highballs for the end, and at a time when you are exhausted so your arms are most likely to give up, aaaggghh - splat! The last four problems are testing and very hard, with moves that are going to undo those previously confident and well cranking biceps. I wouldn't describe it as dangerous though, because you can see quite clearly the challenge in front of you; the hard climbs - look hard! You also find that the landings from halfway up the highballs are mostly very good and allow you to back off in comfort and relative safety. It's the finishes of many climbs that demand nerve and practical competence, but on the other hand, not super human climbing techniques. The technical nasties are discovered in the first part of the circuit that intermingles with the orange and black problems. We have stolen the technical slab of black (2), because it is lovely and pleasant at 5a+, and far too easy for the black circuit. (15) is the first problem which thumps in a hard move to finish and checks out your positive approach. (23) is the first highball and certainly lives up to its highball status, exiting becomes – exciting. A rest after problem (27) is a wise move, to refuel before looking at the finishing sector. Problems (28-35) then work as a warm up for the finishing cascade of highballs. Double mats, with several spotters are a very good precaution here for the finishing blocks. For the ultimate adrenaline attack, you climb the circuit on your own in winter- onsight – just when its getting dark ,and when it's quite damp and with lovely green footholds. Then for sure, you'll be shaking by the pool.

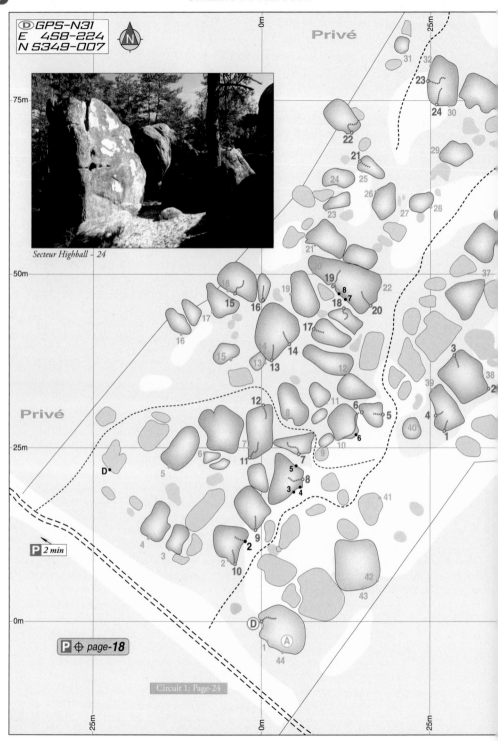

GPS-N31
E 458-224
N 5349-007

75m

Secteur Highball - 24

Privé

50m

Privé

25m

D

P 2 min

0m

P ⊕ page-18

Circuit 1: Page-24

25m

0m

25m

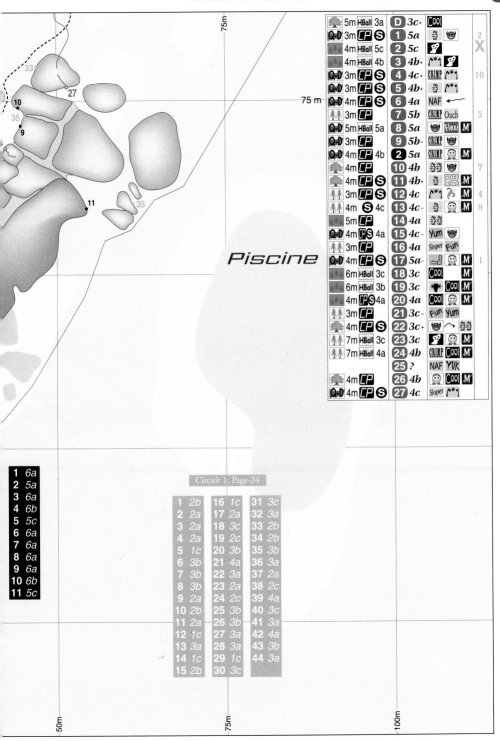

Piscine

		#			
5m HBall 3a		D	3c+	COOL	
Q-D 3m CP S		1	5a		2 X
4m HBall 5c		2	5c		
4m HBall 4b		3	4b+		
Q-D 3m CP S		4	4c	CRIMP	10
Q-D 3m CP S		5	4b+		
Q-D 4m CP S		6	4a	NAF ←	
3m CP		7	5b	CRIMP Ouch	5
Q-D 5m HBall 5a		8	5a	Flexi M	
Q-D 3m CP		9	5b-	CRIMP	
4m CP 4b		2	5a	CRIMP M	
4m CP		10	4b		7
4m CP S		11	4b+	M	
3m CP S		12	4c	M	4
4m S 4c		13	4c-	M	9
5m CP		14	4a		
Q-D 4m CP S		15	4c-	Yum	
3m CP		16	4a	Sloper Fun	
Q-D 4m CP S		17	5a-	M	1
6m HBall 3c		18	3c	COOL M	
6m HBall 3b		19	3c	COOL M	
4m CP S 4a		20	4a	COOL M	
3m CP		21	3c-	Fun Yum	
4m CP S		22	3c+		
7m HBall 3c		23	3c	M	
7m HBall 4a		24	4b	CRIMP COOL M	
		25	?	NAF YUK	
4m CP		26	4b	COOL M	
Q-D 4m CP S		27	4c	Sloper	

1	6a
2	5a
3	6a
4	6b
5	5c
6	6a
7	6a
8	6a
9	6a
10	6b
11	5c

Circuit 1: Page-24

1	2b	16	1c	31	3c
2	2a	17	2a	32	3a
3	2a	18	3c	33	2b
4	2a	19	2c	34	2b
5	1c	20	3b	35	3b
6	3b	21	4a	36	3a
7	3b	22	3a	37	2a
8	3b	23	2a	38	2c
9	2a	24	2c	39	4a
10	2b	25	3b	40	3c
11	2a	26	3b	41	3a
12	1c	27	3a	42	4a
13	3a	28	3a	43	3b
14	1c	29	1c	44	3a
15	2b	30	3c		

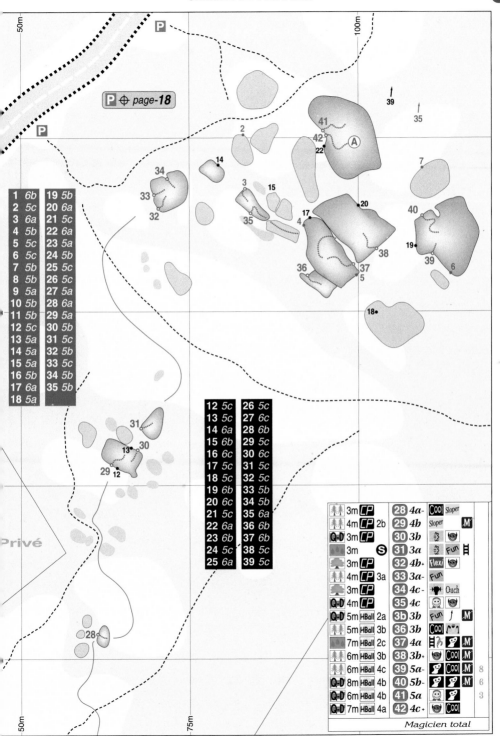

1	6b
2	5c
3	6a
4	5b
5	5c
6	5c
7	5b
8	5b
9	5a
10	5b
11	5b
12	5c
13	5a
14	5a
15	5a
16	5b
17	6a
18	5a

19	5b
20	6a
21	5c
22	5b
23	5a
24	5b
25	5c
26	5c
27	5a
28	6a
29	5a
30	5b
31	5c
32	5b
33	5c
34	5b
35	5b

12	5c
13	5c
14	6a
15	6b
16	6c
17	5c
18	5c
19	6b
20	6c
21	5c
22	6a
23	6b
24	5c
25	6a

26	5c
27	6c
28	6b
29	5c
30	6c
31	5c
32	5c
33	5b
34	5b
35	6a
36	6b
37	6b
38	5c
39	5c

P ⊕ page-18

Privé

3m CP		28	4a-	COOl Sloper	
4m CP 2b		29	4b	Sloper .M.	
Q-D 3m CP		30	3b		
3m S		31	3a	Fun	
3m CP		32	4b+	Flexi	
4m CP 3a		33	3a-	Fun	
3m CP		34	4c-	Ouch	
Q-D 4m CP		35	4c		
Q-D 5m HBall 2a		3b	3b	Fun	.M.
5m HBall 3b		36	3b	COOl	.M.
7m HBall 2c		37	4a	.M.	
6m HBall 3b		38	3b+	COOl .M.	
6m HBall 4c		39	5a-	COOl .M.	8
Q-D 8m HBall 4b		40	5b-	.M.	6
Q-D 6m HBall 4b		41	5a		3
Q-D 7m HBall 4a		42	4c+	COOl	
				Magicien total	

Rouge 10 ~ 3c; Marc Fourcade

FRANCHARD CRÊTE SUD - (D+/Rouge)

Franchard a sans aucun doute le paysage le plus élégant et l'un des cadres les plus sympas de la forêt. Pour visiter la crête sud de Franchard il faut suivre le magnifique sentier qui se nomme Route Amédée. Vous trouverez le début du circuit grâce aux deux blocs jumeaux à droite du sentier. Le circuit mérite bien sa couleur rouge, il est sympa, mais ne doit pas être sous-estimé. Les passages les plus hauts ne cèdent pas si facilement et il faut donc toujours garder la tête froide. Il y a seulement 26 voies sur ce circuit cependant peu de grimpeurs le quittent en demandant plus de divertissement. Ils repartent en général claqué, épuise et parfois même tremblant. Pour les grimpeurs de haut niveau, les passages seraient probablement faciles, cependant ce circuit est destiné à ceux qui souhaitent passer des circuits bleu

Rouge 1 - Very nasty, gnarly and frightening - Yum!

aux circuits rouge et à tous ceux qui souhaitent un défi physique et mental. Ce n'est pas un circuit très populaire et il y a donc peu de trace de magnésie et seulement un peu de lichen sur certains blocs. Cependant il testera votre habileté à vu. Bien que les rochers paraissent verts les prises essentielles sont propres. Il y a une large sélection de dalles d'où le nom crimpomania. Le (19) détruira vos doigts et sera une expérience mémorable. Le rétablissement sur le (16) est diabolique. Le (23) est la pièce de résistance, suspendu par une main à l'envers, à 5 mètres de haut, vous devez mettre votre pied au-dessus de votre tête pour le coincer dans une fissure. C'est extravagant, c'est délirant, c'est marrant, c'est Franchard Crête Sud – un conseil, laissez votre cerveau à la maison.

Rouge 7 - 5b; Patrice Moiselet

Rouge 6 – 4a; Isabelle Hamon

Franchard has without doubt, the most elegant scenery and finest setting of all the Fontainebleau outcrops, highlighted by the subtlety of the glade that you pass through from the parking on the way to Cuisinière. When you visit the south ridge (Crête Sud) of Franchard, you luckily take the beautiful Route Amédée, which in golden morning sunshine provides serenity on a different scale. Finding the start of this circuit along this track would be a real headache if it weren't for the perfectly positioned twin boulders to the right of the main track. This circuit is definitely a red grade for sure; a friendly one, but not one to be underestimated or taken lightly. The high problems don't give in that easily, and you have to keep a cool head at all times. This isn't the circuit to panic on, unless you want your spotters to have a heart attack. There are only 26 problems, a mere sniff of a circuit you might think. But rarely do you see climbers leaving the finish of the circuit needing any more entertainment; the words shattered, exhausted, and perhaps quivering, are more usual descriptive niceties that accompany the parting boulderer who originally thought this to be a lightweight challenge. For the top class boulderer, the problems would be a breeze, however, this is a circuit for those climbers making the transition from blue circuits to red, and for those wanting both a physical and mental challenge. It is the perfect arena for our magician challenge since the circuit is not on the touriod-climber trail, and is therefore rarely chalked up. It has the odd bit of lichen to dissuade the frail, and really does test you on-sight ability both low down and high up! It does give nice clues however, since mostly only good climbers usually visit this spot? The rock may be green, but the vital holds will be perfectly clean, such is the way with higher level climbing – no scrabbling around here. There is a wonderful selection of slabs on this circuit – hence our name crimpomania; (6) will test both your skill and nerve, (19) will excruciate your tips and will be sure to remain a very, memorable, experience! The mantel at (16) is about as mean and diabolical as they come. The Piéce de Resistance must surely be taken by (23), the sort of problem that the health and safety brigade would not allow to be built, or even climbed. How often do you hang only by one hand, upside down & 5 metres up, and then put your foot above your head to jam it in a crack. It's outrageous, it's wild, it's fun, it's Franchard Crête Sud – leave the brain at home.

Rouge 14 - 5c-; Isabelle Hamon

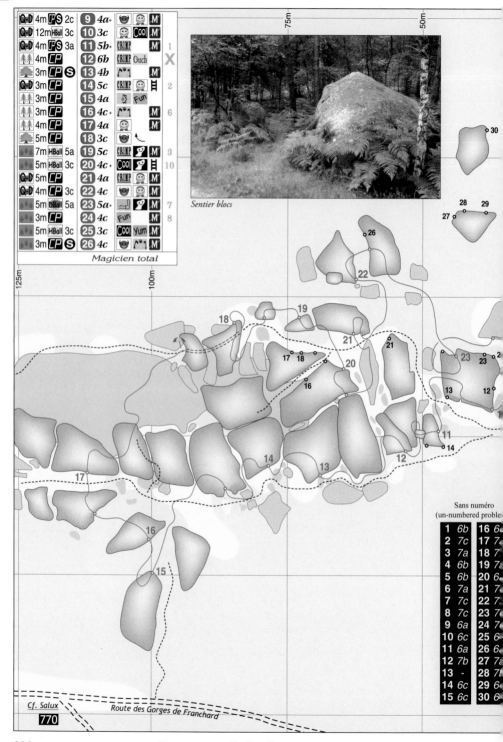

Sentier blocs

Q-D 4m FS 2c	9 4a+			M
Q-D 12m HBall 3c	10 3c		Cool	M
Q-D 4m FS 3a	11 5b+	CRIMP		1
4m CP	12 6b	CRIMP	Ouch	X
3m CP S	13 4b	^*1		
Q-D 3m CP	14 5c	CRIMP		2
3m CP	15 4a		Fun	
3m CP	16 4c+	^*1		6
4m CP	17 4a			M
5m CP	18 3c			
7m HBall 5a	19 5c	CRIMP		3
5m HBall 3c	20 4c+	Cool		10
Q-D 5m CP	21 4a	CRIMP		M
Q-D 4m CP 3c	22 4c			
5m DBall 5a	23 5a+			7
3m CP	24 4c	Fun		8
5m HBall 3c	25 3c	Cool	Yum	M
3m CP S	26 4c		^*1	M

Magicien total

Sans numéro (un-numbered proble

1 6b	16 6
2 7c	17 7
3 7a	18 7
4 6b	19 7
5 6b	20 6
6 7a	21 7
7 7c	22 7
8 7c	23 7
9 6a	24 7
10 6c	25 6
11 6a	26 6
12 7b	27 7
13 -	28 7
14 6c	29 6
15 6c	30 6

Cf. Salux 770 Route des Gorges de Franchard

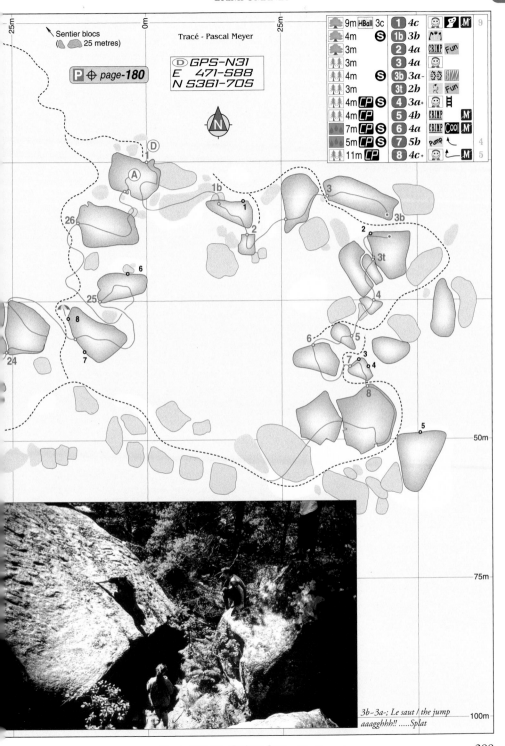

Sentier blocs
(◖◗ 25 metres)

Tracé - Pascal Meyer

P ⊕ page-**180**

Ⓓ **GPS–N31**
E **471-588**
N **5361-705**

N

🌲 9m	HBall	3c	**1**	4c	😊	💨	M'	9
🌲 4m	Ⓢ		**1b**	3b	🏃			
🌲 3m			**2**	4a			CRIMP Fun	
🌲 3m			**3**	4a				
🌲 4m	Ⓢ		**3b**	3a-	🤸	BW		
🌲 3m			**3t**	2b	🤸	Fun		
🌲 4m	CP	Ⓢ	**4**	3a+	😊	▤		
🌲 4m	CP		**5**	4b	CRIMP		M'	
🪨 7m	CP	Ⓢ	**6**	4a	CRIMP COOl	M'		4
🪨 5m	CP	Ⓢ	**7**	5b	Pump ↘			5
🌲 11m	CP		**8**	4c+	😊	↘	M'	

D

A

1b

26

1

2

3

3b

6

2

3t

25

4

8

24

7

6

5

7

3

4

8

50m

5

75m

*3b-3a-; Le saut / the jump
aaagghhh!! .....Splat*

100m

Un nom sympa pour un excellent circuit offrant une grande diversité de passages sur de jolis blocs. Il se divise en deux parties. La première est un petit regroupement de blocs bien ombragé à seulement 200m du Diplodocus. La deuxième partie suit des blocs éparpillés à travers la lande et les arbres, rejoignant presque la fin du circuit bleu à Rocher Fin. La première partie du circuit a récemment été revue et offre maintenant 3 passages pour permettre de bien vous échauffer avant le (4) et ses grattons. Même si vous êtes fatigués, nous vous conseillons de poursuivre sur la deuxième partie du circuit, car les voies sont excellentes en particulier les 7 dernières. Le niveau du circuit est TD- ce qui est parfait car les passages ne sont pas trop difficiles. C'est un circuit mentalement éprouvant et il vous faut un bon niveau de compétences sur certaines voies assez hautes. Vous serez parés avec un bon crash pad et une parade. La plupart des aires de réception sont bonnes, mais attention il y a de nombreuses difficultés en haut des blocs qui testeront vos nerfs et vos bras. Assurez-vous que la personne qui vous pare soit bien attentive. Le circuit est assez technique. Le rétablissement du (8) est assez facile à vu si toutefois vous pouvez le faire sur une largeur d'un centimètre. Le dernier groupe de blocs permet de finir le circuit en beauté. Il est cependant dommage que les prises du (39) soient difficiles à atteindre et que pour la majorité des grimpeurs, il soit nécessaire de faire un jeté pour débuter. Le dernier passage ne laisse aucun répit et vaut la peine d'être tenté lorsque vous êtes très fatigués. Il y a un circuit jaune assez populaire qui se mélange au bleu mais malgré cela c'est un site qui reste très calme.

Bleu 8 - 5a+; Sandy Ogilvie

A fun name for an excellent circuit, one that offers a whole mixture of different problems on sweet boulders, and with nice variations in palatability. It happily breaks into two parts; the first being a small concentration of boulders only 200m from Diplodocus, and mostly shaded by trees. The second part follows scattered boulders across open moorland and trees, almost reaching the end boulders of the blue circuit at Rocher Fin. After the busy concentration of the first half you may be in two minds about the small trek for the rest of the problems; make the effort since they are very good and the whole circuit climaxes with 7 thumping problems to finish. The first part of the circuit was recently redesigned and now works very well, with 3 good problems to warm you up nicely - before the crunching crimper at (4). The circuit is now given a current rating of TD- which is perfectly descriptive, since there aren't any really hard problems – except (23), which can be taken just as nicely on the right to the top of the boulder at a casual 5a. It is a mentally demanding circuit as a whole, and you do need a good level of competence on some of the high problems. With a spotter and crash pad you are well prepared. Many of the landings are quite good but be warned, there is sustained difficulty 'high up,' so be prepared to test your nerves in places alongside your forearms – making sure your spotter is very attentive. A few of the problems can certainly be dispatched with big power, but mostly this circuit is about technicality. The mantelshelf on (8) is so obvious that it is 'ever so easy' to on-sight – well, so long as you can mantle on a 1cm ledge of course. When you know how to do the roof at (11) you will drift up it, but doing it on-sight will most probably pump you solid. Most problems are easy to view from adjacent boulders, so you should do well here attempting the magician status. The last group of boulders really finishes the circuit well, it's just a pity that (39) is a bit reachy and needs a dyno start for most. The last problem is full on, and best when you are completely exhausted, slapping desperately - for anything. The problems alone will present a formidable challenge to most climbers – grades here don't come easily. There's a reasonably popular yellow circuit that mixes in with the blue at the start, but even with that said, it's generally a quiet place to come.

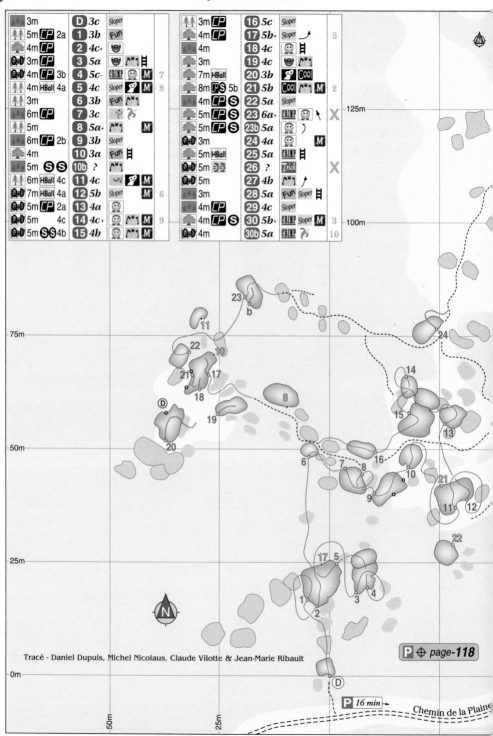

Tracé - Daniel Dupuis, Michel Nicolaus, Claude Vilotte & Jean-Marie Ribault

P ⊕ page-118

P 16 min → Chemin de la Plaine

Bleu 21 - 5b; Sandy Ogilvie

1 - 24
2a-3b

Diplodocus - 200m

Bleu 35 ~ 3c+; Wobbly   *Secteur 39 - 40*

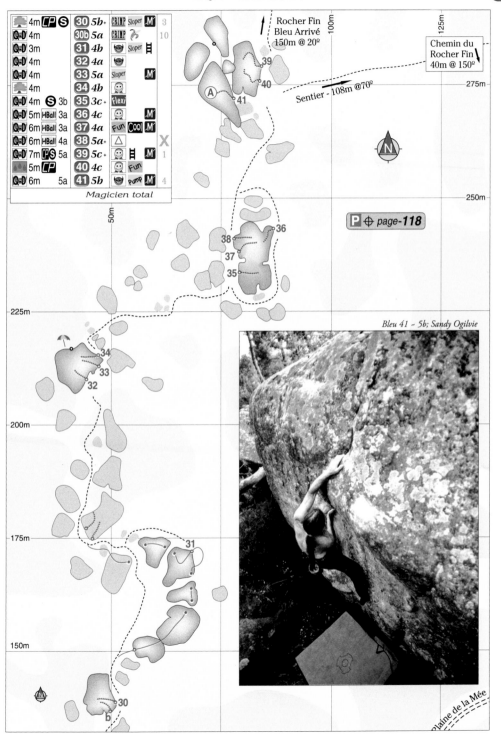

🍀 4m **CP** S	**30** 5b+	CRIMP Sloper	M'	3
Q-D 4m	**30b** 5a	CRIMP ?		10
Q-D 3m	**31** 4b	Sloper	II	
Q-D 4m	**32** 4a			
Q-D 4m	**33** 5a	Sloper	M'	
🍀 4m	**34** 4b			
Q-D 4m S 3b	**35** 3c+	Flexi		
Q-D 5m HBall 3a	**36** 4c		M'	
Q-D 6m HBall 3a	**37** 4a	Fun Cool	M'	
Q-D 6m HBall 4a	**38** 5a+	△		X
Q-D 7m PS 5a	**39** 5c+	II	M'	1
5m **CP**	**40** 4c	Fun		
Q-D 6m 5a	**41** 5b	Pump	M'	4
Magicien total				

Rocher Fin
Bleu Arrivé
150m @ 20°

Chemin du
Rocher Fin
40m @ 150°

Sentier - 108m @70°

N

P ⊕ *page-118*

39
40
A 41

38 36
37
35

34
33
32

31

30
b

Bleu 41 - 5b; Sandy Ogilvie

Plaine de la Mée

5 - 6a; Olivia Hsu

Il y a peu de différence entre un circuit rouge facile et un bleu difficile. Malgré tout ce circuit attire peu de grimpeurs et c'est un site qui reste donc très tranquille. Cuisinière est réputée pour la difficulté de

ses passages, Karma étant par exemple le 8a le plus connu de Fontainebleau, situé seulement à 2 mètres du dernier passage du circuit rouge. Les grimpeurs de haut niveau visitent ce site durant les mois les plus froids c'est pourquoi en été c'est un lieu très tranquille. Vous serez surpris par les conditions, en effet le circuit est situé sur une colline couverte de pins. Bien que les blocs paraissent verts, les arbres qui offrent une excellente couverture, les garde secs même lorsqu'il bruine légèrement. Après une bonne averse, nous vous conseillons de grimper sur le haut

de la colline car les blocs y sèchent plus rapidement. C'est l'un des meilleurs circuits de Fontainebleau. Il y a environ 30 passages avec des techniques très variées. Tel le circuit rouge d'Isatis, il y a des voies sympas pour s'echauffer mais attention au (5) qui demande beaucoup de puissance. Si vous n'avez pas des mains très musclées nous vous conseillons d'éviter le (14) et de faire le (15b) car il est plus divertissant. La faille du (21) est un véritable test qui nécessite plus d'un essai surtout si vous n'êtes pas très grand. Ce circuit est comme une drogue, une fois terminé vous n'aurez qu'une envie c'est d'y revenir sans cesse.

Franchard Cuisinière

FRANCHARD - CUISINIÈRE - (TD-/Rouge)

11 - 5c; Arnaud Janinn

21 – 5c; James Bacon

There isn't a lot of difference between an easy red circuit and a hard blue, in fact there isn't any! However, because this circuit is red, it attracts less climbers to the area and you are rewarded with a more tranquil day out. Cuisinère is an area famous for hard problems, Karma – being the most famous 8a in Font, and only 2 metres from the final problem on the red circuit. Because most top level climbers only operate here in the frosty months, you can often have the place to yourself in summer when the red circuit is easily do-able. You will be constantly surprised at the conditions here. It is situated on a hill which is covered in a very open pine forest. The whole area looks green and slimy in anything other than sunshine. The tree canopy however does provide some excellent sun shade, and surprisingly, keeps the rocks pretty dry in even a slight drizzle. None of the holds on the problems are green however, and it does dry out quite quickly. If there has been a real downpour, try the top of the hill where the boulders dry out a lot quicker. This is one of the greatest circuits in Font, and is excruciating in demanding complete, all round capability. There are only 30 problems on it, but you are very likely to find your nemesis here and fail on a problem if you don't have the technique. Just like the red circuit at Isatis, there are some happy and fun soft touches to warm you up, but the power needed for (5) is raw and unforgiving. Try it as a 'ground up' for the on-sight, saving the traverse as a harder alternative when you know how to finish it. There are several problems where leaving the ground dynamically is handy, if not essential. At (11) you will need to crimp like a demon – and stay right of the number to experience the full red difficulty; at least you are rewarded by (12), a magical problem. Some local Font climbers have developed titanium fingers, so if you are climbing wall bred, give (14) a miss and opt for our 15b, which is far more fun and entertaining. Just looking at the wide crack at (21) will be disheartening if you are going for the magician challenge, a test piece that will eat up attempts – and especially if you are not very tall. The circuit finishes nicely with some pleasant smaller problems. It's a very addictive circuit, when you've completed it, you'll never stop coming back – for that quick easy tick!

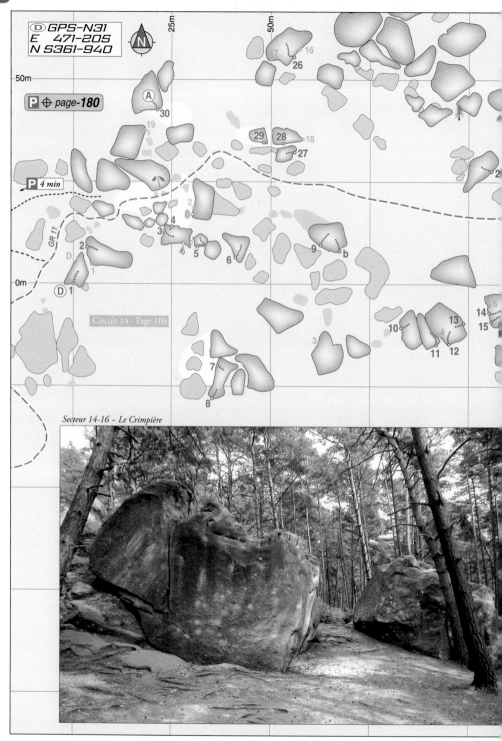

D GPS-N31
E 471-205
N 5361-940

P ⊕ page-**180**

50m

P 4 min

Circuit 14 - Page 108

Secteur 14-16 - Le Crimpière

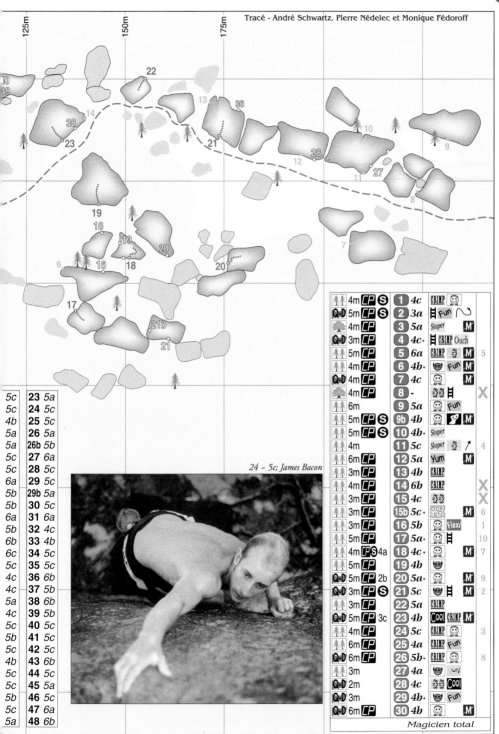

Tracé - André Schwartz, Pierre Nédelec et Monique Fédoroff

125m 150m 175m

24 - 5c; James Bacon

5c	23 5a
5c	24 5c
4b	25 5c
5a	26 5a
5a	26b 5b
5c	27 6a
5c	28 5c
6a	29 5c
5b	29b 5a
5b	30 5c
6a	31 6a
5b	32 4c
6b	33 4b
6c	34 5c
5c	35 5c
4c	36 6b
4c	37 5b
5a	38 6b
4c	39 5b
5c	40 5c
5c	41 5c
5c	42 5c
4b	43 6b
5c	44 5c
5c	45 5a
5b	46 5c
5c	47 6a
5a	48 6b

4m	1	4c	CRIMP
Q-D 5m	2	3a	Fun
4m	3	5a	Sloper
Q-D 3m	4	4c+	CRIMP Ouch
5m	5	6a	CRIMP · 5
4m	6	4b+	Fun
Q-D 4m	7	4c	
4m	8	-	
6m	9	5a	Fun
5m	9b	4b	
5m	10	4b+	Sloper
4m	11	5c	Sloper · 4
6m	12	5a	Yum
3m	13	4b	CRIMP
4m	14	6b	CRIMP
3m	15	4c	
3m	15b	5c+	
3m	16	5b	Flexi · 6
5m	17	5a+	· 1 · 10
4m 4a	18	4c+	· 7
5m	19	4b	
Q-D 5m 2b	20	5a+	· 9
Q-D 3m	21	5c	· 2
3m	22	5a	CRIMP
Q-D 5m 3c	23	4b	COOl CRIMP
4m	24	5c	CRIMP · 3
6m	25	4a	CRIMP Fun
Q-D 6m	26	5b+	CRIMP
3m	27	4a	· 8
Q-D 2m	28	4c	COOl
Q-D 3m	29	4b+	Fun
Q-D 6m	30	4b	

Magicien total

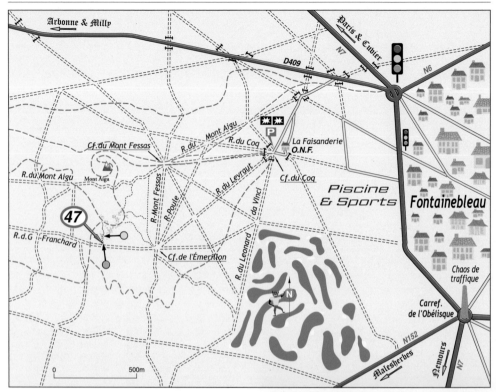

Circuit	Cot.	Ang.	Prob-Var	Bois	Expo	Info	
MONT AIGU - GORGES DU HOUX (p 316)							
⬤	PD	2a-3b		35		CP	Fun
⬤	AD+	2c-4b		48&(19)		CP	Fun
⬤	TD-	3c-6b		56		SP	😊
♦	ABO	6a-8a		69		Zzz	😊

La Grotte Serment - sentier Denecourt circuit Bleu

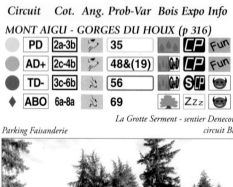

Parking Faisanderie

Bleu 7 - 4b+; Jingo

Bleu 46 ~ 5b; Jingo　　　　　　　　　　　　　　　　　　　Bleu 47 ~ 5c+; Jingo

Le Mont Aigu n'a rien à voir avec l'Aiguille du Midi et n'a pas non plus la taille d'un volcan, mais c'est une colline plutôt grande à seulement quelques kilomètres de Fontainebleau et avec de superbes vues. L'accès au circuit n'est pas très rapide et nécessite environ 14 minutes de marche le long d'un sentier, mais en final vous êtes récompensé par un site très propre et très calme qui bénéficie de blocs d'excellente qualité comme ceux que l'on trouve à Isatis et Cuisinière. Le cadre ressemble un peu à celui de Hautes Plaines avec des chênes et des hêtres en bas de la colline et des pins en haut. Ceci explique que les blocs sèchent de manière très différente sur ce circuit et qu'il fasse éviter quelques passages sur la partie la plus basse lorsque le temps est humide. Bien que le haut du circuit sèche plus rapidement la majorité des passages sont exposés Est et sont à l'ombre l'après-midi. Nous avons appelé ce circuit le volcan puisqu'il bouillonne tranquillement avec quelques petites éruptions à 5a avant de terminer en une cascade d'éruption de passages de niveau 5. C'est un magnifique circuit qui vous fera travailler dès le premier passage. Il est possible que vous utilisiez vos 10 chutes pour le défi du magicien avant même d'avoir atteint le (12), ce dernier étant un rétablissement horrible. Après le (42) le circuit est un crescendo de passages fantastiques. Sur le haut du plateau il y a d'autres blocs et les restes d'un circuit bleu cependant vous serez certainement trop fatigués après avoir fais les 56 voies du circuit pour les essayer. C'est toutefois une bonne manière de retourner au parking.

Mont Aigu is hardly the Aiguille du Midi, nor is it a volcano as a map would suggest, but it is a sizeable hill only a few kilometres away to the west from the centre of Fontainebleau, and has superb views. Being so close to the town, you could imagine it suffering from litter and general abuse. Fortunately there is no quick walk in, the thirteen minute hike along the straight track rewards you with a litter free area, deep in the wilderness and calm. Mont Aigu marks the eastern most point of the Franchard sandstone ridge, and benefits from the superb quality rock that you also find at Isatis and Cuisinière. It's ambience is also similar to Hautes Plaines, where the rocks are set in thick deciduous Oak and beech trees at the bottom, then in pine trees at the top with a airy open feel. This geography does make the circuit unbalanced in its ability to dry out after rain, so be prepared to skip a few problems if the lower part is damp. Even though the top half of the circuit will dry quicker, most of the hard problems face east and get afternoon shade. We call this circuit the Volcano, since it bubbles away with some occasional tiny 5a minor eruptions, before you rise up to the final high area and get a cascading eruption of grade 5 problems. It's a fabulous circuit that keeps you on your toes from the very first problem. With only ten falls in your magician bag, you could use them all up before you even reach problem (12). This is the mantelshelf from hell that will confound and spit off those not supple or perfected in the art of gaining friction on a damp and often greasy top slab. The circuit is full of 4c problems that if read incorrectly, don't give you a second chance before you slither off. It's also a crimpers delight, so long as you know which holds to use. The circuit after (42) is a crescendo of fabulous problems, we only just kept (47) in the magic list since a good dyno solves the problem and doesn't make it too hard. If you are close on the magic tick, be careful with the last problem, when you know how, it isn't very hard. On the top plateau there are many more boulders and the remnants of another blue circuit, but you will most probably be a touch tired after 56 problems, it makes a nice circular way back to the car though.

Bleu 12 - 5a+; Jingo

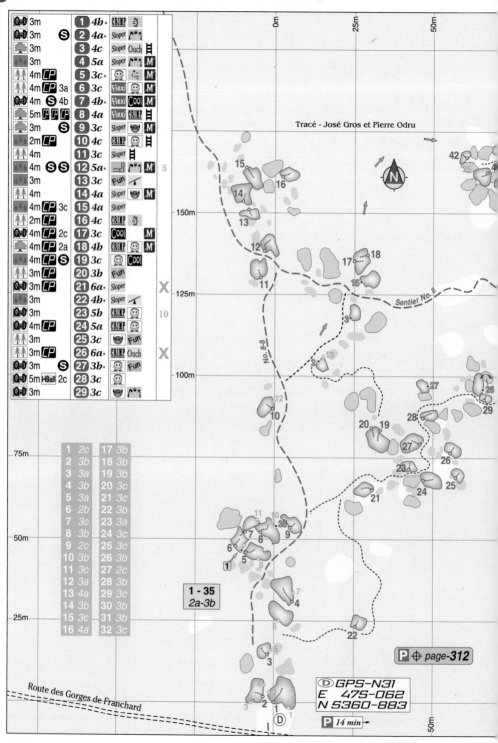

Tracé - José Gros et Pierre Odru

de vue
Aigu
metres

P 12 min

150m   175m

52
51
50
49
48
47
45
44
46

La Grotte du
Serment

53
55
54
56
48

36
38
39
37
35
34
33
33
32
30
31
25

bleu 53 ~ 5b+; Jingo

32	3c	
33	4b	
34	4a	
35	4b	
36	3b	
37	3c	
38	3b	
39	3c	
40	3b	
41	3a	
42	3c	
43	4a	
44	4a	
45	3c	
46	4b	
47	3c	
48	3c	

Approach	No.	Grade	Symbols
4m	30	4c	M
4m	31	4b	Ouch
Q-D 4m CP	32	4b+	Fun M
4m CP	33	4a	
Q-D 3m CP	34	5a	
4m CP	35	5b	CRIMP COOL M
Q-D 4m S	36	4a	Sloper Fun
3m S	37	5b	Sloper
Q-D 3m CP	38	4c+	
Q-D 5m CP 2a	39	4c	
4m	40	6b	Sloper
Q-D 4m CP	41	4b	COOL
Q-D 3m CP	42	5a	CRIMP Flexi
4m CP	43	5c	CRIMP COOL M
Q-D 4m CP CP	44	5b-	Sloper
Q-D 4m CP S	45	4c+	Sloper
Q-D 4m S 5b	46	5b	Sloper M
Q-D 4m CP	47	5c+	M
4m	48	3b	Fun
Q-D 4m CP	49	4c+	
Q-D 3m S 5a	50	5a	M
Q-D 3m S 5b	51	5b	Sloper M
Q-D	52	NAF	
Q-D 4m CP	53	5b+	M
Q-D 4m	54	4b	
6m HBall 2a	55	4c+	M
9m CP S	56	5a	Fun M

Magicien total

9 2
7
X
4 8
1
6
3

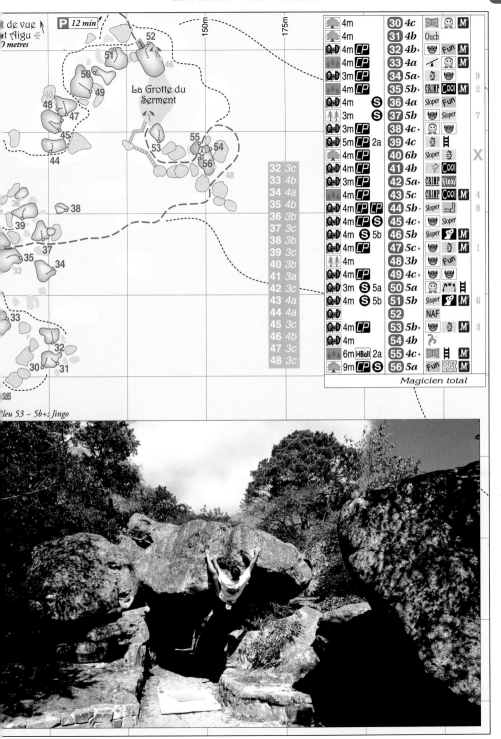

Evitez d'aller à Jean des Vignes depuis le parking de St Jerome et par la colline de Rocher des Souris. La vue que vous aurez sur Cul de Chien depuis le haut de la colline est cependant la meilleure de la forêt. La brusque marche vous préparera psychologiquement pour le circuit "Le Pressoir". Les blocs sont situés en bas de la colline et bénéficient du soleil matinal ce qui est agréable en hiver. En été par contre les bloc restent chauds malgré l'ombre des pins. Il y a peu de blocs sur ce site mais ils offrent des passages assez bas tous regroupés sur un seul circuit. Il faut de nombreux efforts pour avoir des résultats notables sur ce circuit c'est la raison pour laquelle nous l'avons appelé le pressoir.

Il y a une bonne sélection de jolies voies dans des niveaux de difficulté assez bas. Nous recommandons une parade pour les passages les plus difficiles car les sorties vous mettront souvent en situation difficile. Pour ceux qui grimpent en salle et qui souhaitent s'améliorer, c'est l'endroit idéal pour essayer les sorties difficiles, ce qui vous permettra par la suite de finir vos 7a aisément. Il m'a été assez difficile de donner des cotations sur ce circuit et il m'a semblé juste par exemple de donner 6a à un passage qui n'a qu'un seul mouvement toutefois difficile. Le (34) est soit facile ou difficile et ne peut donc recevoir de cotation. C'est le site idéal pour un jour d'hiver car vous n'aurez pas froid surtout si vous avez l'ami de Jean dans votre poche, un flacon de "Marc de Bourgogne."

Bleu 32 - 5a; Carsten Joiko

Bleu 34 ~ 6a+; Carsten Joiko

You might walk to Jean-des-Vignes, directly from the parking at Croix St. Jerome and over the hill of Rocher des Souris, but it is the sort of mistake you only make once. Your view however from the top of the hill, is the finest that you get of the Cul de Chien area in relation to the rest of the forest. The fir trees hide the steepness and height of this quite impressive hill, which leaves you breathless but completely warmed up. The bluntness of the walk will prepare you well for the psychological attack needed to succeed, whilst being mangled by 'Le Pressoir' circuit. The boulders are set at the bottom of the hill and get lovely morning sunshine to warm them up comfortably in winter. In summer however, it can be infuriating in the afternoon since the rocks although shaded by pine trees, stay warm. You will need to start adding numbers to the grades on the slippery-greasy top outs. There are only a small collection of boulders here and they offer low problems (but fortunately not as low as Rocher des Potets) Consequently, there is only one circuit which squeezes in problems of all different standards and explains why there is such a wide variation in grades. I didn't find any vines, or bump into Jean either, but we decided to call this circuit the Pressoir (Wine Press), because you need to put in some high quality effort to produce worthwhile results. It isn't a circuit that gives into a light hearted approach, although there is a good selection of lovely elegant problems in the lower grades. With such a varying standard of problems, it seems pointless in linking them together as a continuous circuit, and especially as you need a spotter for nearly all of the harder problems due to the compromising positions with a lot of the top outs. The boulders aren't very high, but usually demand you to make some contortion that would leave you spinning out of control if you don't quite manage to pull over. For any indoor trained climber wanting to improve, it is an ideal place to practice gnarly top outs, then you can always exit your 7a's in style. I found grading here difficult, problem (6b) is only one move – but a hard one, and giving it 6a- is fair, but a very easy tick (for some). As for (34), it's ungradeable anyway, it's either easy or hard – success or failure. It's a great location for a cold winters day and will keep you nice and warm, especially if you have Jean's friend 'Marc de Bourgogne' in your hip flask.

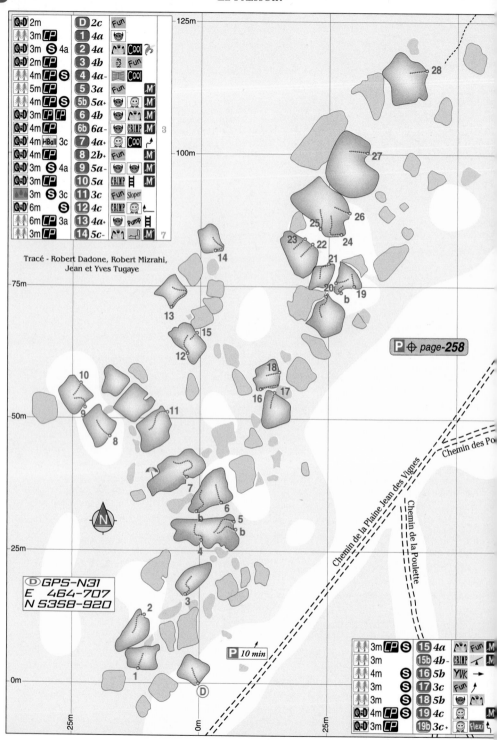

Q-D	2m		D	2c	Fun
	3m	CP	1	4a	
Q-D	3m	S 4a	2	4a	COOL
Q-D	2m	CP	3	4b	Fun
	4m	CP S	4	4a+	COOL
	5m	CP	5	3a	Fun
	4m	CP S	5b	5a+	
Q-D	3m	CP CP	6	4b	
Q-D	4m	CP	6b	6a-	CRIMP
Q-D	4m	HBall 3c	7	4a+	COOL
Q-D	4m	CP	8	2b+	Fun
Q-D	3m	S 4a	9	5a-	
Q-D	3m	CP	10	5a	CRIMP
	3m	S 3c	11	3c	Fun Sloper
Q-D	6m	S	12	4c	CRIMP
	6m	CP 3a	13	4a+	Pump
	3m	CP	14	5c-	

Tracé - Robert Dadone, Robert Mizrahi,
Jean et Yves Tugaye

P ⊕ page-258

Ⓓ GPS-N31
E 464-707
N 5358-920

P 10 min

Chemin de la Plaine Jean des Vignes
Chemin de la Poulette
Chemin des Po

	3m	CP S	15	4a	Fun
	3m		15b	4b-	CRIMP
	4m	S	16	5b	YVK
	3m	S	17	3c	Fun
	3m	S	18	5b	
Q-D	4m	CP S	19	4c	
Q-D	3m	CP	19b	3c+	Flexi

4m **CP**	**20** *4c*	CRIMP	
3m **S**	**21** *4a*		
4m HBall 5b	**22** *5b*		CRIMP 10
4m **F S** 3a	**23** *3c*		
6m **CP S**	**24** *4b*		**M**
4m **CP**	**25** *3c*	Fun	
3m **S**	**26** *5b*		
4m **S**	**27** *5a-*		
3m **CP**	**28** *6a-*		4
5m **CP**	**28b** *6b*	Sloper	1
2m	**29** *5c-*		5
4m	**30** *5c*	Sloper	6
2m	**30b** *3b*	Fun	
5m	**31** *5a*	YUK	X
4m **S**	**32** *5a*	Sloper **M**	
5m **CP S**	**33** *3b*	COOl Fun	
3m **S**	**34** *6a+*	Trick	2
5m **S**	**34b** *5c*	**M**	8
4m HBall 3b	**35** *3b*	COOl	

Magicien total

Bleu 5b – 5a+; Carsten Joiko

L'éléphant est l'un des blocs les plus connus du monde entier grâce à son côté mélancolique, sa jolie forme mais aussi parce qu'il marque le départ de 3 circuits superbes. Le site est jonché de blocs géants et de précipices énormes. Éléphant décrit le massif au sud de la colline qui descend sur une plage de sable. Il y a de nombreux blocs de petite taille qui donnent des passages courts et difficiles avec de bonnes aires de réception. Cependant le circuit est intimidant, effrayant, et demande une bonne technique. Vous aurez besoin de faire une pause mentalement et physiquement sur ce circuit afin d'éviter toute erreur qui pourrait avoir des conséquences désastreuses. Le circuit bleu offre un incroyable défi de commande de soi et d'habileté. Il y a au total 80 passages ce qui est beaucoup pour une seule journée. Nous avons donc arrêté le circuit à 50 voies ce qui paraît plus logique. Ce circuit est très dangereux car il y a de nombreux mouvements difficiles à 7 ou 8 mètres de haut qui vous feront chuter la tête la première si vous ne les réussissez pas. Le circuit fonctionne très bien et vous fait grimper des passages incroyables. Faire la totalité du circuit est un défi difficile qui effraiera de nombreux grimpeurs. Bonne tremblote.

Bleu 17 - 4c;
Frank Van de Wal

Bleu 36 – 5b; Olivier Bridou

Bleu 34 ~ 5a+; Olivier Bridou

Éléphant is one of the best known boulders to climbers from all over the world, partly due to the enigmatic and melancholic mood of its lovely shape, but also because it marks the start of three great climbing circuits of world class merit. Additionally, is not just the shape of the boulder which gives this area such a meaningful name, for here not only is the Éléphant boulder on the big side, but the whole area is strewn with giant blocks and precipices that are on the immense side. Éléphant describes the area on the south side of the hill that descends into a giant sandy beach. Conveniently there are many small blocks in this sector dumped in the sand that give ideal short, hard problems - and typically with good landings. Many climbers may remark that Éléphant is a nice place with happy sandy landings, 'oh yes, I've done the blue circuit there.' This usually means they have done the 5 smallest problems at the bottom in the sandy area. The complete circuit however, takes on an entirely different character; one of intimidation, fear, and demanding technical climbing. You will need to take time out on this circuit for a mental break as well as a physical rest; it is 'not' a place where you can afford to make a mistake on many of the problems without dire consequences. The blue circuit is a tremendous challenge of both climbing skill and mental control. The entire circuit lasts for over 80 problems and circumnavigates the whole hill. At this length it is too demanding for a single day – and especially as a non-suicidal on-sight challenge. The problems on the north side are rarely well marked, face north and are best reserved for those who like esoteric quietness. We have stopped the circuit at 50, which seemed ideal for a single day and before it goes up onto the top plateau and joins the excellent yellow circuit. This really is a dangerous circuit because you do have to make some tricky moves, and very high up at 7-8m, whilst in positions that would leave you tumbling backwards head first if you blew it. It is a proper continuous circuit that works brilliantly, taking you up and down some incredibly high and invigorating problems! To complete this entire circuit is a good tick and a difficult challenge that will simply freak out most climbers, good trembling.

Éléphant   *Bleu 50 ~ 5a; Jan Steinfatt*

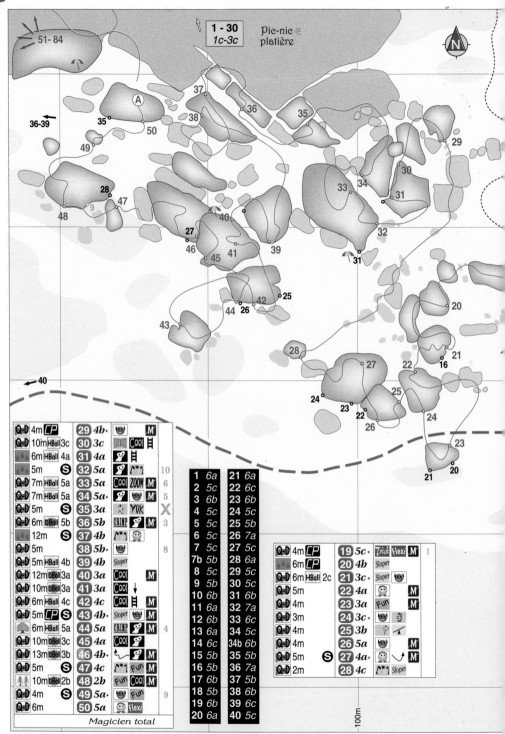

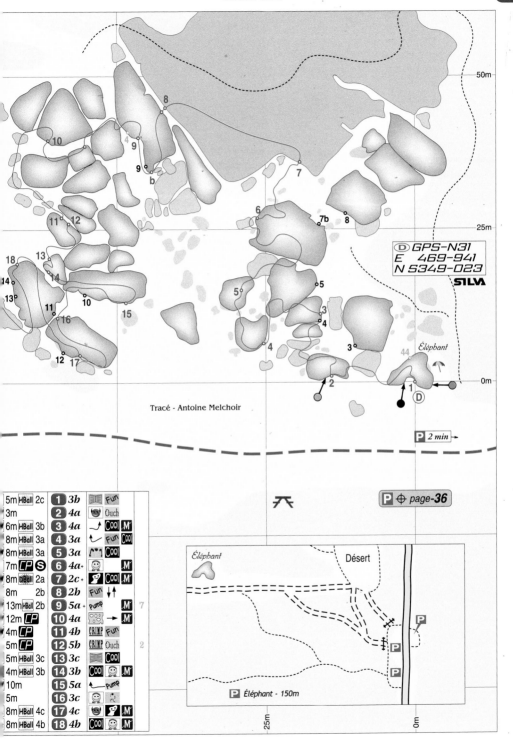

Tracé - Antoine Melchoir

GPS-N31
E 469-941
N 5349-023

SILVA

Éléphant

44

P 2 min

P ⊕ page-36

5m HBall 2c	**1** *3b*	Fun		
3m	**2** *4a*	Ouch		
6m HBall 3b	**3** *4a*	Cool M		
8m HBall 3a	**4** *3a*	Fun Cool		
8m HBall 3a	**5** *3a*	Cool		
7m CP S	**6** *4a+*		M	
8m DBall 2a	**7** *2c*	Cool M		
8m 2b	**8** *2b*	Fun ↓↑		
13m HBall 2b	**9** *5a*	Pump M		7
12m CP	**10** *4a*	→ M		
4m CP	**11** *4b*	CRIMP Fun		
5m CP	**12** *5b*	CRIMP Ouch		2
5m HBall 3c	**13** *3c*	Cool		
4m HBall 3b	**14** *3b*	Cool M		
10m	**15** *5a*	Pump		
5m	**16** *3c*			
8m HBall 4c	**17** *4c*	M		
8m HBall 4b	**18** *4b*	Cool M		

Éléphant

Désert

P

P

P

P Éléphant - 150m

25m

0m

Si vous avez déjà visité le site d'Angles sur Anglin dans l'ouest de la France et que vous avez apprécié les voies de niveau 7 à la Guignoterie, alors vous aimerez ce massif puisque l'escalade y est pratiquement identique. Bien sûr les passages sont plus petits et les prises sont de grès et non de calcaire, cependant les mouvements sont très similaires et il y a de nombreuses variantes sur les murs et les dévers. Il y a sur le côté sud de la crête du Long Rocher une forêt qui donne de l'ombre sur la plupart des passages difficiles. Sur le haut de la crête il y a un long couloir au milieu d'un plateau de grès où il peut faire très frais ou trop chaud selon la position du soleil. De nombreux passages sont encore fléchés en jaune, orange et vert ce qui indique une bonne variété de voies pour ceux qui sont prêts à les chercher. Il y a

Rouge 34 – 5b; Jingo

de nombreux circuits rouge difficiles dans la forêt qui pour la plupart sont une collection de passages difficiles mis les uns après les autres. Ce circuit reste traditionnel dans le sens où il suit un tracé sympathique à travers la forêt, idéal pour une journée d'escalade et pour faire 34 passages à vu. Vous apprécierez la majorité de ces passages bien que certains soient assez désagréables. Les passages les plus hauts ont leurs mouvements les plus difficiles en haut des blocs et une bonne parade ou un bon crash pad sont recommandés. Lorsqu'il fait chaud, nous vous conseillons de faire les passages qui sèchent le plus rapidement en premier car ils deviennent impossibles à faire lorsque la chaleur est trop forte. C'est un circuit très exigeant, le plus difficile dans ce guide, mais qui j'espère n'est pas trop dur pour être fait à vu.

Bloc 22-23

Rouge 6 ~ 5c; Hot sizzling Jim Bacon

If you've ever been to Angles sur l'Anglin in the West of France and enjoyed cranking up grade 7 routes at La Guignoterie, you will be completely in your element here since the climbing style is almost identical. It's smaller obviously and you find pocketed sandstone here rather than limestone, but the moves are very similar and there are countless variations to some of the pocketed walls and overhangs. The south side of the high ridge of Long Rocher gives an enchanting forest that gives dappled shade to most of the harder problems lower down the hill. The hillside blocs offer a good assortment highly technical problems that really test you on-sight ability. At the top of the ridge there is a sandstone plateau which is knife-cut to give a beautiful long corridor, this varies from cool to boiling, depending on the angle of the sun along it. The separating of some of the blocks from the plateau means that you get a large amount of smooth 3-4m high walls which are perfect for harder level climbing. This said, there are the remnants of yellow, orange and green arrows all around the area to prove that it is a good venue for a mixed group who are willing to look for their own problems. There are a lot of hard red circuits in the forest, but most have been well documented over the years and are more often a collection of hard problems just next to each other – e.g. Isatis. This circuit still remains a circuit in the traditional sense and traces a lovely route through the forest, and makes an ideal day trip to get a perfect list of 34 on-sights. You will find however, that this group of nasty problems could be well labelled the Restaurant of Long Rocher. There of course will be many dishes to your liking, but you may find some quite sharp and disagreeable with your finger strength or forearms. Some of the highball problems have the crux's at the top, making the price you pay for your outing somewhat expensive. (Multiple crash pads are handy here). For those climbers who are moaning that the outing a bit on the soft side, there is a good whine menu of off circuit hard problems. A top tip is to pick off the quick drying problems first on a hot day, they get a bit too hot and sizzling for enjoyment later on. This is a full and demanding circuit, the hardest in the book, but hopefully not off the scale and too hard to on-sight. (Note: By re-tracing the start of the circuit, you get a better warm up before 2 & 3.)

Rouge 3t - 6b; J-J-J-Jim

RESTANT DU LONG ROCHER - (TD/Rouge)

Rouge 27 - 5c; The Magicien at work

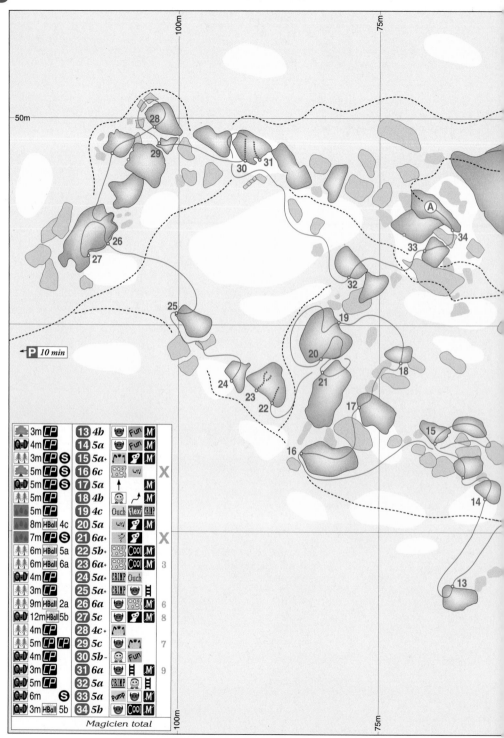

🍀 3m **CP**	**13** *4b*	😊 Fun M'	
Q-D 4m **CP**	**14** *5a*	😊 Fun M'	
🌲 3m **CP** S	**15** *5a-*	⌒⌒1 🐍 M'	
🍀 5m **CP** S	**16** *6c*	▦ ⌣	X
Q-D 5m **CP** S	**17** *5a*	↑ M'	
🌲 5m **CP**	**18** *4b*	😊 M'	
🌲 5m **CP**	**19** *4c*	Ouch Flexi CRIMP	
▦ 8m HBall 4c	**20** *5a*	⌣ 🐍 M'	
▦ 7m **CP** S	**21** *6a+*	😊 👥	X
🌲 6m HBall 5a	**22** *5b-*	▦ Cool M'	
🌲 6m HBall 6a	**23** *6a+*	▦ Cool M'	3
Q-D 4m **CP**	**24** *5a+*	CRIMP Ouch	
🌲 3m **CP**	**25** *5a-*	CRIMP 😊 Ⅱ	
🌲 9m HBall 2a	**26** *6a*	😊 👥 ▦	6
Q-D 12m HBall 5b	**27** *5c*	😊 🐍 M'	8
🌲 4m **CP**	**28** *4c+*	⌒⌒1	
🌲 5m **CP CP**	**29** *5c*	😊 ⌒⌒1	7
Q-D 4m **CP**	**30** *5b-*	😊 Fun	
Q-D 3m **CP**	**31** *6a*	😊 Ⅱ M'	9
Q-D 5m **CP**	**32** *5a*	CRIMP Ⅱ	
Q-D 6m S	**33** *5a*	Pump 😊 M'	
Q-D 3m HBall 5b	**34** *5b*	😊 Cool M'	
	Magicien total		

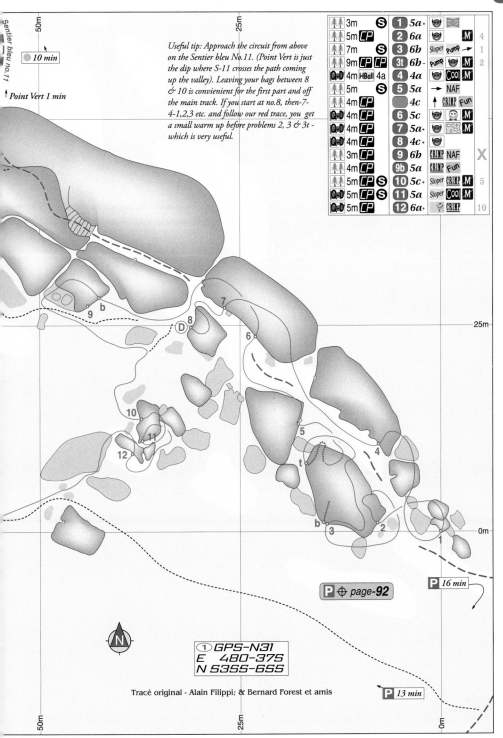

Useful tip: Approach the circuit from above on the Sentier bleu No.11. (Point Vert is just the dip where S-11 crosses the path coming up the valley). Leaving your bags between 8 & 10 is convienient for the first part and off the main track. If you start at no.8, then 7-4-1,2,3 etc. and follow our red trace, you get a small warm up before problems 2, 3 & 3t - which is very useful.

sentier bleu no.11

10 min

↑ Point Vert 1 min

3m	S	1	5a+
5m CP		2	6a
7m	S	3	6b
9m CP CP		3t	6b -
Q-D 4m HBall 4a		4	4a
5m	S	5	5a
			4c
4m CP		6	5c
Q-D 4m CP		7	5a+
Q-D 4m CP		8	4c+
3m CP		9	6b
4m		9b	5a
5m CP S		10	5c+
Q-D 5m CP S		11	5a
Q-D 5m CP		12	6a+

4
1
2

X

5
10

P ⊕ page-92

P 16 min

N

① GPS–N31
E 480-375
N 5355-655

P 13 min

Tracé original - Alain Filippi; & Bernard Forest et amis

HILL WALKING & FELL RUNNING

If you enjoy getting out and about in the Hills and Mountains, don't miss the Jingo Wobbly 'BRITISH' Hill Walking series of books.

These are ideally sized, outdoor pocket books, complete with beautiful maps drawn by David Atchison-Jones.

Fun and reliable books of the highest quality.

The ideal present for anyone that you know. Illustrated with hundreds of colour photos.

JINGO WOBBLY 🔺 WALKING / HILL RUNNING

— ATCHISON'S WALKS —
The Complete Hills of Britain
— VOLUME ONE —
SOUTHERN ENGLAND
CIRCULAR WALKS or Hill Runs with MAPS
· INCLUDES ·
MALVERN HILLS 15 PEAKS CHALLENGE

50 · SHORT MORNING/AFTERNOON RAMBLES · Quick Hill Runs
50 · COMFORTABLE / ALL DAY WALKS · Good Hill Runs
△ 50 · BIG & CHALLENGING HILL WALKS · Tough Hill Runs

JINGO WOBBLY 🔺 WALKING / FELL RUNNING

— ATCHISON'S WALKS —
The Complete Hills of Britain
— VOLUME TWO —
NORTHERN ENGLAND
CIRCULAR WALKS or FELL RUNS with MAPS
· INCLUDES ·
YORKSHIRE THREE PEAKS CHALLENGE

50 · SHORT MORNING/AFTERNOON RAMBLES · Quick Fell Runs
50 · COMFORTABLE / ALL DAY WALKS · Good Fell Runs
△ 50 · BIG & CHALLENGING FELL WALKS · Tough Fell Runs

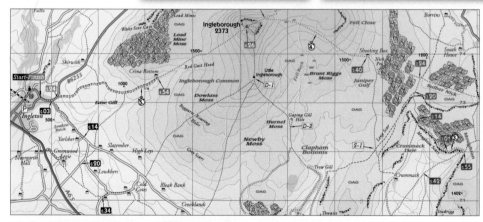

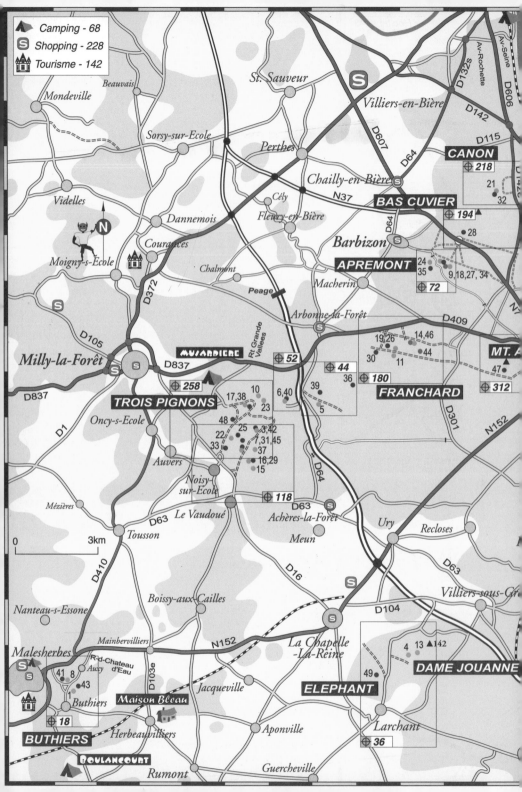